THE
JOURNALS OF KIERKEGAARD

"To read these journals is to live in the intimacy of one of the most extraordinarily original and, at the same time, lovable men in the whole of nineteenth century history. There can be no two opinions about his importance, both as a writer and as a man." *Listener*

"The Journals are the most valuable book that could be made available to those English readers who can yield to the fascination of the strange and disturbing Danish thinker. They constitute the primary source for any understanding of either the man or his thought."
The Times Literary Supplement

"No biography can take the place of these Journals for understanding Kierkegaard's very peculiar position as a thinker."
Edward Sackville West, New Statesman

"There can be very few books in English that admit the reader so intimately to a process of thinking on such a scale, at so many levels, so unflinching and direct." *The Tablet*

For a description of the book and some information about the author, see the back of the book

Religious Books in the Fontana Series

The
Journals of
Søren Kierkegaard

A selection
edited and translated
by Alexander Dru

COLLINS
fontana books

First published by the Oxford University Press 1938
Shortened version first issued in Fontana Books 1958

Contents

INTRODUCTION

Somewhere in the Journal, Kierkegaard remarks that the skipper of a fishing-smack usually knows his whole cruise before leaving port, whereas a man-of-war only receives its orders on the high seas. That is what had happened to him. From 1846 on, it became more and more evident to him that the work which he had written was to end in an unforeseen way. Its whole significance suddenly dawned on him, and he saw that his gifts and talent were to be his vocation. He had understood his mission. This mission was not a self-chosen, self-imposed task, but was implicit in the work he had written. The Revolutions of 1848 had revolutionised his life by confirming his diagnosis of the moral and political situation; the events in Paris, Vienna, and Berlin allowed him to see his position in Copenhagen in a new light.

This new point of view had been pressing in upon him since the beginning of 1846. It was then that he began the series of Note-books, numbered NB 1 to NB 16 which he thought might be published under the title *The Judge's Book*. The earlier Journal was haphazard by comparison with what he calls " the Journal proper," which is in effect the history of the discovery of his mission, the process of simplification and clarification which begins in January 1846 and ends with his death, during his attack on the Established Church in Denmark, in 1855. The earlier note-books, written while he was still unconscious of his mission, allow one to see the raw material of his life, so to say, before his extraordinary destiny had taken shape. This short Introduction is, I need hardly say, limited to giving the reader the main outline of Kierkegaard's life and work so that the Journal should, if possible, be read in comfort.

Those who wish to know more about his thought may use-
fully read *The Mind of Kierkegaard* by Collins, and
Hohlenberg's biography is excellent : Dr. Walter Lowrie's
Short Life is a dual-purpose volume, a sound, overall picture
without frills.

Childhood and Youth

Copenhagen, where Kierkegaard was born on 5th May,
1813, was a small provincial town, the seat of Government
and, at that time, the intellectual centre of Scandinavia,
with its University and its learned Academies—a closely-
knit society which provided Kierkegaard with a clinical
specimen of the social and political, intellectual and
religious currents of the day, which he could consult like
a barometer. There was hardly anyone from the King,
Christian VIII, to the women in the fish-market, whom he
did not know, and there was certainly no one who aroused
more curiosity than the gnome-like figure, with his
umbrella under his arm, who could be seen on his daily
walks about the town.

In appearance he was certainly odd. He was slight,
spindly and with so pronounced a stoop that he was regarded as a hunch-back. The curvature of his spine, which
he thought had been caused by a fall from a tree when
he was a child, made him lean back as he walked, and
gave him a dislocated, mechanical, crab-like gait, so that
every movement appeared to be deliberate. His head was
finely shaped and well-rounded, crowned with a mop of un-
controllable fair hair. The eyes behind his glasses were pale
blue, his nose straight and strong, his mouth large, his
teeth protruding, his chin receding. Unprepossessing and
unimpressive though he was, he had only to begin talking,
and in spite of a rasping voice that easily cracked, he was
altogether transformed. His conversation could be captivating in the highest degree, and he possessed an uncanny, but

not always reassuring, gift of penetrating the minds of others. When Hans Brøchner, later Professor of Philosophy at the University, first met him, he assumed he must be some little clerk from an office. But it was not long before he was disillusioned on that score, and delighted in his company. "His smile," he wrote, after Kierkegaard's death, "and his look, were indescribably expressive. He had a particular way of greeting one at a distance, with a mere look. It was just a little movement of the eyes, and yet it conveyed so much. He could put something infinitely gentle and loving into his gaze, but he could equally goad and tease people to frenzy. With a single look at a passer-by he could, as he expressed it, 'put himself in touch with him.' Whoever met his gaze was either drawn to him or repelled, was either made to feel uncomfortable, or attracted to him. I have walked down whole streets with him while he explained how one could make psychological studies by 'getting in touch' with people; and while he explained his theory he put it into practice with almost everyone."

Seen from the inside, through the pages of the *Journal*, Kierkegaard is all melancholy and the microscopic analysis to which he submitted his thoughts and feelings and experience is in danger of concealing as much as it reveals. For from the outside nothing of this appeared. No one, he triumphantly asserts, ever pitied him. To his contemporaries he was a man of infinite wit whose flashing intelligence dazzled and disturbed; but although his superiority was never in question, he remained an enigma. Far from appearing serious, he gave the impression of taking a frivolous delight in making a mockery of everything they took to heart. "There is nothing," one of the men who knew him well wrote, "spontaneous or straightforward about him. I am surprised he can eat and sleep, etc. Otherwise I acknowledge him to be the most cultured and talented author; but he seems to me like a decrepit old man, or rather like an exceptionally intellectual person with a sickly imagination."

Kierkegaard would not have disagreed. He had never known what it meant to be young, and his genius, he thought, lay in an exceptional compound of opposites, of reflection and imagination and a diseased absence of spontaneity, so that the very qualities which gave him his superiority over others, were at the same time the source of his misery, cutting him off from ordinary life at which he could only assist as an observer, or a spy, he wrote later, in the service of an idea. It was as though his infinitely reflective mind disintegrated experience as it came to him, putting spontaneous reaction beyond his reach. And yet at the same time a vivid imagination enabled him to feel and grasp all that was denied him. "Lacking almost all the requirements for being a man," crippled by the disproportion between body and spirit, he was nevertheless possessed by a vitality which nothing could subdue. Even at the point where he felt that he was on the borderline of madness, his vitality of mind held everything together, piercing the web of explanations in which his reflection tried to imprison him, and finally restoring order. It was this agonising sense of the dislocation between thought and existence which drove him, as he grew up, to search for " the idea for which I can live and die," for the truth which would be the full-blooded union of thought and existence which fate, in the first instance, had denied him.

"From my earliest youth," Kierkegaard writes, " I was in the grip of a profound melancholy." The expression is misleading, and on one occasion at least, he is more precise, and adds, "from my twentieth year." What he meant was that "we are all of us what we are to be by the time we are ten years old :" he was predisposed by his physical weakness, by his malformation and his whole cast of mind to fall into melancholy. But it was only by stages that his singularity turned into isolation, and his isolation was transformed by his imagination into an inescapable fate. The events which determined the course of his life have been discussed *ad infinitum* and the full truth will probably never be known; but the main outline of the great moral and intellectual crisis of his youth is clear enough, and it is possible to follow the steps by which Kierkegaard came to understand the forces of heredity and upbringing by which he was formed. The story is briefly summarised in a group of quotations and comments in which he describes the culminating point as "the great earthquake." They were written on three pages of gilt-edged paper and are given here (p. 39) in the order in which they were written, and not as printed by the editors. Variously interpreted, they give the history of Kierkegaard's development from childhood until the death of his father in August, 1838.

Kierkegaard was anything but a melancholy child. He was, from all accounts, alert, independent and precociously intelligent, "with a tendency to freedom and irresponsibility which prevents him from taking anything seriously." He was perfectly well able to look after himself at school, more than a match for a master who showed any signs of weakness, and never without the physical courage to deal with the boys of his own age, who noticed nothing odd about him except the curious suits he was dressed in and his sarcastic remarks. It was not until much later that he became conscious of being unlike others, and by then he had discovered ample compensation in his home life.

Everything there centred round his father. As the youngest of seven children he was spoilt and allowed a degree of freedom which his brothers and sisters had not known. And as he grew older the natural affinity between him and his father came into play. Everything, it seemed to him in after life, had been done to favour his development and to establish his self-confidence. The autobiographical sketch, "Johannes Climacus" (p. 80) gives a stylised impression of the "insane upbringing" which he cursed and blessed in the same breath as wonderfully suited to his genius, though by developing his natural gifts it encouraged his singularity and made him old before his time. Then and afterwards, his father was the only man with whom he lived on equal terms, whose cast of mind was in many respects like his own, and on whom he could count absolutely for understanding. From him, he says, he learnt the meaning of fatherly love, and so gained some analogy for the love of God. The motto chosen for these years, "Half childish games, Half God in my heart," taken from Goethe, sums up the happy and solid foundations on which his life was built, the sense of freedom and duty and the belief that "one can do what one wills" which supported him through all the trials and crises of his life.

But when the crisis came involving his father, his whole world came crashing about his ears. It is a matter of conjecture when Kierkegaard's suspicion first arose. But whenever it was, he gradually began to notice that the façade of his father's life concealed a different world, that the faith in God which he had been taught, and the Christianity in which he had been reared, were powerless to support the man he loved. He came to see that his father was deeply vulnerable, and that his faith was undermined by "silent despair." This suspicion was explored in every direction, and kept alive by his father's unguarded remarks. When his mother and all but one of his brothers died within a few years, and his father's melancholy could no longer be hidden, Kierkegaard brooded over his suspicions until they acquired the compulsive force of "a frightful foreboding" that in some unexplained way he himself was involved in the fate of the whole family. In 1835 he seems finally to have stumbled on the "secret" that explained everything, and its power over him was doubly increased by the fact that his worst forebodings had been fulfilled. He had discovered the "infallible law" that explained everything and it became an *idée fixe,* something objective, a point on which his sense of isolation could centre and round which his melancholy coagulated.

Kierkegaard's father, Michael Pedersen Kierkegaard, was born in Saeding, a hamlet in the poorest district on the moors of Jutland, where the peasants scraped a bare existence from the soil. As a child, he was often sent out on to the moor to mind the sheep, and it was there, when he was twelve years old, that in his misery and solitude, he climbed on a hill and cursed God. The primitive intensity of thought and emotion which the gesture reveals was never dulled or transformed by education, and the act of rebellion which his grinding poverty had provoked was firmly fixed in his memory when his luck suddenly changed.

When he was about sixteen, Michael Pedersen was sent to assist a cousin in a hosier's business in Copenhagen. He was quick to learn the business and soon took over the management entirely. By the time he was forty he had saved a very substantial sum for a man of his position, and subsequently, in the year of Søren's birth, his capital was unexpectedly increased by a lucky investment. But his material prosperity had already been payed for in spiritual tribulation.

Shortly after the death of his first wife, who died childless, in April 1796, Michael Pedersen wound up his affairs and sold his business. Within a year, in April 1797, he had married his servant, and less than five months later their first child was born. Behind that sequence of events, the death of his first wife, to whom he was devoted, his retirement, and his hurried second marriage, lies the secret on which he began to brood, and which his son was to discover with such tremendous consequences. He had loved his first wife, and to the end of his life continued to regard her as his real wife and himself as responsible in some sense for her death—perhaps she had learnt of his relations with their servant. If Kierkegaard's expressions are any guide, he accused himself of seducing, if not raping, the girl who lived under his roof and under his protection, and who became the mother of his children. Outwardly respected, eminently successful, a close friend of Mynster, the future Primate of Denmark, and widely known for his uprightness and his intelligence, he was inwardly broken by remorse. His vigorous mind was imprisoned in a narrow, disfiguring Protestantism, an arid predestinarian theology and meagre pietism that accentuated the personal dependence of man on God at the price of confining it in an almost mechanistic conception of Divine Providence. To him the chain of cause and effect, of guilt and punishment reached from his first rebellion against God, down through his sensuality to the successive deaths of his children. It was a religion which neither education nor vision had touched; it remained morose, intense, and sterile. In a softened light it was the Christianity which Kierkegaard himself was offered and against which he reacted healthily, though to the end his mind was coloured by it.

By his second wife, Michael Pedersen had seven children, four boys and three girls, the eldest of whom died as the result of an accident in 1819. Two years later, in 1822, his eldest daughter died suddenly. It was ten years later, just as Søren Kierkegaard left school and began going to the University, that his mother and three of his remaining brothers and sisters died within the space of three years. It was this succession of deaths which made such an impression on Michael Pedersen and his two surviving sons. Søren's brother Peter, then lecturing at the University, was himself in the grip of religious melancholy which a grim theology had fastened so firmly on him that at the end of his life, when he had been Bishop of Aalborg for some years, he begged to be relieved of his office, unable to bear the responsibility any longer. The atmosphere in the large house in the main square, where they all three lived, was such that a less sensitive mind than Søren's might well have wondered what lay behind the inheritance of melancholy that had descended upon him.

All three, as Kierkegaard now discovered, had arrived independently at the same conclusion. His father and his brother had come to believe that the father's sins were to be visited on the sons, and that Michael Pedersen was destined, as the deaths of his children had proved, to out-live them all, " a cross on the tomb of all his hopes " and the " outstanding intellectual gifts of our family were only given to us in order that we should rend one another to pieces." Kierkegaard had found the infallible law which explained all the facts; the " great earthquake " shattered his world and left him stranded. " Inwardly torn asunder as I was . . . what wonder then that in desperate despair I grasped at nought but the intellectual side in man, and clung fast to it, so that the thought of my own considerable powers of mind was my consolation, ideas my one joy, and mankind indifferent to me." (p. 40).

The " infallible law " was not merely an explanation of his father's despair; it was a " terrifying, mysterious ex-planation of religion, which a frightful foreboding had played into my hands, which my imagination worked upon, and the scandal which religion became to me." His life which had begun in an idyllic, patriarchal key was suddenly transformed into terror. Instead of submitting like his father and brother and bowing under the weight of the fate they had constructed for themselves, Søren reacted violently and broke with everything which had hitherto protected and supported him, and found release in the new intellectual life that opened out before him at the University. For however firmly " the infallible law " had taken root in his mind, there was the outside world to be explored and new levels of experience to be tasted and tested.

It is at this time that Kierkegaard first appears on the scene rejoicing in his talents and making his superiority felt. He is seen addressing the University Club on a political motion, cutting short a rowdy meeting with his sarcasms and making his *début* in the press. His articles on the Liberal leader, Orla Lehmann, were at once attributed to J. L. Heiberg, the most distinguished *littérateur* of the day —though what the author intended was not quite clear, except to ridicule the Liberals. But neither his father, nor his brother was impressed by his success. They did not share his interest in politics, his enthusiasm for the romantic school, his passion for Mozart or his boundless curiosity in his contemporaries. They only saw him drifting away from home, and speaking and thinking in a cold and critical way to Christianity, while he found as little substance in the stodgy orthodoxy of old-fashioned Protestantism as in the brittle new-fangled rationalistic theology of the young Hegelians like Martensen, his coach. In the hope of bringing him to his senses his father sent him for a holiday to Gilleleje, on the north coast of Zealand, where the first entries in this selection were written in August 1835. For a moment Kierkegaard pulled himself together and the deeper note in his mind sounds through his despair. But on his return to Copenhagen his new state was soon worse than the first.

For the next two years he speaks of himself as " on the path to perdition," but what looked like frivolity and irresponsibility to his father and others and even to himself was a necessary safety-valve. The *Journal* for these years is short and intermittent, hardly more than an echo of his conversation and the carefree mood he adopted in public where he was " never so ungracious as to appear without a freshly picked bouquet of wit." He spent much of his time with a group of seedy æsthetes, Hans Andersen among others, who met regularly in one of the cafés. Among these was P. L. Møller, a gifted young man who supplied the model for the Don Juan character who appears in *Either-Or*, and a drunken, *déclassé* intellectual Johannes Jørgensen. It was probably in their company that he visited a brothel—an incident which suddenly sprang to the forefront of his mind some time afterwards like "lightning announcing a violent storm," at the time when he first met Regine Olsen, the girl to whom he became engaged.

The one man who penetrated his mask, and was not taken in by his nihilism, was the poet and philosopher Poul Martin Møller (not to be confused with P. L. Møller) to whom Kierkegaard afterwards dedicated *The Concept of Dread* where he defines the notion of *Angst* and analyses his own spiritual attitude during these years with special reference to sin and sexuality. In the long dedication Møller is addressed as "the mighty trumpet of my awakening." Møller was almost the only man at the University who sympathised with Kierkegaard's growing irritation with the fashionable philosophy of Hegel, and he suspected rightly enough that the young man whose sardonic comments amused him would, if only he could concentrate his energies, play David to Hegel's Goliath. They were often seen about together, Moller large and easy-going, and Kierkegaard walking him into the gutter as he threw out his ideas and explained his point of view. Møller's early death, in the spring of 1838, touched him deeply and a few days later, he took up his interrupted *Journal* again.

The first sign of change is Kierkegaard's reconciliation with his father. At about this time Michael Pedersen paid his son's debts and made him an allowance which enabled him to leave his father's house and live in rooms. It may have been part of the bargain that Kierkegaard should begin working, and he taught Latin for a time at the school he had attended as a child. To judge by the quotation from Lear (p. 40) headed "twenty-five years old"

it was on the occasion of his legal coming of age that his
father made full amends for the past and confessed his
sins. A week or so later, on 11th May, 1838, Kierkegaard
recorded an experience of "indescribable joy" unique in
the *Journals*. On August 9th his father died and Kierkegaard's period of crisis was over. "The powerful religious
impressions of childhood acquired a renewed power over
me, but softened by reflection." Now that his father was
no longer alive to be put off with excuses, Kierkegaard felt
in duty bound to set to work and take his degree which
during the last eight years he had not attempted to do.
He began working for the theological examination which
would give him the right to preach.

In the spring of 1837, Kierkegaard had visited his friends
the Rørdams, whose daughter Bolette had made an impression on him. It was in their house that he met Regine
Olsen. She was barely fifteen at the time, and for the
next year or two he only saw her occasionally. In her old
age Regine recalled their first meeting clearly, and was in
no doubt that Kierkegaard had decided then and there
that she should be his wife. Immediately after his father's
death he made a pilgrimage to Jutland, carefully noted in
the *Journal,* and on his return began working for his examination. He presented his thesis "On Socratic Irony" in
September, 1840. A few weeks later he asked for Regine's
hand, and they became officially engaged. His self-confidence had returned. He was still under the impression
of his religious experience, and he saw the past through
the haze of his reconciliation with his father. In his happiness he never doubted that he could escape his father,
overcome his isolation and "realise the universal"; marry
and be like others. But no sooner had he spoken than he
felt he had overstepped the mark. And the more he poured
over his dark secret the more certainly he knew that he
could never reveal it and speak of his father's sin, his

mother's dishonour or involve the girl he loved in his exceptional life. It never occurred to him to conceal anything. After a long struggle, during which he hoped she
would break with him, he had finally to tell her he would
not marry. The engagement was broken off in October
1841, and after remaining in Copenhagen for a couple of
weeks, in order to give the impression that he was indifferent to the whole affair and so, if possible, make things
easier for Regine, he took the boat for Stralsund and went
on to Berlin. The possibility that he might still marry
however was not entirely ruled out and he remained in
an agonised state of suspense. "Had I had faith," he
wrote afterwards, " I should have remained with Regine "
—but on another level he had felt " a divine protest " and
believed that his destiny lay elsewhere. Even before he
had become engaged he had asked himself whether he was
to be able to marry Regine or whether perhaps " the orders
are : *further* " : whether fate had other plans for him.

Kierkegaard's Work: The Pseudonyms 1841-1845

From the date of his return to Copenhagen in 1841, to
December 1845, Kierkegaard lived for his work and his
life was arranged accordingly. He was comfortably in-
stalled in a large flat, cared for by his servants, and spared
the worst drudgery by his secretaries. Food and wine,
coffee and cigars interested him, and he fussed about the
temperature of his room, as he could not stand the heat.
His daily walks round the town continued, he was often
seen at the theatre, and when the long summer days came
he hired a carriage and horses and made expeditions into
the surrounding country, where he dined and supped at an
inn, occasionally spending a night or two away. As long
as he was writing his melancholy was in abeyance, and his
whole attention and will were given to the works in hand.

A glance at the chronological table will suggest the speed
at which he worked.

Kierkegaard's work is so large, so complicated and so
strange that the reader is often in danger of not being able
to see the wood for the trees, or perhaps in this case it
would be better to say that the profusion of detail conceals the form; like gargoyles that project, belching their
scorn and ridicule, distracting the eye from the main
features of the building. In reality the structure is large
and simple.

The works fall into two perfectly distinct parts. The
first, written between 1841 and 1845 is a complete *oeuvre,*
self-contained, a *Comédie Humaine* attributed to half a
dozen pseudonyms many of whom re-appear in subsequent
volumes. The second part begins after an interval of about
a year and a half; the works of this period being published
under his own name, and leading directly into the " attack
on Christendom," the last series of pamphlets, which were
cut short by his death. The first period embraces works
concerned with the past into which he put everything he
had seen, read, thought and experienced. The second
period is the unfolding of his mission, the gradual clarification of the aim and end latent in the *oeuvre* : a work
of a different stamp altogether. For the moment, it is the
first part that has to be considered.

The first part of Kierkegaard's work consists of the great
pseudonyms, *Either-Or, Fear and Trembling, Repetition,
The Concept of Dread, Stages on the Road of Life,* and
the two philosophical works, *Fragments of Philosophy* and
the *Concluding Unscientific Postscript.* In addition there
are the eighteen *Religious Discourses* all of which were published under his own name. The pseudonyms, for all the
importance he attached to them, insisting like Balzac on
treating his figures as real, add substantially to the confusion but need not delay us. They gave him freedom of
movement and strangely enough often deceived the public.

With all the intensity at his command, Kierkegaard focused his work at the juncture of thought and existence, of philosophy and Christianity. At first sight everything else seems to go by the board. Church and State, culture and religion (except in its inward, moral aspect), politics and mysticism, are all swept aside and treated as distractions, like geometry to Pascal. His purpose seems to be to isolate the individual in an absolute silence where he will be face to face with the one thing necessary : the fusion of thought and existence, of faith and works. For it is only then that the spirit of man triumphs and he becomes " the individual." That unswerving insistence on the essential repeated in a variety of forms is what makes Kierkegaard's work at once curiously remote, and yet at the same time intensely personal. In one respect he is what he called " an author's author," and yet he never loses the capacity to talk to " the individual," to whom his work is addressed and dedicated, and his vividly inflected language has not been dulled by time. He was both thinker and poet.

The main feature of this part of his work is the polemic against Hegel, a criticism of the whole corpus of post-Christian philosophy from Spinoza to Hegel; an attack on philosophy as such, for its wordy metaphysics and its original sin of divorcing thought from existence. It is also a criticism, on the moral and psychological level, of the humanism of that age, of the world which emerged after the Reformation, which Kierkegaard, for short, calls the Goetheo-Hegelian world. That world, with its rationalist philosophy and its æsthetic humanism is diametrically opposed to the conception of life which he wished to bring to light, for its thought is abstract, and divorced from feeling, while its humanism is æsthetic and ultimately despairing, a flight from existence; it is " the dregs of Christianity."

The critical, almost nihilistic aspect of Kierkegaard's work is so sharp and prominent, his attack on rationalism and humanism so unrelenting, that the constructive part of his work is in some danger of being overlooked. But parallel with it there runs an analysis of " the individual," depicted in a series of scenes and situations, defining the " stages of life " or levels of existence which provides, in one sense, the frame-work of the *oeuvre*. The pseudonyms describe the æsthetic, the ethical and the religious levels of existence with a wealth of psychological detail, Don Juan, Faust and Ahasuerus, the Wandering Jew, providing the skeleton. In every one of these works Kierkegaard starts from a different point and moves towards the moment of decision, the " choice " in *Either-Or* and " the leap of faith " in *Fear and Trembling,* leading up to the *moment* in which decision fuses thought and existence, the *moment* which is the meeting point of time and eternity.

Kierkegaard's insistence on " the choice " and " the leap of faith " are so prominent in his work that, in the context of his attack on rationalism and humanism, they are sometimes allowed to suggest a narrow, fanatical and irrational philosophy of religion. In fact his argument is altogether different. The choice and the leap of faith are not counsels of despair nor a " bet " as in Pascal's argument but a necessary step towards the fusion of thought and existence. Faith and reason are opposed as long as reason is the reason of the rationalist, that is to say isolated from every other faculty in man and consequently divorced from existence. In " the fantastic medium of abstraction " faith is absurd, because existence itself is absurd. It can only be seen as a paradox, since the language of rationalism is of its nature incapable of grasping and expressing existence. But man is not a rational animal and thought which is not the expression of a fully mature and developed personality in whom intellect, will and feeling are harmonised, is thought divorced from existence. It is here that the point of Kierkegaard's attack on Goethe comes to light. The " humanism " of the eighteenth century is a literary concept, a mirage, which for lack of insistence upon existence, conceals the true humanism implicit in the notion of "the individual." The "individual" to Kierkegaard is the humanism open to all men, the level of existence which is attained when all the faculties are purified and brought into harmony through action and decision. "Are the passions heathen, and is reason alone baptised?" is the question which is asked on the title page of his first work, *Either-Or*. It is only when feeling and will are merged with intellect, only when the complete man acts that he can begin to philosophise, and then "the individual" reaches a new level of existence on which he is open to Christianity. Experience does not come to us automatically : it must be *chosen*, just as it must be felt, and only then can it be understood and, given a sufficiently developed language, the language of the imagination (which is the fusion of the three faculties), it can be communicated.

The conclusion to the *Postscript* is that "man only begins to exist in faith." Prior to that act of the will reason and faith will always appear to conflict because reason is incomplete by itself. "Life must be lived forward, but understood backwards" means that there can never be a complete system of philosophy, since man cannot stand outside the movement of life and understand it. It can only be understood in that movement which is continually seized by decision and the action which qualifies thought. Looking towards faith it is seen as the paradox, the absurd, and from the point of view of abstract reason, uninflected by feeling and undetermined by choice, it is the absurd. In the concrete everything is reversed and there is a second form of reflection which performs the opposite task to the first : instead of disintegrating faith, reflection makes it fast. The problem however is not to prove the truth of Christianity beforehand, but to communicate it afterwards, in an appropriate form of dialectics qualified by "passion." The real problem to Kierkegaard is not epistemology, the problem of knowledge, but the problem of communication, of language.

Seen in its broadest lines, Kierkegaard's work involves a shift of emphasis from the objective world of Reason and Culture, to the moral and inward sphere. That is why everything, in the first instance, is obliterated by the intensity with which he manœuvres in order to reach "the choice." But "truth lies in subjectivity" does not mean resting in subjectivity. On the contrary, inwardness or subjectivity *is* the starting point, "the choice" in and through which man becomes "the individual," for whom maturity consists not in cultural humanism with its accent on the externals of personality, but in the depth and richness of the inward life, which is the spring of action. It is that inward action, as Kierkegaard says in one of the very earliest entries in the *Journal,* which means everything, and leads back into the real world to the level of existence where Christianity has meaning. But in the first part of his work Kierkegaard does not go beyond the frontiers of the choice. It was only after he himself had acted decisively, when he was forced out of his work into life by his conflict with his contemporaries, that the significance of his conception of "the individual" dawned upon him and he fully grasped the nature and character of his apology for Christianity. It was then that he understood his mission.

The Metamorphosis

Kierkegaard completed his work in the autumn of 1845 and the *Concluding Unscientific Postscript* was sent to the printers in December. With his vast, though unrecognised, achievement behind him Kierkegaard once again began to think that his melancholy and self-isolation might be overcome. His ambition now was to write *finis* to his work and retire to a country living. He discussed the plan with

Bishop Mynster, his father's friend, who thought well of any arrangement by which so restive a mind could be kept at a distance. But the romantic gesture was hardly practicable. He began to have doubts about his worthiness for the ministry and before he had had time to reach a decision fate intervened. He was not destined to languish in a vicarage.

Just as Kierkegaard had sent off the manuscript of the *Postscript*, P. L. Møller, whom he had hardly seen for the last five or six years, published a violent attack on the author (the pseudonym was "Frater Taciturnitus") of *Guilty?—Not Guilty?* which is a thinly disguised account of Kierkegaard's engagement. Møller was perfectly aware that he had figured in *The Seducer's Diary* and now that Kierkegaard had produced the pendant to it (published at the end of 1844) he took his revenge and held the writer up to ridicule. Møller, who was not without ability as a critic, was trying to live down his reputation in the hope of succeeding the poet Oelenschläger in the Chair of Aesthetics at the University. To this end he used flattery in his more serious articles, but he could not resist the pleasure and profit to be derived from writing anonymously in *The Corsair*—an amusing, gossipy weekly belonging to Meier Goldschmidt, a liberal and enlightened Jew.

Kierkegaard had had his eye on Goldschmidt and *The Corsair* for some time past. He regarded it as lowering the tone and the standard and compromising the reputation of reputable writers such as Heiberg. He had already prepared an article expressing his views, which were shared by everyone, though no one had had the nerve to protest for fear of appearing in its pages. Kierkegaard had up to that time always been singled out by Goldschmidt and Møller for praise; they admired certain parts of his work immensely and felt with a certain justice that Kierkegaard was on their side and against the orthodox reputations it amused them to prick. This was a mistake. Kierkegaard had no intention of allowing his criticism of Heiberg to be used in the levelling down process. His reply to Møller was meant to prevent *The Corsair* from distinguishing between him and men like Heiberg and Gjødwad, the editor of *The Fatherland*, and to force Møller into the open. Heiberg and Gjødwad both thanked Kierkegaard for his article in private, but said nothing, to his irritation, in public, and left him to bear the brunt of it.

Once Møller's association with *The Corsair* had been made public his prospects in Copenhagen were finished. He ultimately went abroad and died in poverty. But not before exploring the possibilities of revenge. Week in week out, for almost a year, Kierkegaard was caricatured, parodied and ridiculed without mercy. Nothing was omitted : his odd appearance, his rounded back, his spindly legs, his ill-fitting clothes, his ridiculous love affair, his incomprehensible jargon, his comfortable life, his high-falutin' Christianity. He was depicted as a megalomaniac. As usual, no one seems to have guessed how deeply Kierkegaard felt these personal attacks, least of all Goldschmidt with whom he continued, when they met on the street, to discuss the rights and wrongs of Frater Taciturnitus, as though Kierkegaard were not involved. His air of treating the matter as a bagatelle convinced everyone.

When finally Kierkegaard cut him in the street, Goldschmidt realised the position and soon after the attacks ceased and the paper was suppressed.

This incident, trifling though it appears, is the dividing line in Kierkegaard's life and work. *The Corsair* affair turned his attention back from his work to the world about him—for the first time he saw his work complete in its historical setting : the historical context of his work revealed it to him in a new light, and he understood his mission.

This change in perspective, first suggested to him by the social and political conditions which *The Corsair* had revealed, occupied him intensely for the next two years. Almost simultaneously with the article against Møller, published in *The Fatherland* like all his newspaper articles, Kierkegaard reviewed a novel by Fru Gyllembourg, Heiberg's mother-in-law, and in the last part (translated under the title *The Present Age*) set down his diagnosis of the times in which he lived, with special reference to Christianity. He could now see the historical situation clearly. His mind then swung back to his own life, and he considered his future. For the first time he realised that his financial independence was threatened and his way of life endangered. He had always spent his money freely and the end was in sight—had he lived a month longer he would have been penniless—and it occurred to him for a moment to apply for a pension. But he had also grasped how important money had been to him by making it possible " to perform a *salto mortale* into a purely spiritual existence." It was at this point that the curious case of a certain Pastor Adler claimed his interest. Adler provided an excellent example of " religious enthusiasm," of a man with a mission without the faintest notion of how enthusiasm would need to be qualified in " the present age." Kierkegaard was fascinated by the spectacle of Adler's *naïveté* and the insoluble problems which it set to Mynster and the Church authorities. Most of what he wrote was left unpublished, but although *The Great Book on Adler* (re-written three times) is a poor book, it shows the direction which his mind was taking and the renewed importance which he gave to social and political conditions—an aspect of his work that is often neglected.

During the first half of 1847 Kierkegaard finished his most important religious work *Works of Love* and by August the meditations of the last year and a half began to bear fruit. "Something is stirring within me" he wrote, "which points to a metamorphosis. For that very reason I dare not go to Berlin, for that would be to procure an abortion. I shall remain quietly at home . . . (and) really think out the idea of my melancholy together with God here and now."

Six months later the metamorphosis which he had suspected culminated in his second conversion. On Wednesday in Holy Week, 1848, all the strands of his thought were drawn together, and for the third time in his life he believed that he was to escape his fate. "My reserve and self-isolation are broken" he exclaims, "I must speak out —Lord give thy grace. It is indeed true as my father said of me, 'you will never become anything as long as you have money'." The spell was broken. At first he assumed that his isolation was to be broken and that he could now take Holy Orders—which would also have solved the financial problem. But almost at once he dismissed the thought and finally understood that his task was not to become like others but to fulfil his mission. In the place of a cruel fate he saw Providence "which had done so much more for me than I ever expected." He could say that he had found the idea for which he could live and die, and could see where his melancholy had entered his soul. "In my melancholy I loved the world. Now I am weaned." He had wanted to be like others. His resignation hitherto had been a shield enabling him to live a purely spiritual existence, more stoical than Christian. Suffering voluntarily accepted and his decision to remain "the exception" opened his eyes to a new world. The metamorphosis had revolutionised his point of view and at one essential point altered the character of his work.

"The communication of Christianity must ultimately end in bearing witness, the maieutic (indirect) method can never be final. For truth from the Christian point of view does not lie in the subject, as Socrates understood it, but in a Revelation which must be proclaimed."

This entry in the *Journal,* read in the light of *The Present Age,* Kierkegaard's view of the world in which Christianity must be proclaimed, defines his mission. For simultaneously with his religious renewal at Easter, 1848, Kierkegaard was confirmed in his diagnosis by the Revolutions of 1848. What he had written in 1846 had been proved correct by events.

"Even now, in 1848, it certainly looks as though politics were everything; but it will be seen that the catastrophe (the Revolution) corresponds to and is the obverse of the Reformation : then everything pointed to a religious movement, and proved to be political; now everything points to a political movement, but it will become a religious movement."

The year of the Communist Manifesto appeared to Kierkegaard to mark the end of an age, of the "Goetheo-Hegelian" period and the bourgeois humanism which he had attacked in his first series of works which now seemed to him to be the prologue to his apology for Christianity. He did not expect a religious revival and still less the triumph of Christianity. On the contrary, the Revolution of 1848 confirmed him in the view that the Revolutionary movement was not merely a change of political *régime* but was the expression of the far more fundamental moral and social revolution which he had analysed in *The Present Age.* Nothing, he had said, least of all humanism "the dregs of Christianity" could halt "the levelling process" which he had first seen at work in *The Corsair.* This analysis, which reads in parts like Nietzsche *avant la lettre,* lays particular stress on the emergence of "the mass man." The victory of communism was the end of the political period which had begun at the Reformation. But little

though Kierkegaard relished the prospect, he believed that
the disappearance of a pseudo-religious culture with which
Christianity had to a large extent been confused, would
help "the individual" to see Christianity not as a
"religion" almost obscured by the culture that had formed
around it, but as a new level of existence.

All those who did not succumb in the process would be
brought up against the final "either-or:" either God or
humanity, either the supreme value of the individual, or
"mass man." In that new world Christianity would be
freed from its cultural associations, from "the rubbish"
of tradition, and become open to "the individual." It
could then be seen for what it was : a new level of existence
where nature is fulfilled by grace. The correctness of his
attack on Hegel stood out more clearly than ever before :

> How often have I shown that fundamentally Hegel
> makes men into heathens, into a race of animals gifted
> with reason. For in the animal world, "the individual"
> is always less important than the race. But it is the
> peculiarity of the human race, that because the individual
> is created in the image of God "the individual" is
> above the race.
>
> This can be wrongly understood and terribly misused :
> *concedo*. But that is Christianity, and *that* is where the
> battle must be fought.

The Second Group of Works
and the Attack on Christendom

The result of the metamorphosis had been to enable Kierkegaard to stand back and see his work as a whole in a new
perspective against the historical background of the age.
The first thing which he saw was that the indirect method
of communication could not be final, since Christianity

is a Revelation which had to be proclaimed. "What" he
had said remained unchanged, but "how" he said it, the
problem of the method of communication, which had
always been his first concern, underwent a transformation.
The link between the two groups is given in the *Journal*
of 1849 where he points out that the conception of subjectivity expressed in the *Postscript* corresponds with his
idea of communication. "The curious thing is" he writes,
"that there is a 'how' which has this quality, that if *it*
is correctly given, then the 'what' is also given; and that
this is the 'how' of 'faith.' Here, quite certainly, we have
inwardness (subjectivity) at its maximum proving to be
objectivity once again." It is the "how" of faith, which
is to say faith lived, that opens the mind to the objective
truth of Revelation, in the same way that Kierkegaard
says elsewhere that any man who becomes "the individual"
will be brought up against the new level of existence which
is Christianity.

From 1848 until 1855 the question uppermost in his mind
was how he was to communicate his thought in order to
fulfil his mission. He could no longer write under pseudonyms and content himself with being a "poet" as he
had been during his first period. He was still "without
authority" and regarded his task as being limited to "making men aware" of the category of the individual, since
that was where the battle was to be fought. But whereas
the illusion which he had fought against in the past was
the Goetheo-Hegelian world, the second phase is an attack
on Christendom, on the Established Church, itself a form
of culture in which Christianity was hardly more than an
ingredient, a spice. *Training in Christianity* is at many
points a repetition of *what* he had said in *Philosophical
Fragments,* but instead of being an attack on Hegel's deification of the State, it is concerned with the deification of
Established Christendom. The great illusion was that Denmark was "a Christian country;" as a culture, Christendom

obliterated the distinction between worldliness and Christianity, between natural and supernatural. In that atmosphere the very notion of "the witness to the truth" and the martyr was unacceptable since they express the conflict between Christianity and the world. "Every time a witness to the truth makes the truth a heart-felt matter of inwardness (and this is the essential business of the witness), and every time a genius makes the truth inwardly vivid with primitive force—then the established order will be offended in him."

To Kierkegaard's relief *Training in Christianity* caused no scandal. As long as Bishop Mynster was alive he clung to the hope that although he was the personification of the *status quo,* Mynster might be persuaded to acknowledge the error of his ways. But when on Mynster's death in 1854 Martensen, who succeeded him, spoke of him as a "witness to the truth," Kierkegaard determined to speak his mind. Mynster, he maintained, had clung to the *status quo,* terrified that if it were touched the spiritual emptiness of Christendom would be revealed, yet equally afraid to preach a distinctive and exclusive Christianity for fear of scandalising and alienating the "official Christians" who in Kierkegaard's view, were blinded by the illusion.

Kierkegaard waited before launching his attack on the State Church until Martensen had been appointed Bishop of Zealand. His first article appeared in January 1855 and the series of pamphlets called *The Instant* appeared between May and October of that year. His aim in these last pamphlets was to supply a "corrective" and this he did with all the violence at his command. He exaggerated without fear, and certainly forgot that he was exaggerating : it is for the reader to catch the truth as it glints in his pages and to remember what Kierkegaard said of Luther, that a "corrective" made into the "norm" is *eo ipso* confusion. What he said was nothing more than what he had said in *Training in Christianity* and in the *Postscript,* and what he had been saying all his life; that truth begins in "the individual," that thought must not be divorced from existence, and that in faith man begins to exist. Everything, to be sure, is strung a tone higher in order if possible "to make men aware," but even if here and there the tone is harsh and the violence excessive, there is also a note of confidence and authenticity. Kierkegaard did not confuse himself with the witness to the truth. "Grateful to Providence I stick to my task which may easily be seen to be infinitely subordinate (to that of the witness), of at least *calling attention* to this category"—the individual. He was confident not of victory against the masses but of having fought in the cause of truth, for the cause of truth was not triumphant—as the Establishment implied —but militant. To be an author had at last become an action and the whole of his life was expressed in the fact that he emerged from his melancholy without falsifying or distorting his gifts and without overstepping the bounds of his personality. He had done everything and risked everything, not forgetting poverty, to reduplicate his thought in existence and by doing so had necessarily come into conflict with the Establishment. Professor Sibbern, who had taught him philosophy, and had followed his career with sympathy up to this time, was unable to conceive how so circumspect and reflective a man, who never acted spontaneously, and who certainly grasped all the consequences of his action, should have ended by causing such a stir that there was a scene at his funeral. Everyone, Kierkegaard had noted in his *Journal*, understood him, and many agreed with him as long as his thought was only expressed in words. As soon as he acted he caused a "scandal." Action, to use his favourite metaphor, made the end of the thread fast, it was the knot that held in existence.

In the middle of October, shortly before the last number of his pamphlets was sent to the printer, Kierkegaard

J.   B collapsed in the street. He was taken to the Frederiks Hospital. He knew he was a dying man. He refused to see his brother Peter, who was of Grundtvig's party and had shown him little enough sympathy. Emil Boesen, his oldest friend, who had become a parson, tried to persuade him to receive communion, but Kierkegaard declined to accept it " from the King's official." He was visited by his brother-in-law Hendrik Lund who always looked after his affairs, and his nephews and his favourite niece, Henriette Lund. One and all were struck by the radiance of his spirits. "He preserved a loving sympathy for others," Brøchner afterwards wrote, " even in the smallest matters, preserved gentleness and even humour, a sense of proportion and a clarity of thought, and above all a calm and peaceful faith, which did not desert him even during the severe suffering of his death-bed."

He died on 11th November, 1855, at the age of forty-two.

CHRONOLOGICAL TABLE

(Where the title of a work is given in italics and without comment, the date is that of publication)

1756		S. K.'s father, Michael Pedersen Kierkegaard, born.
1768	June 18	S. K.'s mother, Anne Sørensdatter Lund, born.
1813	May 5	S. K. born in his father's house, 2 (now 27) Nytorv, Copenhagen.
1821		S. K. sent to school, to the Borgerdydskole in Copenhagen.
1823	Jan. 23	Regine Olsen born.
1828	Apr. 20	S. K. confirmed by J. P. Mynster.
1830	Oct. 30	S. K. entered as student at the University of Copenhagen.
1834	July 31	S. K.'s mother dies.
	Dec. 17	S. K.'s first article in *Kjøbenhavns Flyvende Post*.
	Dec. 29	Death of S. K.'s sister Petrea.
1837	May	S. K. meets Regine Olsen at the Rørdams (119).
1837-1838		S. K. teaches Latin in the Borgerdydskole.
1838	Aug. 9	Michael Pedersen Kierkegaard dies at 2 a.m.
	Sept. 7	*From the Papers of one still living,* ' published contrary to his will, by S. K.' A criticism of Hans Andersen's novel.
1840	July 3	S. K. finishes his theological examination.
	July 19–Aug. 6	The Journey to Jutland.
	Sept. 10	S. K. engaged to Regine Olsen.
1841	Jan. 12	S. K. preaches his first sermon in Holmens Kirke.
	Sept. 16	*On the concept of Irony with particular reference to Socrates* (S. K.'s dissertation).
	Oct. 11	S. K. breaks off his engagement to Regine Olsen.
	Oct. 25	S. K. leaves for Berlin.
1842	Mar. 6	S. K. arrives back in Copenhagen.

1843 Feb. 20 *Either-Or* edited by Victor Eremita.

      May 8   S. K. leaves for Berlin.

      May 16   *Two Edifying Discourses*, by S. K.

1843 May 1   Berlin.

      May 8   S. K. returns from Berlin.

      Oct. 16 *Fear and Trembling*, by Johannes de Silentio; *Repetition*, by Constantin Constantius; *Three Edifying Discourses*, by S. K.

      Dec. 6   *Four Edifying Discourses*, by S. K.

1844 Mar. 5   *Two*   „   „   by S. K.

      June 8   *Three* „   „   by S. K.

      June 13 *Philosophical Fragments, or a Fragment of Philosophy*, by Johannes Climacus, published by S. K.

      June 17 *The Concept of Dread*, by Vigilius Haufniensis; *Prefaces* by Nicolaus Notabene.

      Aug. 31 *Four Edifying Discourses*, by S. K.

      Oct. 16 S. K. moves from 230 (now 28) Nørregade to his house on Nytorv.

1845 Apr. 29 *Three Occasional Discourses*, by S. K.

      Apr. 30 *Stages on the Road of Life*, edited by Hilarius Bookbinder.

      May 13–24 Berlin.

      Dec. 30 Manuscript of the *Final Unscientific Postscript to the Philosophical Fragments* sent to the printer.

1846 Feb. 27 *Final Unscientific Postscript*, by Johannes Climacus, published by S. K.

      Mar. 30 *A Literary Review*, by S. K., containing *The Present Age*.

      May 2–16 Berlin.

      Oct. 2   Goldschmidt gives up the editorship of *The Corsair*.

1847 Mar. 13 *Edifying Discourses of Varied Tenor*, by S. K.

      Sept. 29 *The Works of Love*, by S. K.

      Nov. 3   Regine Olsen married to Fritz Schlegel.

      Dec. 1   *The Book on Adler* completed in its third form.

      Dec. 24 S. K. sells 2 Nytorv for Rdl. 22,000 paid to him and his brother.

1848 Jan. 20 Death of Christian VIII.

	Mar. 23	Rising in Holstein.
	Apr. 23	Battle of Schleswig.
	Apr. 26	*Christian Addresses*, by S. K.
	Nov.	*The Point of view for my Work as an Author* ' as good as finished.' It was published by his brother in 1859.
1849	May 14	*The Lilies of the Field and the Birds of the Air;* second edition of *Either-Or*.
	May 19	*Two Minor Ethico-Religious Essays*, by H. H.
	July 30	*Sickness unto Death*, by Anti-Climacus, published by S. K.
	Nov. 13	*The High Priest—The Publican—The Woman who was a Sinner: Three Discourses before Communion on Friday.*
1850	Aug. 7	*On my work as an author; Two Discourses at Communion on Friday.*
	Sept. 10	*For Self-examination.*
	Sept. 27	*Training in Christianity*, by Anti-Climacus, published by S. K.
	Dec. 20	*An Edifying Discourse.*
1851–1852		*Judge for Yourself*, the second part of *For Self-examination*, published by his brother in 1876.
1854	Jan. 30	Death of Bishop Mynster.
	Feb.	The article against Martensen, ' Was Bishop Mynster a witness to the truth?', written.
	Apr. 15	Hans Martensen, Bishop of Zealand in succession to Mynster.
	Dec. 18	The article against Martensen published.
1855	Jan.–May	Articles arising out of the attack on Martensen.
	May–Oct.	Nos. 1–9 of *The Instant*.
	Oct. 2	S. K. taken to the Frederiks Hospital.
	Nov. 11	Death of S. K.

THE GREAT EARTHQUAKE

CHILDHOOD

Halb Kinderspiel,
Halb Gott im Herzen.
                          Goethe

11   [1835]

Then it was that the great earthquake occurred, the terrible revolution which suddenly forced upon me a new and infallible law of interpretation of all the facts. Then I suspected that my father's great age was not a divine blessing but rather a curse; that the outstanding intellectual gifts of our family were only given to us in order that we should rend each other to pieces : then I felt the stillness of death grow around me when I saw my father, an unhappy man who was to outlive us all, a cross on the tomb of all his hopes. There must be a guilt upon the whole family, the punishment of God must be on it; it was to disappear, wiped out by the powerful hand of God, obliterated like an unsuccessful attempt, and only at times did I find a little alleviation in the thought that my father had been allotted the heavy task of calming us with the consolation of religion, of ministering to us so that a better world should be open to us even though we lost everything in this world, even though we were overtaken by the punishment which the Jews always called down upon their enemies : that all recollection of us should be utterly wiped out, that we should no longer be found.

III   YOUTH   [1835-6]

> Begging—that's not for us!
> Youth on the road of life
> Forcefully seizes the prize.
> *Christian Winter*

IV   [1836-7]

Inwardly torn asunder as I was, without any expectation of leading a happy earthly life ("that I should prosper and live long in the land"), without hope of a happy and comfortable future—as it naturally springs from and lies in the historical continuity of family life—what wonder then that in desperate despair I grasped at nought but the intellectual side in man and clung fast to it, so that the thought of my own considerable powers of mind was my only consolation, ideas my one joy, and mankind indifferent to me.

V   25 YEARS OLD   [1838]

>   So we'll live,
> And pray, and sing, and tell old tales, and laugh
> At gilded butterflies, and hear poor rogues
> Talk of court news: and we'll talk with them too
> Who loses and who wins; who's in, who's out;
> And take upon's the mystery of things,
> As if we were God's spies: and we'll wear out
> In a walled prison, packs and sects of great ones,
> That ebb and flow by the moon.
> *King Lear*

VI   [1838]

What I have often suffered from was that all the doubt, trouble, and anguish which my real self wanted to forget in order to achieve a view of life, my reflective self sought equally to impress and preserve, partly as a necessary, partly as an interesting stage, out of fear that I should have falsely ascribed a result to myself.

Thus, for example when I have so arranged my life that it seems to me as though it were my lot to read for the examination *in perpetuum,* and that my life however long it might otherwise be, is not to reach beyond the point at which I myself once freely broke off, just as one sees feeble-minded people who only remember their childhood and forget all their life that lies in between, or forget everything except one particular moment in their lives—that I should thus, at the thought of being a theological student, be all at once reminded of that happy period of possibility (what might be called one's pre-existence) and my pause therein, more or less like a child who has been given alcohol and so prevented from growing must be. When, now, my active self tries to forget it in order to act, my reflective self would like so much to cling to it because it seems interesting, and would abstract itself from the control of my personal consciousness by raising itself to the power of a universal consciousness.

*   *   *   *   *

THE JOURNAL

July 29. As one goes from the inn through Sortebro across the bare fields that run along the coast, about a mile and a quarter to the north one comes to the highest point in the district, to Gilbjerg. It has always been one of my favourite places. And as I stood there one quiet evening as the sea struck up its song with a deep and calm solemnity, whilst my eye met not a single sail on the vast expanse of water, and the sea set bounds to the heavens, and the heavens to the sea; whilst on the other side the busy noise of life subsided and the birds sang their evening prayer—the few that are dear to me came forth from their graves, or rather it seemed to me as though they had not died. I felt so content in their midst, I rested in their embrace, and it was as though I were out of the body, wafted with them into the ether above—and the hoarse screech of the gulls reminded me that I stood alone, and everything vanished before my eyes, and I turned back with a heavy heart to mix in the busy world, yet without forgetting such blessed moments.—I have often stood there and looked out upon my past life and upon the different surroundings which have exercised their power upon me; and the pettiness which is so often the cause of the numerous misunderstandings separating minds which if they properly understood one another would be bound together by indissoluble ties, vanished before my gaze. Seen thus in perspective only the broad and powerful outline showed, and I did not as so frequently happens to me lose myself in the moment, but saw everything as a whole and was strengthened to

understand things differently, to admit how often I had
blundered, and to forgive others.

As I stood there, without that feeling of dejection and
despondency which makes me look upon myself as the
enclitic of the men who usually surround me, and without
that feeling of pride which makes me into the formative
principle of a small circle—as I stood there alone and forsaken, and the power of the sea and the battle of the
elements reminded me of my own nothingness, and on the
other hand the sure flight of the birds recalled the words
spoken by Christ: Not a sparrow shall fall to the ground
without your Father: then all at once I felt how great and
how small I was; then did those two mighty forces, pride
and humility, happily unite in friendship. Lucky is the
man to whom *that* is possible at every moment of his life;
in whose breast those two factors have not only come to
an agreement but have joined hands and been wedded—a
marriage which is neither a *mariage de convenance* nor a
mésalliance but a tranquil marriage of love held in the
most secret chamber of man's heart, in the holy of holies,
where there are few witnesses but where everything proceeds before the eyes of Him who alone witnessed the marriage in the Garden of Eden—a marriage, which will not
remain unfruitful but bears blessed fruits, as may be seen
in the world by an experienced observer; for like crypto-
gams among plants, they withdraw from the notice
of the masses and only the solitary inquirer discovers them
and rejoices over his find. His life will flow on peacefully
and quietly and he will neither drain the intoxicating cup
of pride nor the bitter chalice of despair. He has found
what the great philosopher—who by his calculations was
able to destroy the enemy's engines of war—desired, but
did not find: that archimedean point from which he could
lift the whole world, the point which for that very reason
must lie outside the world, outside the limitations of time
and space.

Gilleleie, August 1, 1835

What I really lack is to be clear in my mind *what I am to do,* not what I am to know, except in so far as a certain understanding must precede every action. The thing is to understand myself, to see what God really wishes *me* to do; the thing is to find a truth which is true *for me,* to find *the idea for which I can live and die.* What would be the use of discovering so-called objective truth, of working through all the systems of philosophy and of being able, if required, to review them all and show up the inconsistencies within each system;—what good would it do me to be able to develop a theory of the state and combine all the details into a single whole, and so construct a world in which I did not live, but only held up to the view of others;—what good would it do me to be able to explain the meaning of Christianity if it had *no* deeper significance *for me and for my life;*—what good would it do me if truth stood before me, cold and naked, not caring whether I recognised her or not, and producing in me a shudder of fear rather than a trusting devotion? I certainly do not deny that I still recognise an *imperative of understanding* and that through it one can work upon men, *but it must be taken up into my life,* and *that is* what I now recognise as the most important thing. That is what my soul longs after, as the African desert thirsts for water. That is what I lack, and that is why I am left standing like a man who has rented a house and gathered all the furniture and household things together, but has not yet found the beloved with whom to share the joys and sorrows of his life. But in order to find that idea, or better still, in order to find myself, it is no use throwing myself still further into life. And that is just what I have done hitherto. That is why I thought it would be a good thing to throw myself into the study of the law so as to develop my sharpness of mind in the complications of life. Here was a great mass of detail in which I could lose myself; here perhaps I might be able to work out a complete whole from given facts, an organum of theft, following up its darker side (and here a certain spirit of association is also extremely remarkable). I therefore wanted to be a barrister so that by putting myself in another man's rôle I could, as it were, find a substitute for my own life, and find distraction in outward change. That was what I lacked in order to be able *to lead a complete human life* and not merely one of the understanding,* so that I should not, in consequence, base the development of my thought upon —well, upon something that is called objective—something that is in any case not my own, but upon something which grows together with the deepest roots of my life, through which I am so to speak, grafted upon the divine, hold fast to it, even though the whole world fell apart. *That is what I lack and that is what I am striving after.*

It is the divine side of man, his inward action which means everything, not a mass of information; for that will certainly follow and then all that knowledge will not be a chance assemblage, or a succession of details, without system and without a focusing point. I too have certainly looked for such a centre. I have looked in vain for an anchorage in the boundless sea of pleasure and in the depth of understanding; I have felt the almost irresistible power with which one pleasure reaches out its hand to the next; I have felt the sort of meretricious ecstasy that it is capable of producing, but also the *ennui* and the distracted state

*For otherwise how near man is to madness, in spite of all his knowledge. What is truth but to live for an idea? Ultimately everything must rest upon a postulate; but the moment it is no longer outside him, and he lives in it, then and only then does it cease to be a postulate for him.

of mind that succeeds it. I have tasted the fruit of the tree of knowledge, and often delighted in its taste. But the pleasure did not outlast the moment of understanding and left no profound mark upon me. It seems as though I had not drunk from the cup of wisdom, but had fallen into it. I have searched with resignation for the principle of my life, by trying to believe that since all things proceeded according to unalterable laws things could not be otherwise and by dulling my ambition and the antennæ of my vanity. And because I could not adapt everything to my own mind I withdrew, conscious of my own ability, rather like a worn out parson resigning with a pension. What did I find? Not my Self, which was what I was looking for (thinking of my soul, if I may so express it, as shut in a box with a spring-lock which external circumstances, by pressing upon the lock, were to open).—And so the first thing to be decided, was the seeking and finding of the Kingdom of Heaven. But just as a heavenly body, if we imagine it in the process of constituting itself, would not first of all determine how great its surface was to be and about which other body it was to move, but would first of all allow the centripetal and centrifugal forces to harmonise its existence, and then let the rest take its course— similarly, it is useless for a man to determine first of all the outside and afterwards fundamentals. One must know oneself before knowing anything else (γνωθι σεαυτον). It is only after a man has thus understood himself inwardly, and has thus seen his way, that life acquires peace and significance; only then is he rid of that tiresome, illomened fellow-traveller, the irony of life, which shows itself in the sphere of understanding, bidding true understanding begin with ignorance (Socrates) like God creating the world out of nothing.

Although I am still far from having reached so complete an understanding of myself, I have, with profound respect for its significance, tried to preserve my individu-

ality—worshipped the unknown God. Warned by a prema-
ture apprehension I have tried to avoid coming in too close
contact with those phenomena whose power of attraction
would perhaps exercise too great an influence upon me.
I have tried to master them, studied them individually and
examined their importance in men's lives, but at the same
time guarded against going, like the moth, too near the
flame. I have had but little to win or lose from the ordinary
run of men. Partly because everything which occupies
them—so-called practical life—only interests me slightly;
partly because the coldness and lack of interest with which
they treat the more profound and spiritual emotions in man
have estranged me still further. With few exceptions my
associates have not exerted any particular influence upon
me. A life which is not clear about itself inevitably dis-
plays an uneven surface; they have stopped short at particular facts and their apparent disharmony; they were
not sufficiently interested in me to try to resolve them in
a higher agreement or to perceive the inner necessity of
it. Their opinion of me was therefore always one-sided,
and I have, as a result, alternately laid too much, or too
little weight upon their pronouncements. I have now withdrawn from their influence and their possibly misleading
effect upon the compass of my life. And so I stand once
again at the point where I must begin my life in a different
way. I shall now try to fix a calm gaze upon myself and
begin to act in earnest; for only thus shall I be able, like
the child calling itself " I " with its first conscious action,
to call myself " I " in any deeper sense.

But for that patience is necessary, and one cannot reap
immediately where one has sown. I shall bear in mind the
method of the philosopher who bade his disciples keep
silence for three years after which time all would come
right. One does not begin feasting at dawn but at sunset.
And so too in the spiritual world it is first of all necessary
to work for some time before the light bursts through and

the sun shines forth in all its glory. For although it is said that God allows the sun to shine upon the good and the wicked, and sends down rain upon the just and the unjust, it is not so in the spiritual world. And so the die is cast—I cross the Rubicon! This road certainly leads me *to strife*; but I shall not give up. I will not grieve over the past —for why grieve? I will work on with energy and not waste time grieving, like the man caught in the quicksands who began by calculating how far down he had already sunk, forgetting that all the while he was sinking still deeper. I will hurry along the path I have discovered, greeting those whom I meet on my way, not looking back as did Lot's wife, but remembering that it is a hill up which we have to struggle.[1]

Sept. "What!" he said to himself, "the man who penetrates his brother's most secret thoughts, does not that fatal gift bring him to the frightful condition which came upon the Wandering Jew, who wandered through the gay tumult of the world without joy, without hope, without pain, in dull indifference, which is the *caput mortuum* of despair, as though through a dreary and disconsolate desert?"[2]

Oct. 9. The same thing happens to Christianity, or to becoming a Christian, as to all radical cures, one puts it off as long as possible.

Oct. 13. There is a curious connection between Protestantism and the modern political point of view: it is a struggle for the same thing, the sovereignty of the people, which is why it is also interesting to note that the real royalists, in so far as they have not got one view on one subject and an essentially different one on another subject,

[1]S.K. returned to Copenhagen sometime before August 14.
[2]E. T. A. Hoffmann: *Meister Floh.*

which in an individual should both be based upon the same principle—lean towards Catholicism.

The real beauty of Lemming's playing (he is a Danish musician; I heard him at the University Club) was that he *stroked* the guitar. The vibrations became almost visible, just as when the moon shines on the sea the waves become almost audible.

1836

Jan. It is a very curious thing about superstition. One would expect that the man who had once seen that his morbid dreams were not fulfilled would abandon them for the future; but on the contrary they grow even stronger just as the love of gambling increases in a man who has once lost in the lottery.

Feb. People understand me so little that they do not even understand when I complain of being misunderstood.

March. The difference between a man who faces death for the sake of an idea and an imitator who goes in search of martyrdom is that whilst the former expresses his idea most fully in death it is the strange feeling of bitterness which comes from failure that the latter really enjoys; the former rejoices in his victory, the latter in his suffering.

The three great ideas (Don Juan, Faust and the Wandering Jew) represent, as it were, life outside religion in its three-fold direction, and only when those ideas are merged in the individual and become mediate, only then do morals and religion appear; that is my view of those three ideas in relation to my dogmatic standpoint.

A man walked along contemplating suicide; at that very moment a slate fell and killed him, and he died with the words : God be praised.

I have just returned from a party of which I was the life and soul; wit poured from my lips, everyone laughed and admired me—but I went away—and the dash should

be as long as the earth's orbit ————————————————
——————————————————and wanted to shoot myself.

'Sdeath, I can abstract from everything but *not from myself*. I cannot even forget myself when I am asleep.

Is it true that I should not laugh at my own jokes?

The omnipresence of wit.

Exactly how can one explain the inclination, which manifests itself in people who are in some sense or other fallen, to throw themselves into life instead of shunning it. J. Jørgensen for example, says that when he is drunk he feels an almost irresistible urge to be with people, to go wherever there are crowds.

Aug. 25. When Goethe had accomplished the transition involved by a return to classical antiquity, why did the age not follow him, why did it not follow Hegel, why does it have no effect? Because they both limited it to an æsthetic and speculative development, but the political development had also to go through its romantic movement and that is why all the romantics of the newer school are—politicians.

Oct. 8. The extraordinary way in which something long forgotten suddenly bursts into consciousness is really remarkable; for example, the recollection of something wrong of which one was hardly conscious at the moment of acting—Lightning announcing a violent storm. They do not come forward, they literally burst forth with tremendous power, demanding to be heard. And that, generally speaking, is how we are to understand the passage in the

Gospels : that on the day of judgment man will be held responsible for every idle word he has spoken.

What Schleiermacher calls " Religion " and the Hegelians " Faith " is at the bottom nothing but the first immediate condition for everything—the vital fluidum—the spiritual atmosphere we breathe in—and which cannot therefore with justice be designated by those words.

The old man whom I met in the theatre who had been going to *Don Juan* for thirty years (Tradition).

Jan. 17. There are many people who reach their conclusions about life like schoolboys; they cheat their master by copying the answer out of a book without having worked out the sum for themselves.

At every step philosophy sloughs a skin into which creep its worthless hangers-on.

If something is really to become depressing the foreboding that there is something wrong must first of all develop in the midst of the most favourable circumstances, one does not become conscious oneself of anything so wrong; but it must lie in the family history, then the all-consuming power of original sin shows itself, which can grow into despair and have far more terrible effects than the fact whereby the truth of the foreboding is confirmed. That is why Hamlet is so tragic. That is why Robert le Diable, driven by a terrifying foreboding, asks why it should be that he does so much evil.—The blessing is changed into a curse—it is a highly poetic move to make the girl, who alone is in a position to know what is behind Robert le Diable's assumed madness (his penance)—dumb.

Feb. A certain foreboding seems to precede everything which is to happen, but just as it can act as a deterrent, so too it can act as a temptation, awakening in man the thought that he is, as it were, predestined; he sees himself led on to something as though by consequences which he cannot influence at all. One must therefore be very careful with children, never believe the worst, or, as the result of an ill-timed suspicion, or a chance remark (the infernal-machine which sets fire to the tinder which is in every soul)

induce that state of anxiety in which innocent but weak
souls are easily tempted to believe themselves guilty, to
despair, and so take the first step towards the goal fore-
shadowed by the alarming foreboding—a remark which
gives the kingdom of evil, with its stupefying, snake-like
eye, an opportunity of reducing them to a state of spiritual
impotence. Woe to him by whom the scandal cometh
applies in this case too.

It made a terrible impression upon me the first time I
heard that the *indulgences* contained the statement that
they remit *all* sins : *" etiam si matrem virginem violasset."*
—I still remember the impression it made upon me when
some years ago, filled with a youthful and romantic enthusiasm for a *master-thief*, I went so far as to say that it
was only the misuse of powers, and that such a man might
still be converted, and father said very solemnly : " there
are offences which one can only fight against with God's
continual help." I hurried down to my room and looked
at myself in the glass (cf. F. Schlegel's Works, Vol. VII,
p. 15)—or when father said, as he often did, that it would
be a good thing to have " a venerable confessor to whom
one could open one's heart."

When one first begins to reflect upon Christianity it must
certainly have been an occasion of scandal to one before
one enters upon it, one must even have wished that it had
never come into the world or at least that the question
had never arisen in one's consciousness. That is why one
is sickened by all the chatter of fussy go-betweens about
Christ being the greatest hero, etc. etc., the humorous interpretation is far better.

May 8. Oh God, how easily one forgets such resolutions !
Once again I turned back to the world for some time, de-
posed in my inmost self, to dominate there. Oh, what does

it help a man to win the whole world and injure his soul.
To-day again (May 8) I tried to forget myself, not in the
noise and bustle of the world, that substitute is no help,
but by going to the Rørdams[1] and talking with Bolette and
by trying (if possible) to get my demoniacal wit to remain
at home, the angel which, as I deserve, stands with a sword
of fire between me and every innocent girl—I thank thee,
O Lord, that when thou overtookest me thou didst not let
me go mad at once,—I have never been so afraid of it,
and I thank thee for having once more inclined thine ear
towards me.

Again the same scene to-day—nevertheless I got out to
the Rørdams—merciful God, why should that inclination
awaken just now—Oh, how I feel that I am alone[2]—Oh,
cursed be that arrogant satisfaction in standing alone—
all will despise me now—but thou, O my God, take not
thy hand from me now—let me live and better myself.

July 9. I stand like a lonely pine tree egoistically shut
off, pointing to the skies and casting no shadow, and only
the turtle-dove builds its nest in my branches.

Sunday, July 9, in the gardens of Frederiksberg after a
visit to the Rørdams.

I am a Janus bifrons; I laugh with one face, I weep
with the other.

July 13. I have often wondered how it could be that I

---

[1]The family in which Kierkegaard first met Regine Olsen.

[2]Regine Olsen believed that this entry was the result of their first
meeting and the impression which they made upon one another. " He
immediately made a very strong impression upon her, which, however,
she concealed. She still remembered that he talked continuously, that
the words poured forth and that his conversation was captivating in the
highest degree, but after the passage of many years she could not
remember the content." Raphael Meyer: *Kierkegaardske Papirer,
Forlovelsen*, 1904.

had such a strong disinclination to note down individual remarks; but the more I get to know individual great men in whose writings one does not sense the kaleidoscopic shaking up of the same set of ideas (perhaps the example of Jean Paul has made me unnecessarily anxious on that score) and the more I recollect that a writer as spontaneous as Hoffman kept notes and that Lichtenberg recommends it, the more interested I am in discovering why something in itself entirely blameless should become unpleasant and almost revolting to me. The reason evidently was that in each case I had before me the possibility of publication, which would probably have necessitated a fuller treatment and not wishing to be bothered with it, and weakened by that abstract possibility (a sort of literary hiccoughs and nausea) the aroma of the conceits and moods evaporated. I believe on the contrary that it is a good thing, by making frequent notes, to let my thoughts appear with the umbilical cord of their first mood, and to forget as far as possible the use to which they might be put, since in any case I shall never use them by looking up my note-books; by thus expectorating myself as though in a letter to a close friend, I gain a double advantage, the possibility of knowing myself later on, and a certain fluency in writing, the same freedom of articulation in the written word which I have to some extent in the spoken, the knowledge of a number of lesser traits which up till now I have passed by with a hasty glance, and finally one other advantage if, as Hamann says, it is true that some ideas occur only once in a lifetime. Practice of this kind, behind the scenes, is essential to all those who are not so gifted that their development is, in a sense, public.

Thanks, Lichtenberg, thanks! for having said that there is nothing so feeble as the conversation of learned literary men who have never thought for themselves but know a thousand historical-literary facts.* " It is almost like a reading from a cookery book when one is hungry." Oh thanks for that voice in the wilderness, for that comfort, which sets the imagination working like the cry of a wild bird in the silence of the night; I imagine it was written after a protracted session with one of those learned jades, which perhaps robbed him of some happy moments. Unfortunately in my copy I found a mark which has disturbed me; for I already see some journalist or other going carefully through the work in order to fill the papers with aphorisms, with or without Lichtenberg's name; and that has, unfortunately, robbed me of some of the surprise.

Oct 7. How dreadful it is when everything historical vanishes before a diseased probing of one's own miserable history! Who is to show us the middle course between being devoured by one's own reflections, as though one were the only man who ever had existed or ever would exist, and —seeking a worthless consolation in the *commune naufragium* of mankind? That is really what the doctrine of an *ecclesia* should do.

*Like Leporello they keep a list, but the point is what they lack; while Don Juan seduces girls and enjoys himself —Leporello notes down the time, the place and a description of the girl.

1838

Nulla dies sine linea

Jan. 1. Irony is an abnormal growth; like the abnormally enlarged liver of the Strassburg goose it ends by killing the individual.

If I am a weed in literature—well, then at least I am what is called "Proud Henry."

April. Once again a long time has gone by in which I have not been able to concentrate upon the slightest thing —I will now try to get started again.
Poul Møller is dead.[1]

April 1. This morning in the cool fresh air I saw half a dozen wild geese fly away, first of all they rose directly above me, then further and further away till at last they divided into two flocks and formed two arches like eyebrows over my eyes which now looked into the land of poetry.

April 22. If Christ is to come and take up his abode in me, it must happen according to the title of to-day's Gospel in the Almanac : Christ came in through locked doors.

The politicians accuse me of always contradicting; but therein they are my masters; for they always have one person more whom they contradict—namely, themselves.

The paradox is really the *pathos* of intellectual life, and

[1]Poul Martin Møller died on March 13. With this entry the *Journal* begins again.

just as only great souls are exposed to passions it is only the great thinker who is exposed to what I call paradoxes, which are nothing else than grandiose thoughts in embryo.

May 19. *Half-past ten in the morning.* There is an indescribable joy which enkindles us as inexplicably as the apostle's outburst comes gratuitously : " Rejoice I say unto you, and again I say unto you rejoice."—Not a joy over this or that but the soul's mighty song " with tongue and mouth, from the bottom of the heart :" " I rejoice through my joy, in, at, with, over, by, and with my joy "—a heavenly refrain, as it were, suddenly breaks off our other song; a joy which cools and refreshes us like a breath of wind, a wave of air, from the trade wind which blows from the plains of Mamre to the everlasting habitations.

July 6. *Idées fixes* are like cramp in the foot—the best cure is to stamp on it.

July 7. God creates out of *nothing,* wonderful, you say : yes, to be sure, but he does what is still more wonderful : he makes saints out of sinners.

July 9. How I thank you, Father in Heaven, that you have preserved my earthly father here upon earth for a time such as this when I so greatly need him, a father who, as I hope, will with your help have greater joy in being my father a second time than he had the first time in being so.

July 9. I mean to labour to achieve a far more inward relation to Christianity; hitherto I have fought for its truth while in a sense standing outside it. In a purely outward sense I have carried Christ's cross, like Simon of Cyrene.

Aug. 11. My father died on Wednesday (the 9th) at

2 a.m. I had so very much wished that he might live a few years longer, and I look upon his death as the last sacrifice which he made to his love for me; for he did not die from me but *died for me* in order that if possible I might still turn into something. Of all that I have inherited from him, the recollection of him, his transfigured portrait, not transfigured by the poetry of my imagination (for it did not require that) but explained by many an individual trait which I can now take account of—is dearest to me, and I will be careful to preserve it safely hidden from the world; for I feel clearly that at this moment there is only one (E. Boesen) to whom I can in truth talk about him. He was a " faithful friend."

Dec. 31. The Lord cometh, even though we have to wait for him, he cometh even though we grow as old as Anne, as grey as Simeon (that second Noah), but we must wait for him in *his* house.

1839

ad se ipsum

Jan. 1. The same miracle which astonished all those present at the marriage feast in Cana repeats itself in the life of every Christian: Thou hast served the bad wine first and last of all the good, people will agree in saying, particularly those who have felt how the world serves the good first and afterwards the bad.

Jan. 3. In truth I feel at this moment the terrible truth of the words Psalm 82, 6: I have said, Ye are gods; and all of you are children of the most High. But ye shall die like men, and fall like one of the princes.

Jan. 6. Father in Heaven! When the thought of thee wakes in our hearts let it not awaken like a frightened bird that flies about in dismay, but like a child waking from its sleep with a heavenly smile.

Jan. 7. What is so confusing about us is that we are at once the pharisee and the publican.

Feb. 2. Thou sovereign of my heart ("Regina") treasured in the deepest fastness of my breast, in the fullness of my thought, there, where it is equally far to heaven and to hell,—unknown divinity! Oh, can I really believe the poet's tales, that when one first sees the object of one's love, one imagines one has seen her long ago, that all love like all knowledge is remembrance, that love too has its prophecies in the individual, its types, its myths, its Old Testament. Everywhere, in the face of every girl I see

61

traces of your beauty, but it seems to me that I should
have to possess the beauty of all of them in order to draw
out a beauty equal to yours; that I should have to circum-
navigate the world in order to find the place I lack and
which the deepest mystery of my whole being points towards—and at the next moment you are so near to me,
so present, filling my spirit so powerfully that I am transfigured for myself, and feel that it is good to be here.

Thou blind god of love! Wilt thou reveal to me what
thou seest in secret? Shall I find what I am seeking, here
in this world, shall I experience the conclusion of all my
life's eccentric premises, shall I fold you in my arms—or :

are the orders " FURTHER "?

Hast thou gone before me, thou my *yearning*, dost thou
beckon to me, transformed, from another world? Oh, I
will cast everything from me in order to be light enough
to follow thee.

May 12. I can say of my sorrow what the Englishman
says of his house : my sorrow is my castle.

May 13. I can only presume that it is God's will that I
should read for my exam and that it is more pleasing to
him that I should do so than by burying myself in some
research or other, I should reach a clearer understanding
of something or other; for obedience is dearer to him than
the fat of rams.

May 14. God in heaven, let me really feel my nothingness, not in order to despair over it, but in order to feel the
more powerfully the greatness of thy goodness.

(That wish is not, as the scoffer in me would say, an
epicureanism, as when the *gourmand* starves so that the
food will taste all the better.)

May 21. At the present time my existence is like that of a piece on the chess board, of which the opponent says : that piece cannot move—like a deserted spectator, for my time is not yet come.

July 20. What in certain cases we call " spleen," the mystics know under the name *tristitia* and the Middle Ages under the name *acedia* (ακηδια, dullness). *Gregor moralia in Job* xiii, p. 435 : *virum solitarium ubique comitatur acedia . . . est animi remissio, mentis enervatio, neglectus religiosae exercitationis, odium professionis, laudatrix rerum secularium.* That Gregory should pick out the virum *solitarium* shows a wide experience, for it is a sickness to which the isolated man at his highest degree is exposed to and the sickness is most correctly described and the *odium professionis* is rightly emphasised, and if we take that symptom in a slightly more general sense (not about the confession of sins in church, which would also oblige us to take *solitarius* to mean an indifferent member of the church) as an unburdening of oneself, experience would not leave us in the lurch were we to ask for examples. And it shows a deep knowledge of human nature that the old moralists should have included " *tristitia* " among the *septem vitia principalis.* That is what my father called : *a silent despair.*

And now for a year's time, for a mile's distance in time, I will dive below ground like the Guadalquivir;—but I shall come up again !

July 21. Now that I have read his latest handiwork with its political notions I understand why Herz was so anxious to talk with me.[1] Only it is a pity that he has left

[1] Herz's novel *Moods and Conditions* was published in Copenhagen in 1839. The Translator, one of the principal characters, is a description of S. K. as a young man.

out The Translator's satirical ideas which he certainly thinks he can do without spoiling the general lines; but I think that they were the best things in it, and ought certainly not to be left out, if only on account of the dramatic interest of The Translator's character, but there are presumably good reasons for doing so; Herz is not the man for that.

Aug. 8. If only I could finish my examination soon so that I could once again be a *quodlibetarius.*

I am always accused of using long parentheses. Reading for my examination is the longest parenthesis I have known.

The Journey to Jutland

Kallundborg, July 19. On board the ferry. It is terrible how boring conversations in general are when one has to be with people for long; the same remark was repeated again and again, just as toothless old folk turn their food over and over in their mouths, till in the end one had to spit it out. There were four parsons on board, and although the crossing lasted for eight to nine hours (an eternity to me), the experienced travellers found it unusually short, which gave each of the parsons in turn an opportunity of remarking, first of all that no skipper liked to have a parson on board, because it brought contrary winds and that the truth of the remark was now disproved, and then at the end of the crossing in full chorus, to establish it as a principle that the saying about contrary winds was un-true. It was in vain that I spread every inch of hearing-canvas to catch a breath of wind; there was a dead calm; from the four quarters one only heard that no skipper wanted parsons on board (which goes to show what a doubtful blessing the freedom of the parish is, for although there was absolute freedom of parishes on board the smack, and I could have listened to whichever parson I liked, I was no better off). Since each of the parsons seemed equally interested and justified in appropriating that story, naturally no one of them would grant another a *privilegium exclusivum.*—I had hoped to be sea-sick, or at least that all the other passengers would be sea-sick.

I feel so dull and so completely without joy, my soul is so empty and void that I cannot even conceive what could satisfy it—oh, not even the blessedness of heaven.

To thee, O God, we turn for peace . . . but grant us too the blessed assurance that nothing shall deprive us of that peace, neither *ourselves,* nor our foolish, earthly desires, nor my wild longings, nor the anxious cravings of my heart.

The terrible thing about the absolute spiritual incapacity from which I am suffering at the present time is that it is coupled with a consuming desire, with a spiritual passion, —and yet so formless that I do not even know what I long for.

I sit here quite alone (I have often been just as much alone but I have never felt so conscious of it) counting the hours until I see Saeding. I can never remember any change in my father and I shall now see the places where as a poor child he watched the flocks and for which, as a result of his descriptions, I have felt such home-sickness. What if I were to fall ill and be buried in the churchyard of Saeding! Extraordinary thought. His last wish is ful-filled[1]—is that to be the whole meaning of my earthly life? Great heavens! The task cannot be so small when compared to all that I owe him. I learnt from him the meaning of fatherly love and so was given some idea of divine fatherly love, the one unshakable thing in life, the true archimedean point.

To stand outside the door of this little place[2] in the late evening light, in the aroma which hay always gives out; the sheep coming home make the foreground; dark skies broken by a few violent patches of light, such as are always seen before a wind—in the background rises the moor— if only I could remember the impression of this evening clearly.

[1] S. K. had taken his degree.
[2] S.K.'s aunt's house in Saeding.

Just as people say : *nulla dies sine linea,* so I can say of this journey : *Nulla dies sine lacryma.*

The heaths of Jutland must of all places be suited to develop the spirit powerfully; here everything lies naked and uncovered before God, and there is no room for the many distractions, the many little crevices where consciousness can hide and where seriousness has such difficulty in running down one's scattered thoughts. Here consciousness must firmly and scrupulously close itself around itself. And on the heaths one may say with truth : " Whither shall I flee from thy presence?"

It seems as though I were to experience contrasts good and proper. After having stayed with my poor aunt for three days, almost like Ulysses's stable-companion with Circe, the very first place I come to is so stuffed with Counts and Barons as to be frightening. I spent the night in Them and the morning and afternoon with Count Ahlefeldt, who invited me to Langeland. The only friend I found to-day was Rosenørn my old and distinguished friend.

On the way to Aarhuus I saw a very funny sight : two cows harnessed together cantered past us, the one jogging gaily along and swinging its tail with a fine dash, the other was more prosaic and depressed at having to take part in such emotions.—Are not most marriages like that?

End of Journey

It requires moral courage to grieve; it requires religious courage to rejoice.

Nov. 15. There is a world of difference between the proud courage which dares to fear the worst and the humble courage which dares to hope for the best.

1841

My Lord God, give me once more the courage to hope; merciful God let me hope once again, fructify my barren and infertile mind.

My doubt is terrible.—Nothing can withstand it—it is a cursed hunger and I can swallow up every argument, every consolation and sedative—I rush at 10,000 miles a second through every obstacle.

It is a positive starting point for philosophy when Aristotle says that philosophy begins with wonder, not as in our day with doubt. Moreover the world will learn that the thing is not to begin with the negative, and the reason why it has succeeded up to the present is that it has never really given itself over to the negative, and so has never seriously done what it said. Its doubt is mere child's play.

For the rights of understanding to be valid one must venture out into life, out on the sea and lift up one's voice, even though God hears it not, and not stand on the shore and watch others fighting and struggling—only then does understanding acquire its *official sanction,* for to stand on one leg and prove God's existence is a very different thing from going on one's knees and thanking him.

My relation to "her"[1]
August 24, 1849. Infandum me jubes, Regina, renovare dolorem

Regine Olsen—I saw her first at the Rørdams. I really saw her there before, at a time when I did not know her family. (In a certain sense I feel a responsibility towards Bollette Rørdam. Earlier on she made a certain impression upon me and I perhaps the same impression upon her; but in all innocence, purely intellectual.)

Even before my father died I had decided upon her. He died (Aug. 9, 1838). I read for my examination. During the whole of that time I let her being penetrate mine.

In the summer of 1840 I took my theological examination.

Without further ceremony I thereupon called at their house. I went to Jutland and even at that time I was perhaps fishing for her, e.g. by lending them books in my absence and by suggesting that they should read certain passages.

In August I returned. The period from August 9 till the beginning of September I used in the strict sense to approach her.

On September 8 I left my house with the firm purpose of deciding the matter. We met each other in the street outside their house. She said there was nobody at home. I was foolhardy enough to look upon that as an invitation, just the opportunity I wanted. I went in with her. We stood alone in the living room. She was a little uneasy. I asked her to play me something as she usually did. She did so; but that did not help me. Then suddenly I took the

---

[1]This account of his engagement was sent to Regine Olsen on S. K.'s death with all the papers relating to their engagement. They were edited under her supervision, but not published until after her death, by Raphael Meyer in 1904 under the title *Kierkegaardske Papirer: Forlovelsen*.

music away and closed it, not without a certain violence, threw it down on the piano and said : " Oh, what do I care about music now! It is you I am searching for, it is you whom I have sought after for two years." She was silent. I did nothing else to make an impression upon her; I even warned her against myself, against my melancholy. When, however, she spoke about Schlegel I said : " Let that relationship be a parenthesis; after all the priority is mine." (N.B. It was only on the 10th that she spoke of Schlegel; on the 8th she did not say a word.)

She remained quite silent. At last I left, for I was anxious lest someone should come and find both of us, and she so disturbed. I went immediately to Etatsraad Olsen. I know that I was terribly concerned that I had made too great an impression upon her. I also feared that my visit might lead to a misunderstanding and even harm her reputation.

Her father said neither yes nor no, but he was willing enough as I could see. I asked for a meeting : it was granted to me for the afternoon of the 10th. I did not say a single word to persuade her. She said, Yes.

I immediately assumed a relation to the whole family, and turned all my virtuosity upon her father whom, moreover, I have always loved.

But inwardly; the next day I saw that I had made a false step. A penitent such as I was, my *vita ante acta,* my melancholy, that was enough.

I suffered unspeakably at that time.

She seemed to notice nothing. On the contrary her spirits were so high that once she said she had accepted me out of pity. In short, I have never known such high spirits.

In one sense that was the danger. If she does not take it more to heart, I thought, than her own words betray : " if she thought I only came from force of habit she would

break off the engagement at once "; if she does not take
it more to heart, then I am saved. I pulled myself together again. In another sense I must admit my weakness,
that for a moment she vexed me.

Then I set my whole strength to work—she really gave
way and precisely the opposite happened, she gave herself
unreservedly to me, she worshipped me. To a certain extent I myself bear the guilt of that. While I perceived
the difficulty of the position only too clearly, and recognised
that I must use the maximum of strength in order if possible to burst through my melancholy, I had said to
her: " Surrender to me; your pride makes everything
easier for me." A perfectly true word; honest towards her,
melancholy and treacherous towards myself.*

And now of course my melancholy woke once more. Her
devotion once again put the whole " responsibility " upon
me on a tremendous scale, whereas her pride had almost
made me free from " responsibility." My opinion is, and
my thought was, that it was God's punishment upon me.

I cannot decide clearly what purely emotional impression she made upon me. One thing is certain : that she
gave herself to me, almost worshipping me, asking me to
love her, which moved me to such an extent that I was
willing to risk all for her. How much I loved her is shown
by the fact that I always tried to hide from myself how
much she had moved me, which however really has no
relation to the passions. If I had not been a penitent, had
not had my *vita ante acta,* had not been melancholy, my

---

*To some extent she suspected my condition, for she
often answered : " You are never happy; and so it is all
one to you whether I remain with you or not." She also
once said to me : that she would never ask me about anything if only she might remain with me.

union with her would have made me happier than I had
ever dreamed of being. But in so far as I was what, alas,
I was, I had to say that I could be happier in my unhappiness without her than with her; she had moved me
and I would have liked, more than liked, to have done
everything for her.

But there was a divine protest, that is how I understood
it. The wedding. I had to hide such a tremendous amount
from her, had to base the whole thing upon something
untrue.

I wrote to her and sent her back the ring. The letter
is to be found word for word in the "psychological experiment."[1] With all my strength I allowed that to become
purely historical; for I spoke to no one of it, not to a single
man; I who am more silent than the grave. Should the
book come into her hands I wanted her to be reminded of
it.

What did she do? In her womanly despair she overstepped the boundary. She evidently knew that I was
melancholy; she intended that anxiety should drive me to
extremes. The reverse happened. She certainly brought me
to the point at which anxiety drove me to extremes; but
then with gigantic strength I constrained my whole nature
so as to repel her. There was only one thing to do and
that was to repel her with all my powers.

During those two months of deceit I observed a careful
caution in what I said directly to her from time to time:
Give in, let me go; you cannot bear it. Thereupon she
answered passionately that she would bear anything rather
than let me go.

I also suggested giving the appearance that it was she
who broke off the engagement, so that she might be spared
all offence. That she would not have. She answered: if
she could bear the other she could bear this too. And not
unsocratically she said: In her presence no one would let

[1] A part of *The Stages* by Frater Taciturnitus.

anything be noticed and what people said in her absence remained a matter of indifference.

It was a time of terrible suffering : to have to be so cruel and at the same time to love as I did. She fought like a tigress. If I had not believed that God had lodged a veto she would have been victorious.

And so about two months later it broke. She grew desperate. For the first time in my life I scolded. It was the only thing to do.

When I left her I went immediately to the Theatre because I wanted to meet Emil Boesen. (That gave rise to what was then said in Copenhagen, that I had looked at my watch and said to the family that if they had anything more in their minds would they please hurry up as I had to go to the theatre.) The act was over. As I left the stalls Etatsraad Olsen came up to me and said "May I speak to you?" We went together to his house. "It will be her death, she is in absolute despair." I said "I shall calm her down; but everything is settled." He said, "I am a proud man and I find it difficult to say, but I beg you, do not break with her." He was indeed a noble-hearted man; I was deeply moved. But I did not let myself be persuaded. I remained with the family to dinner. I spoke to her as I left. The following morning I received a letter from him saying she had not slept all night, and asking me to go and see her. I went and tried to persuade her. She asked me : "Are you never going to marry?" I answered, "Yes, perhaps in ten years time when I have sown my wild oats; then I shall need some young blood to rejuvenate me." That was a necessary cruelty. Then she said, "Forgive me for the pain I have caused you." I answered : "It is for me to ask forgiveness." She said : "Promise to think of me." I did so. "Kiss me," she said. I did so but without passion. Merciful God !

And so we parted. I spent the whole night crying on my bed. But the next day I behaved as usual, wittier and in better spirits than ever. That was necessary. My brother told me he wanted to go to the family and show them that I was not a scoundrel. "If you do so I will put a bullet through your head," which is the best proof of how deeply concerned I was.[1] I went to Berlin. I suffered greatly. I thought of her every day. Until now I have kept my promise and have prayed for her at least once and often twice a day, in addition to the other times I might think about her.

When the bonds were broken my thoughts were these : either you throw yourself into the wildest kind of life—or else become absolutely religious, but it will be different from the parsons' mixture.

I only remained in Berlin six months. Actually my intention was to remain away a year and a half. The fact that I came back so soon must have attracted her attention. And indeed it did, and she waited for me after Mynster's sermon on the first Sunday after Easter. But I rejected her advances. My intention was to repel her. I did not want her to think that I had been thinking of her whilst I was away. Moreover I knew from Sibbern that she herself had said that she could not bear seeing me. Now that was not the case as I truly saw; but I was obliged to think that she could not bear speaking to me.

For the rest, it would seem she took the most decisive step in her life under my auspices. Shortly before her engagement to Schlegel she discovered me in a Church. I did not avoid her look. She nodded to me twice. I shook my head. That meant "You must give me up." She nodded again and I nodded in as friendly a manner as possible. That meant "You have retained my love."

Then, after she had become engaged to Schlegel (1843),

[1] In a letter to Emil Boesen S. K. forbade Boesen to contradict all the stories about the engagement which were being told to his discredit, and refers to the above episode. It was Professor Sibbern who had spoken sharply to Peter Kierkegaard.

she met me in the street and greeted me in as friendly and confiding a way as possible. I did not understand her, for I had not heard about the engagement. I only looked enquiringly at her and shook my head. She certainly thought I knew about the engagement and was asking for my approval.

When the banns of marriage were published (1847) I was present in the church.

1841

Oct. 25.[1] . . . You say, "what I have lost or rather what I have deprived myself of," what I have lost, oh, how should you know or understand it. When it is mentioned the best thing you can do is to remain silent—and how should anyone know it better than I who have made the whole of my tremendously reflective soul into as agreeable a frame as possible for her pure depths—my dark thoughts—my melancholy dreams, my brilliant expectations—and above all my inconstancy, in short all that brilliance by the side of her depths—and when I reeled from looking down into her infinite devotion, for there is indeed nothing so infinite as love—or when her feelings did not sink into the depths—but danced above in the easy play of love—

What I have lost, the only thing I loved; what I have lost, in the eyes of men my word of honour; what I have lost, what I still and always shall, and without fearing that shock, stake my honour, my happiness, my pride in—being faithful. . . . Yet at the present moment as I write

[1]S.K. broke off his engagement on October 11 and on October 25, 1841, sailed for Berlin. He was seen on to the boat by his brother and Emil Boesen.

this, in a cabin shaken by the double movement of a steam-packet, my soul is as shaken as my body.

And in the one case in which I so much desired to act, it is melancholy to see myself assigned as my only activity what is usually left to women and children—to pray.

You say: she was beautiful. Oh what do you know about it; I know it, for her beauty cost me tears—I myself bought flowers with which to adorn her, I would have hung all the adornments of the world upon her, though only as they served to bring out all the hidden beauty within—and as she stood there in all her array—I had to go—as her joyful look, so full of life, met mine—I had to go—and I went out and wept bitterly.

How great is womanly devotion.—But the curse which rests upon me is never to be allowed to let anyone deeply and inwardly join themselves to me. God in heaven knows how often I have suffered when with childish glee I thought out a plan which I thought would really please her, and then had to make it a principle never to carry out anything in the joy of the moment, but wait until understanding and shrewdness had forbidden it, for fear of drawing her nearer to me. My relation to her may, I truly believe, be called unhappy love—I love her—I own her—her only wish is to remain with me—her family implore me—it is my greatest wish—and I have to say no. In order to make it easier for her I will, if possible, make her believe that I simply deceived her, that I am a frivolous man, so as if possible to make her hate me; for I believe that it would always be more difficult for her if she suspected that the cause was melancholy—how like are melancholy and frivolity.

How my pride is humbled because I am not able to return to her. I had set all my pride on being faithful to

her, and yet I dare not be so. I am not accustomed to be-
smirching my honour—it has always been a point of honour
with me to remain faithful. And yet in her eyes I am a
deceiver, and that is the only way of setting right again
what I have done wrong. I have held my ground with a
terrible consistency, in spite of all my own inner desires, for
I do not heed the outward temptations of men who would
interfere with me. And yet there is still a fear which tortures me. Supposing she really becomes convinced that I
deceived her, supposing she falls in love with someone else,
which I must naturally wish for in many ways—supposing
she then suddenly discovers that I really loved her, that I
had done so out of love for her, inwardly convinced that
it must end badly or that with the greatest joy in the
world, and thanks to God, I would share my happiness
with her and not my sorrow—then the last would be worse
than the first.

I saw a pretty girl to-day—but it does not interest me
any more—I do not wish it—no husband can be more
faithful to his wife than I am to her. At the same time it
is good for me; those little romances distracted me a good
deal.

Passion is the real thing, the real measure of man's
power. And the age in which we live is wretched, because
it is without passion. If, as the good Jonas Olsen[1] wrote
in that memorable note, he really could hate as none has
hated before, then I should consider myself fortunate in
having been contemporary with him, fortunate in having
become the object of that hate,—that is a real fight.

Here in Berlin a Demoiselle Hedevig Schulze, a Vien-
nese singer, plays the part of Elvira. She is quite pretty,
and acts her part vigorously,—in her movements, stature,

[1]Regine Olsen's brother.

dress (black silk dress, bare neck, white gloves), she bears a striking resemblance to a young lady I once knew.

. . . And when God wishes to bind a man to him he calls his most faithful servant, his most trustworthy messenger, and it is sorrow, and says to him : hasten after him, overtake him, do not leave his side (. . . and no woman can attach herself more closely to the man she loves than sorrow).

Letter to his brother.   *Berlin, Feb.* 27, 1842.

Dear Peter,

Schelling drivels on quite intolerably. If you want to form some idea what it is like then I will ask you to submit yourself to the following experiment as a sort of self-inflicted punishment. Imagine Parson R.'s meandering philosophising, his entirely aimless, haphazard knowledge, and Parson Hornsyld's untiring efforts to display his learning, imagine the two combined and in addition an impudence hitherto unequalled by any philosopher; and with that picture vividly before your poor mind go to the workroom of a prison and you will have some idea of Schelling's philosophy and the temperature one has to hear it in. Moreover, in order to intensify it he has conceived the idea of lecturing for longer than usual, and so I have decided not to attend his lectures for as long as I meant to. The question is, which is the better idea. . . . Consequently I have nothing more to do in Berlin. My time is too precious to allow me to take in drop by drop what I should hardly have to open my mouth to swallow all at once. I am too old to attend lectures and Schelling is too old to give them. His whole doctrine of potency betrays the greatest impotence. . . .

Disjecta Membra[1]

The nature of original sin has often been considered, and yet the principal category has been missing—it is *dread,* that is what really determines it; for dread is a desire for what one fears, a sympathetic antipathy; dread

[1] S. K. returned to Copenhagen on March 6, 1842.

is an alien power which takes hold of the individual, and yet one cannot extricate oneself from it, does not wish to, because one is afraid, but what one fears attracts one. Dread renders the individual powerless, and the first sin always happens in a moment of weakness; it therefore lacks any apparent accountableness, but that want is the real snare.

Woman has more dread than man; that is why the serpent chose her for his attack and deceived her through her dread.

Johannes Climacus
or
De omnibus dubitandum est
a story

His home did not offer many diversions, and as he almost never went out, he early grew accustomed to occupying himself with his own thoughts. His father was a very severe man, apparently dry and prosaic, but under his frieze coat he concealed a glowing imagination which even old age could not dim. When occasionally Johannes asked his permission to go out, he generally refused to give it, though once in a while he proposed instead that Johannes should take his hand and walk up and down the room. At first glance this would seem a poor substitute, and yet, as with the frieze coat, there was something totally different concealed beneath it. The offer was accepted, and it was left entirely to Johannes to determine where they should go. So they went out of doors to a nearby castle in Spain, or out to the seashore, or about the streets, wherever Johannes wished to go, for his father was equal to anything. While they went up and down the room his father described all that they saw; they greeted passers by, carriages rattled past them and drowned his father's voice; the cake-woman's cakes were more enticing than ever. He described so

accurately, so vividly, so explicitly even to the least details,
everything that was known to Johannes and so fully and
perspicuously what was unknown to him, that after half
an hour of such a walk with his father he was as much
overwhelmed and fatigued as if he had been a whole day
out of doors. Johannes soon learned from his father how
to exercise his magical power. What first had been an epic
now became a drama; they talked while walking up and
down. If they went along familiar ways, they watched
one another sharply to make sure that nothing was overlooked; if the way was strange to Johannes, he invented
something, whereas his father's almighty imagination was
capable of shaping everything, of using every childish whim
as an ingredient in the drama which was being enacted.
To Johannes it seemed as if the world were coming into
existence during the conversation, as if his father were our
Lord and he were his favourite, who was allowed to inter-
pose his foolish conceits as merrily as he would; for he
was never repulsed, his father was never put out, he agreed
to everything, and always to Johannes's satisfaction. . . .

While thus there was being developed in him an almost
vegetative tendency to drowse in imagination, which was
in part æsthetic, in part more intellectual, another side of
his soul was being strongly shaped, namely, his sense for
the sudden, the surprising. This was not accomplished by
the magic means which commonly serves to rivet the attention of children, but by something far higher. His father
combined an irresistible dialectic with an all-powerful
imagination. When for any reason his father engaged in
argument with anyone, Johannes was all ears, all the more
so because everything was conducted with an almost festive
orderliness. His father always allowed his opponent to state
his whole case, and then as a precaution asked him if he
had nothing more to say before he began his reply.
Johannes had followed the opponent's speech with strained
attention, and in his way shared an interest in the out-

come. A pause intervened. The father's rejoinder followed,
and behold! in a trice the tables were turned. How that
came about was a riddle to Johannes, but his soul delighted
in the show. The opponent spoke again. Johannes could
almost hear his heart beat, so impatiently did he await
what was to happen.—It happened; in the twinkling of an
eye everything was inverted, the explicable became inexplicable, the certain doubtful, the contrary evident.
When the shark wishes to seize its prey it has to turn over
upon its back, for its mouth is on its underside; its back
is dark, its belly is silver-white. It must be a magnificent
sight to witness that alternation of colour; it must sometimes glitter so brightly as to hurt the eyes, and yet it is
a delight to look upon. Johannes witnessed a similar alternation when he heard his father engage in argument. He
forgot again what was said, both what his father and what
the opponent said, but that shudder of soul he did not forget.

. . . What other children get through the fascination
of poetry and the surprises of fairy-tales, he got through
the repose of intuition and the alternations of dialectic.
This was the child's joy, it became the boy's game, it became the youth's delight. So his life had a rare continuity;
it did not know the various transitions which commonly
mark the different periods of growth. When Johannes grew
older he had no toys to lay aside, for he had learned to
play with that which was to be the serious business of his
life, and yet it lost thereby nothing of its allurement.

. . . Wherever he surmised a labyrinth, there he must
find a way. If once he began such an enterprise, nothing
could make him leave off. If he found it difficult, if he
grew tired before having finished, he used to adopt a very
simple method. He shut himself up in his room, made
everything as festive as possible and then said in a loud
and clear voice, *I will it.* He had learned from his father
that one can do what one wills; and his father's life had

not discredited this theory. This experience had imparted to Johannes' soul an indescribable sort of pride. It was intolerable to him that there should be anything one could not do if only one willed it. But his pride was not at all indicative of a feeble will; for when he had said those energetic words he was ready for anything, he then had a still more lofty goal, namely, to penetrate by sheer will the jungle growth of difficulty. This was again an adventure which aroused his enthusiasm. So his life was at all times romantically adventurous, although for his adventure he did not need forests and distant travel, but only what he possessed—a little room with one window.

Although his soul was early attracted to the ideal, yet his trust and confidence in reality was in no wise weakened. The ideal which he was nourished upon lay so close to him, all came about so naturally, that this became his reality, and again in the reality around him he might expect to discover the ideal. His father's melancholy contributed to this. That his father was an extraordinary man was something Johannes got to know later. That he astonished him, as no other man did to the same degree, he knew; but he was acquainted with so few people that he possessed no scale with which to measure him. That his father, humanly speaking, was something out of the ordinary was the last thing he would learn in the paternal house. Once in a while, when an old friend visited the family and entered into a confidential conversation with his father, Johannes would hear him say, " I am good for nothing, cannot accomplish anything, my one wish is to find a place in a charitable institution."[1] That was not a jest, there was no trace of irony in his father's words, on the contrary there was a gloomy seriousness in them which alarmed Johannes.

. . . Johannes, whose whole view of life was, so to say, hidden in his father, inasmuch as he himself saw only very

[1]The episode is historical and the friend Bishop Mynster.

little, found himself involved in a contradiction, which baffled him for a long time, the suspicion that his father contradicted himself, if not in other ways, at least by the virtuosity with which he could triumph over an opponent and put him to silence. So Johannes's confidence in reality was not weakened; he had not imbibed the ideal from writings which taught him that the glory they describe is, indeed, not to be found in the world; he was not formed by a man who knew how to make his knowledge precious, but rather to make it as unimportant and worthless as possible.

My judgment on Either-Or

There was once a young man, as fortunately gifted as an Alcibiades. He went astray in the world. In his need he looked around him for a Socrates, but among his contemporaries he found none. Then he prayed the gods to change him into one. And behold! He who had been so proud of being an Alcibiades was so shamed and humbled by the grace of the gods that at the very moment of receiving that of which he might have felt proud, he felt himself to be less than all others.

If I have proved nothing else with *Either-Or* at least I have proved that a work can be written in Danish literature without the warm embraces of sympathy, without the incitement of expectation, that one can work against the current, that one can be industrious without showing it, that one can collect one's thoughts in silence while almost every duffer of a student considers one an idler. Though the book itself were meaningless its genesis would be the neatest epigram I have composed on a garrulous philosophic age.

Experience, it is said, makes a man wise. That is very

silly talk. If there were nothing beyond experience it would simply drive him mad.

If people insist on calling my crumbs of wisdom sophistry I should just like to draw their attention to the fact that it lacks at least one of the characteristics, according to the definitions of both Plato and Aristotle: that one earns money with it.

Esquisse

In his early youth a man once let himself be carried away while in a state of intoxication, and visited a prostitute. The whole thing is forgotten. Now he wants to marry. Then comes dread. The possibility of his being a father, that somewhere in the world there might be living a creature owing its existence to him, tortures him day and night. He cannot confide in anyone, he has not even any absolute assurance of the fact.—It must therefore have occurred with a prostitute, in the wild recklessness of youth; had it been a little love affair or a real seduction one could not imagine his being ignorant, but it is precisely his ignorance which is the disturbing element in his torture. On the other hand his doubt could only really appear when he falls in love, precisely because of the thoughtlessness of the whole affair.

After my death no one will find among my papers a single explanation as to what really filled my life (that is my consolation); no one will find the words which explain everything and which often made what the world would call a bagatelle into an event of tremendous importance to me, and what I look upon as something insignificant when I take away the secret gloss which explains all.

1843

The day after my arrival I was very bad, ready to sink at the knees.

In Stralsund I almost went mad hearing a young girl playing the pianoforte, among other things Weber's last waltz over and over again. The last time I was in Berlin it was the first piece I heard in the Thiergarten, played by a blind man on the harp.[1]

It seems as though everything were intended to remind me of the past; my apothecary, who was a confirmed bachelor is married. On that point he explained several things to me : one only lives once; one must have someone to whom one can explain oneself. I was struck by how much there was in what he said, particularly when it is said without affectation.

In the Hotel Saxen I have a room giving on to the water, where the baths are. Good Lord, how it reminds of the past.—In the background is the church—and when it strikes the sound penetrates to the very marrow of my bones.

Berlin, May 17, 1843.

Had I had faith I should have remained with Regine. Thanks and praise be to God, I now see that. I was near to losing my mind in those days. Humanly speaking I behaved rightly towards her, I ought perhaps never to have got engaged, but from that moment I behaved honestly

[1]This is the second journey to Berlin, described in *The Repetition*. S.K. left for Berlin on May 8.

towards her. From an æsthetic and chivalrous point of view I loved her in a far higher sense than she loved me; for otherwise she would never have treated me proudly or afterwards frightened me with her cries. I have just begun a story called *Guilty—Not Guilty,* it could of course contain things which would astonish the world; for I have experienced more poetry in the last year and a half than all the novels put together, but it is impossible for me, and I do not wish my relation to her to be volatilised into poetry, it has quite a different reality. She has not become a fairy princess and if possible she shall be my wife. Oh God, that was my one desire and I have had to relinquish it.

(*A page torn from the Journal*)

. . . it would certainly have happened. But where marriage is concerned everything is not sold as it stands when the hammer falls, and the point, here, is a little honesty about the past. Here again my chivalry is clear.

Had I not honoured her above myself, as my future wife, had I not been prouder of her honour than of mine, then I should have remained silent and have fulfilled her desire and mine, and have been married to her—there are so many marriages that conceal their little tale. That I did not want; in that way she would have become my concubine; I would rather have murdered her.—But if I had had to explain myself then I would have had to initiate her into terrible things, my relation to my father, his melancholy, the eternal darkness that broods deep within, my going astray, pleasures and excesses which in the eyes of God are not perhaps so terrible, for it was dread that drove me to excess, and where was I to look for something to hold on to when I knew, or suspected that the one man I revered for his power and strength had wavered.—

I must take up my Antigone again. The problem will

be to develop and motivate the foreboding of guilt psychologically. To that end I have been thinking of Solomon and David,[1] Solomon's youthful relationship to David; for it is quite certain that both Solomon's intelligence (that which was paramount in it) and his sensuality are consequences of David's greatness. Earlier he had suspected David's tremendous agitation, not knowing what guilt there could be upon him, and yet saw that profoundly God-fearing man give his repentance so ethical an expression; for it would have been another thing had David been a mystic. These conceptions, these suspicions kill all energy (except in the form of imagination), awaken the intelligence and that combination of imagination and intelligence, where the factor of the will is lacking, is really sensuality.

It is really curious about my little secretary Hr. Christensen. I bet it is he who is scribbling in various forms in the papers and in the supplements; for I often hear an echo of my ideas, not as I am in the habit of writing them, but as I throw them out in conversation. And I who treated him so kindly, paid him well, talked to him hours together, for which I paid him, simply in order that he should not feel hurt and humiliated because his poverty made it necessary for him to be a copyist; I initiated him into the whole thing, cast a veil of mystification over everything, made the time as agreeable for him as possible.—The little article in the supplement which appeared several days before *Either-Or* is certainly by him. It was really not very nice of him. He could have confided in me and told me he wanted to write; but his authorship has a bad conscience. He notices that I have changed a little, though I was just as polite and kind to him. On the other hand I have put a stop to his curiosity and his sniffing about my room; one must keep him at à distance; how I loath plagiarists.

[1]The third autobiographical insertion, *Solomon's Dream* describes ' the earthquake.' *Solomon's Dream* in *Guilty—Not Guilty.*

I could perhaps reproduce the tragedy of my childhood, the terrifying, mysterious explanation of religion which a frightful foreboding played into my hands, which my imagination worked upon, and the scandal which religion became to me—all in a novel called "the mysterious family." It would begin on a completely idyllic, patriarchal note so that no one suspected anything until suddenly the word sounded which translated everything into terror.

Nullum exstitit magnum ingenium sine aliqua dementia is the worldly expression of the religious proposition : whom God blesses in a religious sense he *eo ipso* curses in a worldly sense. It has to be so, the reason being firstly, the limitations of existence, and secondly the duplicity of existence.

It is perfectly true, as philosophers say, that life must be understood backwards. But they forget the other proposition, that it must be lived forwards. And if one thinks over that proposition it becomes more and more evident that life can never really be understood in time simply because at no particular moment can I find the necessary resting-place from which to understand it—backwards.

1844

I was born in 1813, in that mad year when so many other mad bank-notes were put into circulation,[1] and I can be best compared to one of them. There is something about me which points to greatness, but because of the mad state of affairs I am only worth little.

And sometimes bank-notes of that kind are the misfortune of a whole family.

Let no one misunderstand all my talk about passion and pathos to mean that I am proclaiming any and every uncircumcised immediacy, all manner of unshaven passion.

The hardest trial of all is when a man does not know whether the cause of his suffering is madness or guilt. While in other cases freedom is what he fights with, in this case it has become dialectical in its own most terrible contrary.

Where feelings are concerned the same thing happens to me that happened to the Englishman who got into financial difficulties because no one could change his £100 note.

In *Aus meinem Leben* Goethe is nothing but a talented defender of solecisms. At no single point has he realised the idea; but (whether the subject is girls, love or Christianity) there is one thing he can do, talk himself out of everything.

If Hegel had written the whole of his logic and then said,

[1]The inflation which enriched S. K.'s father.

in the preface, that it was merely an experiment in thought in which he had even begged the question in many places, then he would certainly have been the greatest thinker who had ever lived. As it is he is merely comic.

N.B. God can only show himself to man in miracles, *i.e.* as soon as he sees God he sees a miracle. But by himself he is incapable of seeing miracles for the miracle is his own annihilation. The Jews expressed that pictorially by saying that to see God was death. It is truer to say that to see God, or see miracles happens by virtue of the absurd, for reason must stand aside.

It seems quite extraordinary to me to read Cap III of Book III of Aristotle's *de anima*. It is a year and a half since I began my little essay: *de omnibus dubitandum est* in which I made my first attempt at a bit of philosophical writing. The motivating concept which I used was: error. Aristotle does so too. At that time I had not read any Aristotle and only part of Plato.

It is however the Greeks who are my consolation, the cursed mendacity which came into philosophy with Hegel, that eternal hinting and deceiving, and blustering and dilution of some point or other in the Greeks.

Trendelenburg be praised; one of the most honest thinking philologists I know.

May 14, 1845.   *Arrival in Berlin.*

The only character on board whom one could make any use of was a young lad wearing a velvet cap tied on with a kerchief, and a striped smock over his coat, and a stick hanging by a string to one of the buttons. Frank, honest, travelling, interested in everything, naïve, shy, and yet confident. By combining him with a melancholy traveller (like Herr Hagen) one could produce a fine melancholy effect.

It is curious that *The Corsair* has never thought of representing people in the classical style, naked, with a figleaf.

A drawing of Hercules for example, or something in that style, and underneath : Pastor Grundtvig.

A possible conclusion to all
the pseudonymous works
by
Nicolaus Notabene

I shall now tell an honoured public how it happened that I became an author. The story is quite simple, for there is no question of my having had a vision, a dream or the inspiration of genius, or anything of the kind to which to appeal. I had spent some years of my life as a student in a sort of idleness, certainly reading and thinking a bit, but my indolence always had the upper hand completely; then one Sunday afternoon, four years ago, I was sitting out in a café in the Frederiksberg Gardens smoking my cigar and looking at the servant-girls and suddenly the idea struck me : you go on wasting your time without profit; on every side one genius after another appears and makes life and existence, and the historical means of con-veyance and communication with eternal happiness, easier and easier—*what do you do?* Could you not discover some way in which you too could help the age? Then I thought, what if I sat down and made everything difficult? For one must try to be useful in every possible way. Even if the age does not need ballast I must be loved by all those who make everything easy; for if no one is prepared to make it difficult it becomes all too easy—to make things easy. From that moment I found my entertainment in that work. I mean the work has been amusing, for in another sense I did not find it entertaining, but had to sink money in it. Nor can one really ask people to pay in order to have things made difficult; that would be to make it still more difficult. No, really those who make things easy should support me out of their profits. They have more-over made good use of me and straightway assumed that I did it for their sakes, simply so that they should have something further to make easy.

When a skipper sails with a smack he usually knows his whole cruise beforehand; but a man-of-war only gets its orders at sea—that is what happens to genius, he is out on the deep before he gets his orders, we others know more or less what we have to do.

Monologue

When one reads Luther one gets the impression, rightly enough, of a sure and certain mind, of one who speaks with a decision that is "authoritative" (he preached with authority—εξουσια Matt. vii. 29). And yet it seems to me there is something disturbing about his certainty, which is in fact uncertainty. It is common knowledge that a particular state of mind often tries to conceal itself beneath its opposite. One encourages oneself with strong words, and the words become even stronger because one is hesitant. That is not deception, but a pious wish. One does not even wish to express the uncertainty of fear, one does not wish (or dare) even to name it, and one forces out the very opposite mood in the hope that it will help. Thus Luther makes paramount use of that which is used with such moderation in the New Testament: the sin against the Holy Ghost. In order to encourage himself and the believer he makes immediate and draconian use of it on every occasion. With the result that ultimately there is not a single man who has committed the sin against the Holy Ghost, not only once but many times. And the New Testament says that it cannot be forgiven; so what then?—I know full well that most people will cross themselves when I compare Luther's assurance with that of Socrates. But is that not simply because the majority of men have a greater understanding of and leaning towards disturbing? Luther, as is well known, was shaken by the lightning which killed his friend beside him; in the same way his expressions always sound as though the lightning were continuously striking down behind him.

Just as the top layer in a case of herrings is crushed and spoilt, and the fruit next to the crate is bruised and worthless, so too in every generation there are certain men who are on the outside and are made to suffer from the packing case, who only protect those who are in the middle.

Happily I am neither marked out by fortune nor among the admired, for much as I am willing to rejoice with them and pay them my tribute, I am little desirous of being one of them, because that kind of existence is at variance with the universal and distressing in relation to the unfortunate.

There is a bird called the stormy-petrel, and that is what I am, when in a generation storms begin to gather, individuals of my type appear.

1846

The " Final Postscript "

Jan. The whole manuscript was delivered to the printer, lock, stock and barrel, *circa medio* Dec., 1845.—" A first and last explanation " was written down hastily on a page of the original manuscript but was put on one side to be finished and was only sent to the printer at the last moment, so as not to lie about the printer's office. I would not allow a foot-note to a passage about the pseudonymous works to be printed simply because it was written during the printing. The falsehood, gossip and vulgarity that surround one on all sides make one's position difficult enough at times, make me perhaps all too nervously anxious to have the truth on my side, down to the smallest details; what's the good?

Feb. 7. My idea is now to prepare myself for Holy Orders. I have prayed to God for several months to give me further help, for it has been clear to me for a long time past that I ought not to continue any longer as an author, which I either wish to be entirely and absolutely, or not at all. For that reason I have not begun anything new while correcting the proofs, but only the little review of *The Two Ages,* which is, moreover, finished.[1]

How terrible about the man who once as a little boy, while herding sheep on the heaths of Jutland, suffering greatly, in hunger and in want, stood upon a hill and cursed God—and the man was unable to forget it even when he was eighty-two years old.

[1]From which *The Present Age* is translated.

De occultis non judicat ecclesia.

Dare I conceal the guilt? And yet dare I reveal it myself? If God wishes it to be revealed, then to be sure he can do so, and this idea of informing against myself may, what is more, be playing the part of providence.

To-day an accusing memory passed by. Supposing, now, the accusation came to light. I could go far away, live in a foreign country, a new life far from the memory, far from every possibility of its being revealed. I could live hidden—No, I must remain on the spot and continue to do everything as usual, without a single prudential measure, leaving everything to God. Terrible, how it can develop a man to remain on the spot, formed only by possibility.

The new development in our age cannot be political, for politics is a dialectical relation between the individual and the community in the *representative* individual; but in our times the individual is in the process of becoming far too reflective to be able to be satisfied with merely being *represented.*

The immediate person thinks and imagines that when he prays, the important thing, the thing he must concentrate upon, is that *God should hear* what HE *is praying for.* And yet in the true, eternal sense it is just the reverse: the true relation in prayer is not when God hears what is prayed for, but when *the person praying* continues to pray until he is *the one who hears,* who hears what God wills. The immediate person, therefore, uses many words and, therefore, makes demands in his prayer; the true man of prayer only *attends.*

Why did Socrates compare himself to a gad-fly?

Because he only wished to have ethical significance. He did not wish to be admired as a genius standing apart from others, and fundamentally, therefore, make the lives of

J.

D

others easy, because they could then say, "it is all very fine for him, he is a genius." No, he only did what every man can do, he only understood what every man can understand. Therein lies the epigram. He bit hard into the individual man, continually forcing him and irritating him with this 'universal.' He was a gad-fly who provoked people by means of the individual's passion, not allowing him to admire indolently and effeminately, but demanding his self of him. If a man has ethical power people like to make him into a genius, simply to be rid of him; because his life expresses a demand.

The time will come when it will be considered just as bad taste to give results (now so much in demand and so popular) as it was at one time to point a moral. The man who cannot discover the result for himself with the help of the road never discovers it at all, he only imagines he does.

In relation to their systems most systematisers are like a man who builds an enormous castle and lives in a shack close by; they do not live in their own enormous systematic buildings. But spiritually that is a decisive objection. Spiritually speaking a man's thought must be the building in which he lives—otherwise everything is topsy-turvy.

Everything depends upon making the difference between quantitative and qualitative dialectic absolute. The whole of logic is quantitative or modal dialectic, since everything is and everything is one and the same. Qualitative dialectic is concerned with existence.

The phrase "while this and that happened something else happened," always implies that the first was something which lasted longer, and it can therefore be used so that the second thing only took a moment within the first

"while." One says: While Cicero was Consul this and
that happened; while Pitt was minister, etc. And so it gave
the effect of being an excellent parody when one read in
the papers: while Grundtvig spoke the people from Fyen
arrived. They themselves are naturally of no importance;
the point lay in the idea one got of the fantastic length
of Pastor Grundtvig's speech,—*while* he spoke (while Cicero
was Consul). For instance, one might say: *while* Grundtvig spoke the French fleet put to sea and conquered Algiers.

Report[1]

March, 1846

March 9. The *Final Postscript* is out; the pseudonyms
acknowledged; in a few days *A Literary Review* goes to the
press. Everything is in order; now I have only to keep
calm and remain silent, confident that *The Corsair* will
support my whole undertaking negatively, just as I should
like. At the present time I am situated as correctly as
possible in literature from the ideological point of view, and
am at the same time situated in such a way that to be an
author becomes an action. The idea of breaking with *The
Corsair* in order to prevent any direct approach, just when
I had finished with authorship and, by acknowledging all
the pseudonyms, ran the risk of becoming a sort of
authority, was a very happy thought. [Earlier on nothing
could be done, every minute of my time was taken up
working for my idea. It is quite admirable that just when
someone might imagine, and perhaps even rejoice mali-
ciously, that I am acting precipitously—I am more calculating, more circumspect than ever. The best help in all

[1]With this memorandum begins the series of note-books numbered
NB[1] to NB[36] which continue down to within a year of S. K.'s death.
The memorandum was written between March and May or June.

action is—to pray, that is true genius; then one never goes wrong.] Furthermore, at the same moment that I come out polemically against the age, I owe it to the idea and to irony to prevent any possible confusion with the ironical bad spirits with which *The Corsair* attends on the dance floor of vulgarity. And here once again, as so often before, something more results which, in spite of all my reflection, is not due to me but to providence. The things which I do after the greatest possible consideration, I so often understand far better afterwards, not only their ideological significance but the fact that that was exactly what I should have done.

Nevertheless my life at the present time is exhausting; I am convinced that not a single person understands me. At the most even an admirer would grant that I bore all the gossip with a certain dignity, but he would never dream that I desired it. On the other hand if hasty, thoughtless people were to understand why I must desire it, by virtue of the idea of double reflection, they would conclude : *ergo* he does not suffer at all, is not touched by all these lies and expressions of vulgarity. As though one could not decide freely to take upon oneself every kind of unpleasantness, if the idea so commands.

The article against P. L. Møller was written in fear and trembling; I devoted the holidays[1] to it and did not fail to go to Church, or to read my sermon in order to supply the regulating counter-balance. So too the article against *The Corsair*. On the other hand they were written in the right spirit, for had I shown any passion then a few people would have found a way of assuming a direct relation to me. It was amusing and psychologically capital to see how quickly P. L. Møller understood the signal and came out in *The Corsair*. He came forward, bowed respectfully, and then retired where he belonged.

The thing that has pained me is moreover not the vul-

[1]Christmas, 1845.

garity of it all, but the clandestine participation of the better people. For I might also like to make myself intelligible to a single man, to my reader. But I may not do that; I should be betraying the idea. It is precisely when I have won, when vulgarity is at its most impertinent, that I may not say so. Finally I am responsible perhaps for certain people being confused by my unshakable consistency. I cannot alter things. My duty is to remain silent.

The last two months have been rich in things for me to observe. How true, what I said in my dissertation, that irony makes things manifest. My ironic leap into *The Corsair* in the first place makes it quite clear that there is no idea behind *The Corsair*. From that point of view it is dead, even though it were to get two or three thousand more subscribers. It tries to be ironical and does not even understand irony. In fact it would have been an epigram on my life if it had ever had to be said : at the time he lived there was a blundering ironical paper, by which he was praised; no, stop—he was insulted and demanded that himself—furthermore my ironical leap into *The Corsair* makes the surroundings manifest in all their inconsistency. Everyone went about saying that it counted for nothing, who bothers about *The Corsair*, and so on. And what happens : when somebody behaves in this way he is accused of thoughtlessness, people say he deserves everything he gets (and consequently it counts for that much), because he himself was the occasion of it; they hardly dare go down the street with me—for fear of appearing in *The Corsair*. Moreover the self-contradiction has deeper roots; for out of Christian envy they rather want the paper to continue, each man hoping he will not be attacked. They say of the paper that it is contemptible, that it counts for nothing, while the individual attacked is awed into silence and into not being angry; *ergo* the paper must continue.

In the first place the public can indulge its envy and thus has the impertinent pleasure of watching the person

attacked—whether he is affected or not, and then has the
opportunity of lying, by saying that he is affected, that he
may conceal it but is nevertheless affected. The last form
of slander is the most agreeable of all. And this occurs in
a small country like Denmark, where it dominates everything—and is supposed to be a mere nothing! How well
cowardice and contemptibleness suit one another if united
in wretchedness. And when the whole thing finally goes to
pieces Goldschmidt will get the blame; and the public is
exactly the same—the world has indeed become a fine
place!

Two things in particular occupy me : (1) that, whatever
the cost, I should remain intellectually true, in the Greek
sense, to my life's idea; (2) that religiously it should be as
ennobling as possible. For the second I pray to God. I
have always been isolated, now I have a proper opportunity
of improving myself. Indeed, my solitary secret is not a
cause of grief to me, but is precisely why I have power to
change what is grief into that which serves my idea, without its suspecting anything of the kind. This life is certainly satisfying, but it is also terribly exhausting. One gets
to know men from such a pitiful side, and it is so sad that
what looks well from a distance should always be misunderstood by contemporaries! But religion, once again, is the
salvation; in religion there is sympathy with all, not a
prosy sympathy with party friends and adherents, but an
infinite sympathy with each one—in silence.

But it is undeniably instructive to be placed in so small
a town as Copenhagen, as I am. To work with all one's
might, almost to despair, to endure all the tortures of the
soul and the suffering of my inner life, to pay out money
in order to publish books—and then literally not to find
ten men who can read them properly, while undergraduates
and other authors find it easy to make it almost ridiculous
to write a large volume. And then to have a paper which
everyone reads, which is privileged, as a result of being con-

temptible, to say everything, even the most distorted lies
—which "counts for nothing," though everyone reads it;
and then all the crowds of envious people who, by saying
the very opposite, help to disparage. Ever and ever again
to be the one subject of conversation and interest. Even
the butcher's boy almost thinks himself justified in being
offensive to me at the behest of *The Corsair*. Undergraduates grin and giggle and are delighted that someone
prominent should be trodden down; the dons are envious
and secretly sympathise with the attack, help to spread it
abroad, adding of course that it is a crying shame. The
slightest thing I do, even if I simply pay a visit, is lyingly
distorted and repeated everywhere; if *The Corsair* gets to
know of it then it is printed and read by the whole population. In that way the person I visit is embarrassed, is
almost angry with me, and one cannot very well blame him.
In the end the only thing will be to withdraw and only go
about with those I dislike, for it is really a shame to go
about with the others.

So it continues, and when I am dead people's eyes will
be opened, they will marvel at what I have desired, at
the same time behaving in the same way to someone else,
who is probably the only man who understands me.

God in heaven, if there were not deep within a man a
place where all this can be completely forgotten in communion with thee, who could endure it.

But the days of my authorship are past. God be praised.
I have been granted the satisfaction of bringing it to a
conclusion, of myself understanding when it is fitting that
I should make an end, and next after the publication of
Either-Or I thank God for that. That this, once again, is
not how people will see it; that I could actually prove in
two words that it is so : I know quite well and find quite in
order. But it has pained me; it seemed to me that I might
have asked for that admission; but let it be.

If only I can manage to become a priest. However

much my present life may have satisfied me I shall breathe more freely in that quiet activity, allowing myself an occasional literary work in my free time.

It is really curious how men, whom I otherwise look upon as honest, and who in other respects are not my enemies, lie monstrously, and are hardly conscious of it themselves, when they really get into a passion. Passion has an extraordinary power. How foolish, then, is the modern seeking after system upon system, as though help was to be found there; no, passion must be purified. At the present time I am incidentally experiencing expressions of it.

Twaddle, rubbish, and gossip is what people want, not action; that is what they think interesting. In *Aus meinem Leben* Goethe relates that *The Sorrows of Werther* created a great sensation and after that time, he says, he never again knew the peace and obscurity which he had known before, because he was drawn into all kinds of relationships and friendships. How interesting and exciting small talk is ! Nothing would have been easier than to have prevented that if Goethe had really had the courage, had he genuinely loved ideas more than acquaintances. Anyone with Goethe's powers could easily have kept people away. But in fact, soft and sensitive as he was, he did not wish it— but he likes to relate it as a story. People like to hear about it because it relieves them from action. If someone were to get up and preach, saying : once, in my early youth I had faith, but then I grew busy in the world, made many acquaintances, was knighted, and since that time I have never really had time to collect my thoughts—people would find the sermon very touching and would enjoy listening to it. If one wishes to succeed, the secret of life is to chatter freely about all one wishes to do and how one is always being prevented—and then do nothing.

One day Professor Molbech was visiting me. He praised my idiosyncrasy, my singular way of life, because it favoured my work. "I shall do the same," he said. Thereupon he told me that that very day he had to go to a dinner party and "there I have to drink wine, and I cannot stand it; but one cannot avoid doing so because people begin at once saying: Oh, just a little glass, Herr Professor, it is good for you." I answered, "Nothing is easier than to prevent that. Do not say a word about not being able to take any wine, for in that way you only egg on a prosy sympathy. Sit down at the table and when the wine is served smell it and then say or express by a look that the wine is not good. Then your host will be angry and will not fuss you." To that Molbech answered, "No, I cannot do that, why should I quarrel with people." I answered: "In order to get your own way; is that not reason enough?" But that is how it goes on. First of all he gossips away with me for an hour and makes a fool of me with all his hot air; then to dinner where he gossips about it—and drinks; then he goes home and feels unwell—and gossips the whole night through about it all to his wife; that is life and being interesting.

It is, after all, possible that in spite of my insignificance before God, in personal humiliation at what I personally have committed, I may be "the gift of God"[1] to my people. God knows they have treated me scurvily enough, like children misusing a beautiful present.

To be the greatest philosopher in Denmark is on the very border line of satire—rather like being the greatest—just think of it—the greatest of the travelling actors—in Odense; or like P. L. Møller's praise of what I have written against Heiberg: "that it was the wittiest thing written against Heiberg."—

[1] Plato, *Apology*.

This is how I have understood myself in my entire literary work.

I am in the profoundest sense an unhappy individuality which from its earliest years has been nailed fast to some suffering or other, bordering upon madness, and which must have its deeper roots in a disproportion between soul and body; for (and that is what is extraordinary) it has no relation to my mind. On the contrary, perhaps because of the strained relation between soul and body my mind has received a tensile strength that is rare.

An old man, himself prodigiously melancholy (wherefore I shall not write down) had a son in his old age upon whom the whole of that melancholy descended in inheritance—but at the same time he had such an elasticity of mind that he was able to conceal it, and because his mind was essentially, eminently sound his melancholy could never obtain power over him, but neither was he able to throw it off, at the most he was able to bear it.

A young girl (who with girlish pride set gigantic forces in motion, and let me suspect a way out from what was begun through a sad mistake, a way out, a way of breaking off our engagement, for at first she only let the forces be suspected as though she did not care in the least about it) put a murder on my conscience; at the most solemn moment, a troubled father solemnly repeats the assurance that it would be the girl's death. Whether she was merely a chatterbox or not does not concern me.

From that moment on I dedicated my life with every ounce of my poor ability to the service of an idea.

Although no lover of confidants, although absolutely averse from talking with others about my inmost self, I nevertheless think and thought that it is the duty of man not to skip such a factor as that of seeking the advice of another man; only it must not become a foolish confidence, but a serious and official communication. I have therefore consulted my doctor as to whether he thought that the discord between the psychical and the physical could be resolved so that I might realise the universal. He doubted it. I asked him whether he thought that acting through my will my mind was capable of reforming and transforming that fundamental disproportion; he doubted it; he would not even advise me to set my whole will power in motion, of which he had some idea, lest I should burst everything asunder.

From that moment I made my choice. That sad discord with its attendant suffering (which without doubt would have driven most of those with sense enough to understand it to suicide) I have always looked upon as my thorn in the flesh, my limit and my cross; I have looked upon it as the high price at which Almighty God sold me an intellectual power which has found no equal among my contemporaries. That does not puff me up for *I am already ground to dust*; my desire has become to me a bitter pain and a daily humiliation.

Without being able to appeal to revelations or anything of the kind, I have understood myself in having to stress the universal in a botched and demoralised age, in making it lovable and accessible to all others who are capable of realising it, but who are led astray by the age to chasing after the unusual and extraordinary. I have understood my duty like the man who, being himself unhappy, so long as he loves man, desires only to help others who are capable of being happy.

But since my task was, at the same time, a humble and a pious attempt to do something good in reparation for what I have done wrong, I have been particularly observant that my effort should not serve the cause of vanity, that above all I should not serve the idea and the truth in such a way as to obtain worldly advantage from it. I am therefore certain that I have worked with true resignation.

During my work I have also constantly believed that I learnt to understand better and better God's will in regard to me : that I bear the agony with which God laid the reins upon me and so perhaps achieve the exceptional.

My merit in literature is that I have set forth the decisive qualifications of the whole compass of existence with such dialectical clarity and so originally as has not, so far as I know, been done in any other literature; neither have I had any books to help me nor upon which to draw for advice. Secondly, the art with which I have communicated it, its form, its logical accomplishment; but no one has time to read and study seriously and to that extent my production is for the moment wasted, like putting exquisite dishes in front of peasants.

End of Report

Berlin, May 5-13, 1846.

A *providence* is no easier to understand (to grasp) than *the redemption* : both can only be believed. The idea of a providence is that God is concerned about the individual and for what is most individual in him, which can at the very most be grasped imaginatively (in the abstract) as an eternal immanent congruence between the finite and the infinite—but not in becoming. The Redemption is the *continued providence* that God will care for the individual in him in spite of the fact that he has lost everything. Nevertheless the redemption is a transition $\varepsilon\iota\varsigma$ $\alpha\lambda\lambda o$ $\gamma\varepsilon\nu o\varsigma$ and to that extent it is also dialectical because of the sign by which it is known; for providence is not known from a sign in the same way that the death of Christ is the sign (the sign of the cross).

Providence and redemption are the categories of despair : I should have to despair if I dared not, if indeed I ought not, to believe. They are not what one despairs over, but what keeps despair away.

The historicity of the redemption must be certain in the same sense as any other historical thing, but not more so, for otherwise the different spheres are confused. The so-called historical factual certainty would have to be either the autopsy of some contemporary person, or of some later person who has it from a dependable man; but if that is valued too highly the essence of faith becomes enervated. In relation to providence there is nothing to which I can cling physically, nor is there any man upon whom I may depend, and moreover I have all the troubled view of existence with all that it knows of the wretchedness of existence, against me: so I believe in a providence. The historical factual assumption necessary for the redemption must only be as certain as all other historical facts, but the passion of faith must decide the matter in the same way as with providence.

The redemptive belief in the forgiveness of sins takes away the intermediary state of dread from the troubled and afflicted, so that his relation to God should be entirely through the intermediary of punishment.

Father in Heaven! Well do we know that thou art everywhere present; and that should anyone at this moment call upon thee from his bed of sickness, or one in great need upon the ocean cry out to thee, or one in still greater need in sin, that thou art near to hear him. But thou art also near in thy house where thy community is gathered together, some perhaps flying from heavy thoughts, or followed by heavy thoughts, but some too coming from a quiet daily life of contentment, and some perhaps with a satisfied longing hidden in a thankful heart enveloped in joyous thoughts—and yet all drawn by the desire to seek God, the friend of the thankful in blessed trust; consolation of the weak in strengthening communion; refuge of the anxious in secret comfort; confident of the afflicted as thou doest count their tears; last comfort of the dying as thou doest receive their souls. So let thyself be found also in this hour; thou who art the father of all let thyself be found with a good gift for everyone who needs it, that the happy may find courage to rejoice at thy good gifts, that the sorrowful may find courage to accept thy perfect gifts. For to men there is a difference in these things, the difference of joy and of sorrow, but for thee O Lord there is no difference in these things : everything that comes from thee is a good and perfect gift.

Immanently (in the fantastic medium of abstraction) God does not *exist*, he only is—God only *exists* for an existing man *i.e.* he can only exist *in faith*. Providence, atonement, etc. only exist for an existing man. When all things are accomplished providence rests in consummation, when all things are accomplished the atonement comes to rest in equilibrium, but they do not *exist*. Faith is therefore the anticipation of the eternal which holds the factors together, the cleavages of existence. When an existing individual has not got faith God *is* not, neither does God *exist*, although understood from an eternal point of view God is eternally.

End of Berlin entries

Report	*Result*

Sept. 7. Wherein lies the annoyance, the vexation? Not, of course *in what* is said (for I have often enough said the same things about myself jokingly) but *to whom* it is said, and because it has produced a street riot, which has landed me in a crowd with whom I can having nothing in common. *In company* with Jewish commercial-travellers, shopworkers, prostitutes, school-boys, butcher-boys, etc. I really cannot laugh at the things which I can very well laugh at in company with Carl Weiss for example. When I laugh with him at my thin legs I thereby presuppose a common

intellectual basis. But to laugh over that with the plebs would be to admit to having a basis in common with them. —And just because that is the case, it has come about in a curious way that the only person here, who can really handle such dialectical problems with irony and satiric ability, cannot take the responsibility of doing so—and that person is myself. I am ready to bind myself to write amusing articles about myself and my legs of a very different kind from Goldschmidt's; but in that case the plebs would not understand them.

Pascal says: it is so difficult to believe because it is so difficult to suffer.

Nov. 5. Perhaps—I do not say more, for I know how difficult it is to judge oneself *in abstracto* if one is to judge truthfully—perhaps I should have succeeded in breaking off my literary work so as to concentrate upon taking an official position, if everything had been as it should have been and it had been clear that I was free when I made my decision. Now that is no longer possible. There is a great difficulty in the way of my becoming a priest. If I undertook it I should certainly run the danger of coming to grief as I did over my engagement. On the other hand it has been made difficult for me to live entirely and peacefully withdrawn in the country, for I am all the same somewhat embittered and as a result I need the enchantment of literary composition in order to be able to forget all the crude trivialities of life.

It becomes more and more clear to me that, constituted as I am, I am never successful in fulfilling my ideals whilst in another sense I become, humanly speaking, more than those ideals. Most people's ideals are great and extraordinary things which they never achieve. I am altogether too melancholy to have such ideals. Other people would laugh at my ideals. For example it is perfectly true to say

that my ideal was to marry and simply live for marriage.
Then, by despairing of being able to achieve so much, I
became an author, and perhaps an author of importance.
My other ideal is to be a country parson, to live quietly
in the country and devote my life to the little circle of
those around me—and then, because I despair of success,
it is quite possible that I shall achieve something which
seems much greater.

When Bishop Mynster advises me to be a country parson
he evidently does not understand me. It is perfectly true
that that is what I desire, but our premises are completely
at variance. He imagines that, in some way or other, I
want to go further along that road, that I want to be something, and that is the whole point, I want to be as little
as possible; that is precisely the idea of my melancholy.
For that very reason it has pleased me to be looked upon
as half mad, though that is only a negative way of being
something unusual. Yet it is still possible that that should
really be my form of existence, in which case I shall never
achieve the lovely quiet and calm existence of being something quite little.

What I have always known within myself, and the reason
why I have never spoken with any other man about my real
concerns, has proved true again in my conversation with
Mynster : it leads to nothing, for since I cannot and dare
not speak of what entirely and essentially constitutes my
inmost life, my conversations with others are almost a
deceit on my part. In relation to Mynster I feel the real
sadness of it all because I honour him so highly.

The whole question of God's goodness and omnipotence
and its relation to evil (instead of distinguishing and saying that while he works good he only permits evil) can
perhaps be explained quite simply in this way. The greatest
good which can be done to any being, greater than any
end to which it can be created, is to make it free. In order

to be able to do that omnipotence is necessary. That will sound curious, since of all things omnipotence, so at least it would seem, should make things dependent. But if we rightly consider omnipotence, then clearly it must have the quality of so taking itself back in the very manifestation of its all-powerfulness that the results of this act of the omnipotent can be independent. That is why one man cannot make another man quite free, because the one who has the power is imprisoned in it and consequently always has a false relation to him whom he wishes to free. That is why there is a finite self-love in all finite power (talent and so forth). Omnipotence alone can take itself back while giving, and this relationship is nothing else but the independence of the recipient. God's omnipotence is therefore his goodness. For goodness means to give absolutely, yet in such a way that by taking oneself back one makes the recipient independent. From finite power comes only dependence, and omnipotence alone can make something independent, can create something out of nothing which endures of itself, because omnipotence is always taking itself back. Omnipotence is not involved in a relation to the other; since there is nothing to which it has any relation, it can give without giving away the very least of its powers : it can make the other independent. And that is what is inconceivable; omnipotence can not only bring forth the most imposing of all things, the world in its visible totality, but it can create the most delicate of all things, a creature independent of it. Omnipotence which can lay its hand so heavily upon the world can also make its touch so light that the creature receives independence. It is only a miserable and worldly picture of the dialectic of power to say that it becomes greater in proportion as it can compel and make things dependent. Socrates knew better; the art of using power is " to make free." But between men that can never happen, though it may always be necessary to stress that it is the greatest good; only omnipotence can do so in

truth. If, therefore, man had even the least independent
existence (in regard to *materia*) then God could not make
him free. Creation out of nothing is once again the expression of omnipotence for being able to make things
independent. It is to him who made me independent, while
he nevertheless retained everything, that I owe all things.
If in order to create man God had lost any of his power,
then he could not have made man independent.

But let us never forget that not everyone who has not
lost his senses thereby proves conclusively that he is in
possession of them.

If I refuse to deify the established order à la Mynster (and therein lies Mynster's heresy) and out of zeal for morality end by confusing it with the bourgeois spirit,— if I do not wish to do away entirely with the category of the *extraordinarius* and again à la Mynster, only understand that they have existed, only understand them after the event : I cannot myself scorn a task which has been so clearly imposed upon me.

Although Mynster is to a certain degree well disposed towards me, and at the bottom of his heart perhaps more so than he would admit, it is evident that he looks upon me as a suspicious and dangerous person.

He therefore wants to have me out in the country. He thinks that up to now all has gone well, but that one must expect anything from a person of character, particularly when the whole system of strings in which he wishes to imprison life is in question. His advice is therefore most consistent from his point of view, and from his point of view it is meant kindly in so far as he does not trouble too much whether a man's deepest traits are harmed somewhat so long as he succeeds, as he considers, in the world.

Mynster has never been out on 70,000 fathoms in order to learn out there, he has always clung to the established order of things and has now quite grown into it. That is what is so glorious about him. I shall never forget him, always honour him, always think of my father when I think of him, and anything further is unnecessary. But Mynster does not understand me; when he was thirty-six years old he would not have understood me; he would have hardened in order not to understand me, so as not to ruin his career; and now he cannot understand me.

But to God all things are possible. From now on, humanly speaking, I must not only be said to be running into uncertainty but to be going to certain destruction— and, in confidence in God, that is victory. That is how I understood life when I was ten years old, hence the terrible polemic which filled my soul; that is how I understood it when I was twenty-five, and now that I am thirty-four. That is why Poul Møller called me the most completely polemical of men.

The difference between a Christian Address and a Sermon.

A Christian Address deals to a certain extent with doubt —A Sermon operates absolutely and entirely through authority, that of Holy Writ and of Christ's apostles. It is therefore neither more nor less than heresy to entertain doubt in a sermon, however well one might be able to handle it.

The preface to my *Christian Discourses,* therefore, contains the phrase : If a sufferer who has also *run wild in many thoughts.*

A Sermon presupposes a priest (ordination);[1] a Christian Address can be by a layman.

I am accused of leading young men to rest satisfied in their own subjectivity. Perhaps, for a moment. But how is it possible to get rid of all the illusions of objectivity such as the public etc. without drawing forth the category of the individual? Under the guise of objectivity people have wished to sacrifice individualities completely. That is the whole question.

The whole development of the world tends to the importance of the individual; that, and nothing else, is the prin-

[1]Ordination is a *character indelebilis*; s.v. vii. 232.

ciple of Christianity. Yet we have not got very far in practice, although that is recognised in theory. That explains why people still consider it proud and haughty and presumptuous to talk about the individual when it is of course the really human attitude, namely, that everyone is an individual.

Sometimes misunderstandings are expressed piously. When the late Bishop Møller says (in the introduction to his *Instructions*) that it would be sad if truth (*in specie* Christianity) were only accessible to a few individuals and not to everyone, he certainly said something true, but at the same time false. For Christianity is certainly accessible to all but—be it carefully noted—only provided everyone becomes an individual, becomes " the individual." But people have neither the moral nor the religious courage. The majority is quite terrified of becoming each one of them, an individual. This is how the question oscillates : At one moment it is pride to preach that opinion of the individual and then, when the individual tries it out, he finds the thought is too great for him, in fact overwhelming.

There is only one mistake in Kant's theory of radical evil. He does not make it clear that the inexplicable, the paradox, is a category of its own. Everything depends upon that. Until now, people have always expressed themselves in the following way : the knowledge that one cannot understand this or the other thing does not satisfy science, the aim of which is to understand. Here is the mistake; people ought to say the very opposite : if *human* science refuses to understand that there is something which it cannot understand, or better still, that there is something about which it clearly understands that it cannot understand it—then all is confusion. For it is the duty of the human understanding to understand that there are things which it cannot understand, and what those things are. Human understanding has vulgarly occupied itself with nothing but understanding, but if it would only take the trouble to understand itself at the same time it would simply have to posit the paradox. The paradox is not a concession but a category, an ontological definition which expresses the relation between an existing cognitive spirit and eternal truth.

Properly understood, every man who truthfully desires a relation to God and to live in his sight has only one task : always to be joyful. Even the best of men, in whom one could place entire confidence, upon whom one could rely entirely, may need advice, or need to be reminded of this and that; I may really be cleverer than he is, really be in the right etc. But none of this is necessary in relation to God—and to begin with such things is in fact to busy oneself with ungodly things, or is rather childish.

"The masses " : that is really the aim of my polemic; and I learnt that from Socrates. I wish to make people aware, so that they do not squander and dissipate their lives. The aristocrats assume that there is always a mass of men lost. But they hide the fact, they live withdrawn and behave as though these many, many men did not exist. That is what is godless in the superiority of the aristo-crats; in order to have things their own way they do not even make people aware.

But I do not want that. I wish to make men aware of their own ruin. And if they will not listen to good then I will compel them through evil. Understand me, or at least do not misunderstand me. I do not mean that I am going to strike them (alas, one cannot strike the masses); I mean to make them strike me. And in that way I all the same compel them through evil. For if they once strike me they will be made aware; and if they put me to death— then they will certainly become aware of their position, and I shall have won an absolute victory. In that respect

I am completely dialectical. There are already many who
say " why bother about Mag. Kierkegaard, I'll teach him."
Alas, but all that about showing me that they do not bother
about me, or bothering that I should know that they do
not bother about me, only proves their dependence.
That is perfectly true if one is indifferent enough. But
people show their respect for me by the very fact of showing me that they do not respect me.

People are not so completely depraved as really to desire
evil, but they are blinded and do not really know what
they are doing. Everything depends upon luring a decision
from them. A child may be rebellious against his father in
small things for a long time, but if once its father can drive
it to a real revolt it is far nearer salvation. That is why
the rebellion of the masses is victorious if one goes out of
its path, so that it never notices what it is doing. The
masses have no real opinions and so if they happen to put
a man to death they are *eo ipso* brought to a standstill,
are called to their senses and are made to think.

The reformer who, as it is said, fights against a powerful
man (a pope, an emperor, any individual man) must aim
at bringing about the fall of the powerful; but the man
who, with more justice, takes arms against the masses,
from whom comes all corruption, must see to it that he
himself falls.

Andersen can tell the story of *The Shoes of Fortune*[1]—
but I can tell the story of the shoes that pinch, or rather I
could tell it, but just because I will not tell it but treasure
it in silence, I can tell a very different tale.

The most thankless life of all is to be an author who
writes for authors. One can divide authors into two classes,
those who write for readers, and the real authors, those

[1]The story referred to is the one in which S. K. appears caricatured
as the parrot.

who write for authors. These latter are unintelligible to the reading public, are looked upon as mad and are almost despised—and in the meanwhile authors of the second class plunder their works and have a tremendous success with what they have stolen and spoilt. And thus the authors of the second class become the worst enemies of the others—it is a matter of some importance to them that no one should discover the real position.

What the age needs is *pathos* (in the same way that scurvy needs greens); but not even the work of drilling an artesian well is more subtle than the calculated dialectics of humour, emotion, and passion, with which I have tried to produce a beneficial gust of feeling. The misfortune of the age is understanding and reflection. No one, however immediately enthusiastic, can any longer help us, because they are consumed by the reflection of the age. That is why it requires a man who could reflect the renunciation of all reflection; a man of thought who could conceal an enthusiasm of the first water under the guise of intelligence, heartlessness, mockery, and wit. In order to defend marriage nowadays one must be able to enchant its licentious inclinations with *The Seducer's Diary,* and the same thing applies everywhere.

Objections to the living become the praise of the dead.

May, 1847.   *Nytorv 2, Copenhagen.*

Dear Peter,
        The birthday upon which you write to congratulate me, and which you say " has, contrary to usual, been in your thoughts several times during these days," has lately also been in my thoughts frequently. I am now thirty-four years old. In a certain sense that happened quite

unexpectedly. It astonished me greatly at the time—yes, now I can say so without being afraid of upsetting myself—that you reached the age of thirty-four. Both father and I were of the opinion that no one in our family would live beyond thirty-four. However little I may otherwise have been at one with father we had, in certain particular ideas, a real meeting point, and in conversations such as those father was always quite enthusiastic about the way I could describe the idea with a vivid imagination, and follow it with rigid consequence. It was an altogether peculiar thing about him that he had most markedly what one least expected, imagination, a really melancholy imagination. The thirty-fourth year was then to be the limit and father was to outlive us all. And now it has not happened—I enter upon my thirty-fifth year. . . . (*There follows a detailed proposition for the sale of the house and the mortgages*). . . .

May 14. There is another respect in which conditions are certain to change, and in the future every effort at reformation, if the man concerned is a true reformer, will be directed against the "masses," not against the government. Government (royal power) is really representation, and to that extent Christian (Monarchy), the dialectic of monarchy is historically both tried and settled. Now we are going to begin at another point, namely upon the intensive development of the state itself. In that way there arises the category: "the individual," the category which is so wedded to my name that I wish that on my grave might be put "the individual."

In this respect I attribute great importance to the troubles which are making the round of Europe this year, they show that the European constitution (just as a doctor talks of a man's constitution) has changed entirely; in the future we shall have internal troubles, *secessio in montem sacrum* etc.

It all fits perfectly into my theory, and one day it will be seen how *precisely I* understood the times—Oh, that is the greatest fault a man can commit; for what the times want is nonsense and half-truths—and then that the truth should be despised.

The difference between men is simply a question of how they say stupid things, the universally human is to say them.

. . . "Mary chose the better part."
What is the better part? It is God, and consequently everything. The better part is everything, but it is called the better part because it must be chosen; one does not receive everything as everything; that is not how one begins, one begins by choosing the better part, which is, nevertheless, everything.

The thing that grips me more and more is my original, my first, my deepest, unaltered opinion that I have honestly not chosen this life because it would be brilliant, but as a penitential consolation in all my wretchedness. I have often enough explained the dialectics of the paradox : it is not higher than the universal but beneath it, and only then again a little higher. But the first, the pressure is so great that the joy which comes from the last cannot be taken in vain. That is the thorn in the flesh.

I have lately begun preparing some lectures on the dialectics of the communication of ethics and religion. In the meanwhile I have convinced myself that I am not fit to give lectures. I am spoilt by working things out in detail; the vegetative luxuriance of my style and my method of presentation and the habit of thinking out every line are much too essential to me. If I were to give lectures I should have to take care that they were thoroughly prepared like everything else, and so read them out : which I cannot be bothered to do. In no other way can I satisfy myself.

The thing that makes my position in public life most difficult of all is that people simply cannot grasp what I am fighting. To make a stand against the masses is, in the opinion of the majority, complete nonsense; for the masses, the numbers, the public, are themselves the powers of salvation, that association of lovers of liberty of whom salvation is to come—from the Kings, Popes, and officials who tyrannise over us. *Ach, du lieber Augustin.* That is the result of having fought for centuries against Kings, Popes, and the powerful, and of having looked upon the people and the masses as something holy. It does not occur to people that historical categories change, that now the masses are the only tyrant and at the bottom of all corruption.—To the masses of course that is absolutely incomprehensible.—The masses are domineering and think themselves secure against retribution, for how is one to catch hold of the masses.—What we, at home, call the opposition still lives on the old rubbish about fighting the tyranny of the government. If a police inspector makes the slightest mistake, for which he is punished by his superiors into the bargain, there is a terrible outcry; but when year after year the public, the masses, the plebs etc. are the occasion of the most disgusting horrors and abuse of power, the opposition dares not mention the fact. Either they are incapable of perceiving that something is horrible because it is done by the idol of the opposition, or they see it and dare not discuss it, because they are cowards.—Nowadays when a man is censured for some trifling wrong but, be it noted, by the King, by someone in authority, he has the sympathy of everyone, he is a martyr. But when a man is intellectually speaking persecuted, ill-treated, insulted day in and day out by the stupidity, inquisitiveness and impertinence of the plebs, then it is nothing at all and everything is as it should be.

There can therefore be no doubt that a sacrifice is necessary at this point. We are so far behind that a lot of victims must be sacrificed in order to make people aware that the situation is quite different from the revolt against the Popes and Kings.

Moreover it shows an incredible narrow-mindedness on the part of the reformers' *judicium* and does them no honour to imagine that a reformation could turn upon overthrowing a single man—for then the world would be a fine world indeed.

No, the ancients understood the problem better, understood that the masses are a dangerous power. And it is to the ancient conditions that history is turning back once again. Europe will not have war; but continual internal disorders (Plebeians—Patricians).

If mankind had not embedded itself, with the momentum of centuries and the passion of habit, in the *idée fixe* that a tyrant is one man, they would easily understand that to be persecuted by the masses is the most grievous of all, because the masses are the sum of the individuals, so that each individual makes his little contribution, while he does not realise how great it becomes when all of them do it.

The philosophers have surely been teaching us long enough that the world has entered upon the period of reflection. That is true and for that very reason no individual (King or Pope) can ever be a tyrant. Tyranny must necessarily become a reflective relationship. And so here once again we come up against the category : the masses, public opinion.

But as I have already said, it will be a long time before the man who opposes the masses can win sympathy over to his side, *i.e.* before anyone will understand the reality of the struggle.

Socrates, in my opinion, is and remains the only reformer I know. The others I have read about may have been enthusiastic and well-meaning but they were at the same time decidedly narrow-minded.

When a man, particularly in adversity, proves himself to have been beautifully constructed, like some fine old instrument, so that with each new adversity not only are the strings unharmed but a new string added, that is a sign that the grace of God is upon him.

God looked upon me in my conscience, and now it is impossible for me to forget that he sees me. And because God looked upon me I had and have to look towards God.

From birth (or from one's earliest years) to be thus marked out as a sacrifice, to be thus painfully placed outside the universal, so that absolutely everyone would have compassion on one (for whilst other men are busy complaining of men's lack of compassion, such a man is only too certain of it) : is the beginning of the demoniacal in a man. Now all depends upon whether such a man is bad—or good. If he is bad he becomes a Gloucester,[1] hating and cursing life, raising himself above the universally human. If he is good then he will do everything for other men, his life as a sacrifice will bring him melancholy satisfaction, yet his life, too, has a condition which he makes, or even if he makes no conditions with God he nevertheless thanks God if he is successful : to be able to hide his wretchedness, to avoid becoming the object of compassion. Of all sufferings none is perhaps so great as to be marked out as the object of compassion, none which tempts man so strongly to rebel against God. It is commonly thought that such a man is dull and of limited intellect, but it would not

[1] *Richard III*, cf. *Fear and Trembling*, Problem III.

be difficult to show that this is the secret which lies behind the lives of some of the greatest minds in history.
But it is kept hidden, and that can be done, for it is as
though God were to say to such a man, so long as he makes
use of his outstanding gifts in the service of the good : I
do not wish you to be thus humbled before men, to be aban-
doned in your unmerited misery, but where I am concerned
it will help you to be conscious of your nothingness.

The majority of men are subjective towards themselves
and objective towards all others, terribly objective sometimes—but the real task is in fact to be objective towards
oneself and subjective towards all others.

If you wish to be and to remain enthusiastic, then draw
the silk curtains of facetiousness (irony's), and so hide your
enthusiasm.

June 9. In a certain sense my whole misfortune lies in
this : had I not had means it would never have been possible for me to preserve the terrible secret of my melancholy. (Merciful God, my father too was terribly unjust
to me in his melancholy—an old man who put the whole
weight of his melancholy upon a child, not to speak of
something even more frightful, and yet for all that he
was the best of fathers.) But then I should never have
become the man I have become. I should have been *compelled* either to go mad or to break through. As it is I have
succeeded in making a *salto mortale* into a purely spiritual
existence. But then again in that way I have become completely heterogeneous from mankind in general. What I
really lack is the physical side and all the assumptions
that go with it.

Had St. Paul an official position? No. Had he any means
of livelihood? No. Did he make a lot of money? No.

Did he marry and have children? No. But in that case St. Paul cannot have been a serious man!

Aug. 14. Curiously enough the journey to Berlin is still in my thoughts. But I cannot go. A man has applied to me regarding the sale of my house. He came so opportunely, really so inexplicably opportunely that I cannot appreciate it enough. In such circumstances I dare not go away. If he were to come in my absence it would distress me indescribably.

Aug. 16. And so the decision is taken; I remain at home. To-morrow the manuscript[1] goes to the printer.—In order to reassure myself that it was not in any way a possible dislike for all the pother connected with going on a journey which prevented me I have, with my habitual suspiciousness of myself, begun a course of baths which I knew to be very distasteful to me. . . .

I now feel the need of approaching nearer to myself in a deeper sense, by approaching nearer to God in the understanding of myself. I must remain on the spot and be *renewed inwardly*. It is quite a different thing from the possibility of setting forth upon a journey abroad of some length, perhaps at the end of the autumn. But it must not bear the impress of emotion or the concentrated excitement of a little expedition to Berlin.

I must come to closer grips with my melancholy. It has until now lain deep down and the tremendous intellectual strain has helped to keep it down. That my work has profited others, that God has approved it and helped me in every way is sure enough. Again and again I thank him for having done infinitely more for me than I ever expected. My consolation is that although no man has any merit before God yet he has nevertheless looked with

[1] *Works of Love.*

approval upon my efforts, and that with his assistance I have borne my terrible suffering to the very end. I know within myself before God that my work as an author, my willingness to obey his sign, to sacrifice every earthly and worldly consideration, will soften for me the impression of what I have personally done wrong. Just because I began my literary activity with a heavy conscience I have taken the greatest care to make it so pure that it might be a small repayment of my debt. That purity, that integrity, that industry is what seems to be madness in the eyes of the world. I know that God looks upon it otherwise, and that it does not follow that my work is so pure in his eyes that I can praise myself for it before him.

But now God wishes things otherwise. Something is stirring within me which points to a metamorphosis. For that very reason I dare not go to Berlin, for that would be to procure an abortion. I shall therefore remain quiet, in no way working too strenuously, hardly even strenuously, not begin on a new book, but try to understand myself, and *really think out the idea of my melancholy together with God here and now*. That is how I must get rid of my melancholy and bring Christianity closer to me. Hitherto I have defended myself against my melancholy with intellectual work, which keeps it away—now, in the faith that God has forgotten in forgiveness what guilt there may be, I must try to forget it myself, but not in distraction, not at a distance from it but in God, I must see to it that in thinking of God I learn to think that he has forgotten it, and thus myself learn to dare to forget it in forgiveness.

Everyone would like to have lived *at the same time* as great men and great events : God, knows how many really live at the same time as themselves. To do that (and so neither in hope or fear of the future, nor in the past) is to understand oneself and be at peace, and that is only possible through one's relation to God, or it is one's relation to God.

Christianity is certainly not melancholy, it is, on the contrary, glad tidings—for the melancholy; to the frivolous it is certainly not glad tidings, for it wishes first of all to make them serious.

A word about myself

I am the ultimate phase of the poetic temper on the way to becoming a sort of reformer on a small scale. I have much more imagination than such a man would have, but then again less of a certain personal power which is necessary in order to appear in that way. With the help of my imagination, which be it noted comes after the dialectical, I can catch all the Christian qualifications at their most accurate and most living. Our times clearly require that. There are certain things which must continually be called to mind or otherwise the standard is lost. It is like the flight of wild birds above the heads of tame ones when those qualifications of the Christian life are recalled which demand the utmost.—But just because I am a poet in that sense, one whose task is to raise the price and if possible to whisper to every individual what the demands could be, I must take particular care not to acquire any followers.

Deep within every man there lies the dread of being alone in the world, forgotten by God, overlooked among the tremendous household of millions upon millions. That fear is kept away by looking upon all those about one who are bound to one as friends or family; but the dread is nevertheless there and one hardly dares think of what would happen to one if all the rest were taken away.

If Christ had been merely a man then Peter would

J.   E clearly not have denied him; Peter was too deep and honest for that. But whereas in general the parsons talk nonsense in the opposite sense and say that it was doubly irresponsible of Peter because Christ was God; one ought to say : no, that is precisely what explains Peter. Had he simply looked upon Christ as a man then he could well have endured the thought that he should be treated thus, and Peter would not have forgotten himself but would have been true to him. But the seeming madness that Christ was God, that he had it in his power to call legions of angels at any moment he wished : that is what utterly over-whelmed Peter. Just as one can lose the power of speech from fright, in the same way all Peter's ideas left him and in that, as it were, apoplectic condition he denied him.

I was brought up on Mynster's Sermons—by my father. There's the rub; for naturally it never occurred to my father to take the sermons other than literally. Brought up on Mynster's Sermons—by Mynster; that's a problem.

Nov. There is no doubt that the present time, and Pro-testantism always, needs the monastery again, or that it should exist. " The Monastery " is an essential dialectical fact in Christianity, and we need to have it there like a light-house, in order to gauge where we are—even though I myself should not exactly go into one. But if there is to be true Christianity in every generation there must be individuals with that need. What would Luther say if he were to look around him now and see that at the present time there were not many whom religion had overwhelmed —that we had all grown so strong—or so weak in religion ! That the few who resembled such men were nowadays directed to a mad-house. What would Luther say to the fact that the class which alone and decisively (*si placet*) represents Christianity, the priests, have become so worldly-minded in the service of the state (not to speak of their inner state) that they have more to do with counting sheep and pigs or à la Augustus with counting men, with attending to the awakening of the apparently dead—rather than with tearing Christendom out of its seeming death, or what is worse still out of its appearance of life. For a seeming death is not so dangerous simply because it has the seeming danger of death; but a seeming life is the most dangerous of all—and without apparent danger.

With the strange freemasonry of poets I can use these words as the motto for part of my life's suffering. *Infandum me jubes* Regina *renovare dolorem*.

The girl has given me trouble enough. And now she is —not dead—but happily and comfortably married. I said that on the same day (6 years ago)—and was called the lowest of lowest cads. Extraordinary!

Alas, yes, I admit it, I have been deeply and inwardly concerned to recognise all of the poor men who knew me, to greet every servant with whom I had even the slightest acquaintance, to remember the last time I saw him, whether he had been ill, and to enquire after him. I have never in my life, not even when I was most preoccupied with an idea, been so busy that I did not find time to stop for a moment if a poor man spoke to me. Is that a crime? I should have been ashamed before God, and my soul would have been troubled, if I had become so self-important that I behaved as though "other men" did not exist. Do these other men not exist for God, and does he not demand that I should not become conceited and self-important but rather that I should acknowledge by my actions that obedience is dearer to God than the fat of rams!

When in regard to communicating something it is self-evident what to communicate means, when it is simply a matter of course and not a moment need be wasted discussing the question, when it is the kind of assumption which does not even need to be mentioned : then, if one has something to communicate, it is as easy as shelling peas. But when an author has an individual conception of what communication is, when perhaps the distinctive characteristic, the reality of his historical importance is concentrated in precisely that; well, then it will be a long affair—O school of patience. Before there can be any mention of understanding anything which he has communicated one must first of all understand him from the point of view of his particular dialectic of communication, and understand everything from that point of view. For that particular dialectic of communication cannot be communicated in the traditional dialectical form. The age will of course require this of him. Oh, how long it will take to be understood, O school of patience. And the more a man understands himself through what he understands, the more easily he will discover that he is not understood— only those who themselves understand nothing can delude themselves into believing that everyone understands them. Oh, the sadness of having understood something true—and then of only seeing oneself misunderstood. Oh, sadness—for what is irony in the mystery of the heart but sadness. Sadness means to be alone in having understood something true and as soon as one is in company with others, with those who misunderstand, that sadness becomes irony.

"The Individual"

A hint[1]

"The individual" is the category through which, from a religious point of view, our age, our race and its history must pass. And the man who stood and fell at Thermopylæ was not as convinced as I am, who stand at the narrow pass "the individual." It was his duty to prevent the hordes from forcing their way through that narrow pass; if they got through he was lost. My duty is, at any rate at first sight, much easier and seems to place me in far less danger of being trodden down; as though I were an unimportant servant who, if possible, was to help the masses trying to go through the narrow pass, "the individual," through which, be it noted, no one can ever go without first becoming "the individual." Yet had I to crave an inscription on my grave I would ask for none other than "the individual"—and even if it is not understood now, then in truth it will be. It was with that category that I worked at a time when everything in Denmark was directed towards the system; now it is no longer so much as mentioned.* My possible importance is undoubtedly linked to that category. My writings may soon be forgotten, like those of many another writer. But if that was the right category, and everything in order with that category, if in this I saw aright, if I understood aright that such was my task, neither pleasurable nor thankful, whether vouchsafed to me in inward suffering such as has certainly rarely

*And now, in 1848!

[1] Afterwards added as an appendix to *The point of view for my work as an author.*

been experienced, or whether in outward sacrifices such as not every man is willing to make—in that case I shall endure and my writings with me.

"The individual"; now that the world has gone so far along the road of reflection Christianity stands and falls with that category. But for that category Pantheism would have triumphed. There will therefore certainly arise men who will know how to distort its meaning in a very different sense (they will not have had to work to bring it to light); but "the individual" is and remains the anchor in the confusion of Pantheism, the hellebore which can sober people and the weight upon which stress can be laid, only that as the confusion grows greater and greater those who are to work with it (at the capstan—or where the weights are put on) must have an increasingly dialectical relation to it. I bind myself to make every man whom I can include in the category "the individual" into a Christian or rather, since no man can do that for another, I vouch for his becoming one. As "that individual" he is alone, alone in the whole world, alone—before God : then it will be easy to obey. Ultimately all doubt has its stronghold in the illusions of temporal existence, such as that one is several people or all mankind, who can in the end thus overawe God (just as the "people" overawe the King or the "public" overawe the alderman) and oneself become Christ. Pantheism is an optical illusion, one of the various notions formed at random by temporal existence, or one of those atmospheric phenomena which it produces and which are supposed to be eternity. The point is however, that this category cannot be taught; the use of it is an art, a moral task, and an art the exercise of which is always dangerous and at times might even require the life of the artist. For that which divinely understood is the highest of all things will be looked-upon by a self-opinionated race and the confused crowd as *lèse majesté* against the "race," the "masses," the "public" etc.

"The individual"; that category has only been used once before and then by Socrates, in a dialectical and decisive way, to disintegrate paganism. In Christianity it will be used once again—in order to make men (the Christians) into Christians. It is not the category which missionaries can use in dealing with heathens when they preach the Gospel, but the category of a missionary in Christendom itself, so as to make the change, which lies in being and becoming a Christian, a more inward change. When he comes the missionary will use that category. For if the age is waiting for a hero it waits in vain. It is far more probable that a man will come who will teach them obedience in divine weakness—by making them rebel against God by putting to death the one who was obedient to God.

Jan. 29. Christ cast out a devil and it was dumb. Have you never been dumb, or known what it is to be dumb. One can go about and be dumb, not wishing to speak : but that is not what is meant. One can play at being mysterious and be dumb : but that is not what is meant. But have you never been so indescribably distressed, that the power of sorrow over your whole being was almost like the powers of nature : then you have experienced what it means to be dumb, experienced the feeling of being unable, even though your life were at stake, to express the agony that rocked deep within you, and selfish of itself made you dumb—in order that you might not rid yourself of it. For that is how infinite sorrow is egotistical; it makes a man dumb in order to keep him in its power.

All this fear of Germany is a fancy, a game, a new attempt to flatter national vanity. A million people who honestly own up to being a small nation, and then if everyone is resolved before God to be what they are : is a tremendous strength; there is no danger there. No, the misfortune is quite another; the misfortune is that this little people is demoralised, divided against itself, disgustingly envious one of another, insubordinate towards everyone in power, petty towards everyone who is something, impertinent and unbridled, incited to a sort of tyranny of the plebs. That produces a bad conscience, and therefore people fear Germany. But no one dares to say where the misfortune lies—and so people flatter all these unhealthy passions and become self-important by fighting against the Germans.

Denmark is facing a loathsome period. Provincialmindedness and ill-natured pettiness fighting among themselves; in the end one will be suspected of being German unless one wears a particular kind of hat, etc., etc. On the other side the Communist rising; everyone who owns a little will be marked out and persecuted through the press.

That is Denmark's misfortune—or the punishment which has come upon Denmark, a people without a true fear of God, a people whose national consciousness is small-town gossip, a people who idolise being nothing, where schoolboys are the judges, a people where those who should govern are afraid and those who ought to obey are impertinent, a people among whom are to be found daily proofs that there is no public morality in the land—a people who can only be saved by a tyrant or a few martyrs.

NB NB   *Wednesday, April* 19, 1848.

My whole being is changed. My reserve and self-isolation is broken—I must speak.

Lord give thy grace.

It is indeed true, what my father said of me: "you will never be anything so long as you have money." He spoke prophetically, he thought that I would lead a riotous and debauched life. But that is just where he was wrong. But with an acuteness of mind and a melancholy such as mine, and then to have had money: what an opportunity for developing all the agonies of self-torture in my heart.

(Just as I had decided to speak, curiously opportunely, my doctor arrived. But I did not speak to him, it was too sudden for me. But my decision to speak stands fast.)

Alas, she could not break the silence of my melancholy,

That I loved her—nothing is more certain—and thus my melancholy received enough to feed upon, oh, it received a terrible addition.* It is essentially owing to her, to my melancholy and to my money that I became an author. Now, with God's help, I shall be myself; I believe that Christ will help me to be victorious over my melancholy, and so I shall become a priest.

And yet in that melancholy I loved the world, for I loved my melancholy. Everything has helped to heighten the tension of my position, her sufferings, all my exertions, and finally the fact that I was derided has, with the help of God, contributed to my breaking through now, finally, when I am obliged to worry about my livelihood.

NB   NB

April 24, 1848, Easter Monday.

No, no, my self-isolation cannot be broken, at least not now. The thought of breaking it occupies me so much, and at all times, that it only becomes more and more firmly embedded.

Yet it consoles me to have spoken to my doctor. I have often felt anxious about myself for perhaps being too proud to speak to anyone. But just as I did so earlier I have done so again. And what had the doctor really to say? Nothing. But for me it was of importance to have respected the human relationship.

*and yet she could not have been mine. I was and am a penitent and my punishment was merely terribly increased by having begun that relationship.

NB NB

May 11. The majority of men (if they find that from
their earliest years it is their lot to bear one suffering or
another, one cross or another, one of those sad limitations
of the soul) begin by hoping, or as they say, believing that
things will go better, that God will make things all right
etc., and then at length, when no change occurs they come
little by little to rely upon the help of eternity, *i.e.* they
resign themselves and find strength in contenting themselves with the eternal.—The deeper nature, or he whom
God has fashioned on a more eternal plan begins at once
by understanding that this is a thing he must bear as long
as he lives, he dares not require of God such an extraordinary paradoxical help. But God is perfect love just
the same, nothing is more certain to him. So he is resigned
and inasmuch as the eternal lies close to him he thus finds
repose, blessedly assured all the while that God is love.
But he must put up with suffering. Then in the course of
time, when he becomes more concrete in the actuality of
life, comes more and more to himself as a temporal being,
when time and its succession exercises its power over him,
when in spite of all his effort it becomes so difficult to live
on with the assistance of only the eternal, when he becomes
a human being in a humbler sense or learns what it means
to be human (for in his resignation he is still too ideal or
too abstract, for which reason also there is something of
despair in such resignation) :—then the possibility of faith
presents itself to him in this form : whether he will believe
by virtue of the absurd that God will help him temporally,
(Here lie all the paradoxes.) So the forgiveness of
sin also means to be helped temporarily, otherwise it
is mere resignation, which can endure to bear the
punishment, though still convinced that God is love. But
belief in the forgiveness of sins means to believe that

here in time the sin is forgotten by God, that it is really true that God forgets.

That means to say, that most people never attain to faith. For a long time they live on in immediateness and finally they attain to a certain amount of reflection, and so they die. The exceptions begin the other way round, from childhood up dialectical, *i.e.* without immediateness, they begin with dialectics, with reflection and in that way live on year after year (just about as long as others live merely in the immediate) and then, at a ripe age, the possibility of faith shows itself to them. For faith is immediateness after reflection.

The exceptions, naturally, have a very unhappy childhood and youth; for to be essentially reflective at an age which is naturally immediate, is the depths of melancholy. But they are recompensed; for most people do not succeed in becoming spirit, and all the fortunate years of their immediateness are, where spirit is concerned, a loss and therefore they never attain to spirit. But the unhappy childhood and youth of the exception is transfigured into spirit.

It is wonderful how God's love overwhelms me—alas, ultimately I know of no truer prayer than what I pray over and over again, that God will allow me and not be angry with me because I continuously thank him for having done and for doing, yes, and for doing so indescribably much more for me than I ever expected. Surrounded by scorn, pestered day in and day out by the pettiness of men, even of those nearest to me, I know of nothing either at home or in my inmost self than to thank and thank God; for I understand that what he has done for me is indescribable. A man —and what is a man before God, nothing, less than nothing; and what is more a poor man who from childhood up has fallen into the most wretched melancholy, an object of dread to himself : and then God helps me and grants me

what he has granted me! A life which was a burden to me
however much I may at times have understood all its fortunate aspects, but which was all embittered for me by the
dark spot which ruined all; and as I understood, if other
men knew the secret of my life, I should from the very
beginning have been the object of their pity and sympathy,
a burden to myself: God takes charge of such lives. He
lets me weep before him in silent solitude, pour forth and
again pour forth my pain, with the blessed consolation of
knowing that he is concerned for me—and in the meanwhile he gives that life of pain a significance which almost
overwhelms me, gives me good fortune and strength and
wisdom for my whole undertaking, in making my life the
pure expression of ideas, or he makes it into that.

For I now see so clearly (once again in renewed joy to
God, a new occasion of thanks) that my life is so arranged.
My life began without immediateness, with a terrible
melancholy, in its earliest youth deranged in its very deepest
foundations, a melancholy which threw me for a time into
sin and debauchery and yet (humanly speaking) almost
more insane than guilty. Thus my father's death really
pulled me up. I dared not believe that the fundamental
misfortune of my being could be resolved: and so I grasped
eternity with the blessed assurance that God is love, even
though I was to suffer thus all my life; yes, with that blessed
assurance. That is how I looked upon my life. Then once
again and sympathetically, I was flung down into the
abyss of melancholy by having to break off my engagement and why, simply because I dared not believe that
God would resolve the fundamental misfortune of my
being, take away my almost insane melancholy, which I
now desired, for her sake and then again for mine, with
all the passion of my soul. It was as difficult as possible
to have to reproduce my own misery. Once again I was
resigned. Thinking only of working to free her I went to
meet a life of this kind but, God be praised, always certain

and with the blessed assurance that God is love, nothing has been more certain to me.

And now, now that in many ways I have been brought to the last extremity, now (since last Easter, though with intervals) a hope has awakened in my soul that God may desire to resolve the fundamental misery of my being. That is to say, now I am in faith in the profoundest sense. Faith is immediacy after reflection. As poet and thinker I have represented all things in the medium of the imagination, myself living in resignation. Now life comes closer to me, or I am closer to myself, coming to myself.—To God all things are possible, that thought is now, in the deepest sense, my watch-word, has acquired a significance in my eyes which I had never imagined it could have. That I must never, at any moment, presume to say that there is no way out for God because I cannot see any. For it is despair and presumption to confuse one's pittance of imagination with the possibility over which God disposes.

Most people really believe that the Christian commandments (*e.g.* to love one's neighbour as oneself) are intentionally a little too severe—like putting the clock on half an hour to make sure of not being late in the morning.

NB

Here again is one of the most important points regarding man's relation to God.

If it were possible to have a physical certainty that God would use one as an instrument (like a king his minister)—how could it be possible not to submit willingly to every sacrifice. But is it possible to have a real certainty, or even a purely immediate certainty of one's relation to God. For God is spirit. One can only have a spiritual relationship to a spirit; and a spiritual relationship is *eo ipso* dialectical.

—How an Apostle understands himself in having been called by a revelation and in having an immediate certainty which cannot in any way be dialectical, I do not understand—but it can be believed. I understand an ordinary man's relation to God and to Christ, Socratically. Socrates did not know with certainty whether he was immortal. (Oh, the rogue, for he knew that immortality was a spiritual qualification and *eo ipso* dialectical, and beyond all immediate certainty. So that even though he did not know to what degree he was immortal—which so many dunces know exactly—he knew what he was saying.) But his life expresses the fact that there is an immortality and that he himself was immortal. The question of immortality, he says, concerns me so infinitely, that I stake everything on that " if."

Mynster has always had a great partiality for " these quiet hours in holy places," because then he can dispense Christianity as one of life's ingredients not as the absolute. . . . For Mynster, however, it would be quite impossible, indeed the most impossible thing of all, to preach in the market-place. Yet this preaching in churches has become an almost heathenish and theatrical thing, and Luther is quite right in insisting that we should not preach in churches. In paganism the theatre was the church—in Christendom the churches have practically become theatres. How so? Why, in this way. It is agreeable, and not devoid of a certain pleasure, to commune with the highest thoughts through the imagination once a week. Nothing more than that. And this has actually become the norm for the sermons in Denmark. Hence the artistic remoteness—even in the clumsiest sermons.

My years of penitence are fast running out. I have nothing to complain of; I understand with God why I suffer—and give thanks. I live, and with God's help I shall die in the belief that when death has carried me away (and this cannot happen before, or else it would not be penitence to the end) he will place the imprint of providence upon my life so that it will help men to become aware of God and to see how thoughtlessly they hinder themselves from leading the highest life, a life in communion with God.

I feel a longing to say nothing more except : Amen. I am overwhelmed by gratitude for all that providence has done for me. How is it possible for things to go so well? Poetically speaking I can only say that there is nothing which has happened in my life of which I cannot say, that is the very thing which perfectly suits my nature and disposition : I lack nothing. I was unhappy in my love; but I simply cannot imagine myself happy unless I were to become a different person altogether. But in my unhappiness I was happy. Humanly speaking, I am saved by one already dead, my father; but I simply cannot imagine myself having been saved by someone living. And so I became an author in exactly the way which suited the latent possibilities of my nature; and then I was persecuted —oh, had that been wanting my life would not have been mine. There is melancholy in everything in my life, but then again an indescribable happiness. But in that way I became myself through God's indescribable grace and support and, as I am almost tempted to say, by his special favour, if that did not mean less to me than the blessed thought, which I believe and which brings me such perfect peace : that he loves all men equally. I have, quite literally, lived with God as one lives with one's father. Amen.

If I could be reconciled with her, that would be my one wish, and a heartfelt joy. But her marriage rests upon me. If I were to give her any certainty as to how she was and is loved : she would regret her marriage. She is held together by the thought that however much she may have seen in me, admired me and loved me, I behaved meanly to her. She was not religious enough to stand by herself with an unhappy love—I have never dared to help her directly, that has cost me suffering enough.

I owe everything, from the beginning, to my father. When melancholy as he was, he saw me melancholy, his prayer to me was : Be sure that you really love Jesus Christ.

The Archimedian point outside the world is an oratory where a man really prays in all sincerity—and he shall move the earth. And it is unbelievable what a man of prayer can achieve if he will close the doors behind him.

From now on the human race will no longer be led on by prophets and judges but forced back by martyrs, who will run headlong against that human discovery, progress. Otherwise there can be no progress : in intensity. The problem is set, once and for all; there is nothing further to add. The thing is to become more inward.

The result of human progress is that everything becomes thinner and thinner—the result of divine providence is to make everything more inward.

I should have been able to bear everything else, would have been able to bear indescribable suffering far more easily, all the attacks upon me (for in that respect I am sufficiently conscious of my superiority)—if my financial future had not tortured me.

The communication of Christianity must ultimately end in "bearing witness," the maieutic form can never be final. For truth, from the Christian point of view, does not lie in the subject (as Socrates understood it) but in a revelation which must be proclaimed.

In Christendom the maieutic form can certainly be used, simply because the majority in fact live under the impression that they are Christians. But since Christianity is Christianity the maieuticer must become the witness.

In the end the maieuticer will not be able to bear the responsibility because the indirect method is ultimately rooted in human intelligence, however much it may be sanctified and consecrated by fear and trembling. God becomes too powerful for the maieuticer and so he is the witness, though different from the direct witness in that he has been through the process of becoming one.

NB NB

It has constantly been maintained that reflection inevitably destroys Christianity and is its natural enemy. I hope, now, that with God's help it will be shown that a godfearing reflection can once again tie the knot at which a superficial reflection has been tugging for so long. The divine authority of the Bible and all that belongs to it has been done away with; it looks as though one had only to wait for the last stage of reflection in order to have done with the whole thing. But behold, reflection performs the opposite service by once more bringing the springs of Christianity into play, and in such a way that it can stand up—against reflection. Christianity naturally remains completely unaltered, not one iota is changed. But the struggle is a different one; up to the present it has been between reflection and simple, immediate Christianity; now it will be between reflection and simplicity armed with reflection.

And that, in my opinion, is sense. The problem is not to understand Christianity but to understand that it cannot be understood. That is the holiness of faith, and reflection is sanctified by being thus used. . . .

Oh, the more I think upon all that has been vouchsafed me the greater my desire for an eternity in which to thank God.

It now seems as though I were to be on good terms with the leading people, and why, partly because they have become polemical; now they themselves are, or think themselves, in the minority, and I, well, if my genius can be said to be related to anything at all then it is to being in the minority.

It is very dangerous to go into eternity with possibilities which one has oneself prevented from becoming realities. A possibility is a hint from God. One must follow it. In every man there is latent the highest possibility, one must follow it. If God does not wish it then let him prevent it, but one must not hinder oneself. Trusting to God I have dared, but I was not successful; in that is to be found peace, calm, and confidence in God. I have not dared : that is a woeful thought, a torment in eternity.

When I sold the house[1] I thought of giving up writing and travelling abroad for two years, and then returning home and becoming a priest. I had in fact made 2,200 Rd. on the deal.

But then the thought occurred to me : you want to travel abroad, but why? In order to break off your work and for the sake of recreation. But surely you know from experience that you are never so productive as when abroad, living as you do in complete isolation, so that you would return from a two-years' journey abroad with an enormous pile of MSS.

[1]Nytorv 2, sold for 22,000 Rd. in December, 1847. S. K. had inherited half; bought the other half from his brother (making 1,000 Rd.) and lived there from 1844-1847.

So I took rooms, a flat which had attracted me particularly for some time back, and which I had often said was the only one I really wanted.

The idea of travelling for two years was all imagination. Particularly since I had a whole work lying ready for publication and, as I have already said, by going abroad I should only have opened the sluice-gates of production.

But it was with the idea of travelling for two years that I bought government bonds with the cash from the sale of my house, which I had otherwise decided to leave lying idle—the stupidest thing I have ever done and which must certainly be looked upon as a sort of lesson; for now I have lost *c.* 700 Rd. on them. For the rest of the cash I afterwards bought some shares on which I have not perhaps lost.

And so I rented the flat; printed *Christian Discourses* and was in the midst of proof-correction when confusion broke loose—Anders[1] was taken from me : and it was a good thing I had the rooms.

I moved in. In the flat I suffered indescribably because of its inadequacy. But on the other hand providence helped me as usual to achieve my desire, though I always grasp at the wrong methods and use the wrong means; the same thing happened again. If anything is to help me to be less productive, to slacken the pace, and in general make me worldly, then it is worldly troubles and inconveniences.

As for the rest, I have written some of the best things I have ever written in this house; and in the meanwhile I had the opportunity of getting used to the thought of gradually stopping my production or in any case of being somewhat more careful about my resources. That would not have happened in an eternity abroad where, far from all disturbances, suffering too a little from melancholy, I throw myself into my work on a tremendous scale.

Last summer I drew Rasmus Nielsen closer to me; that

[1] S. K.'s servant who was called up.

meant decreasing my work and yet doing something towards carrying it out.

If I could travel without becoming productive, travel
and travel for some time, it might perhaps be a good thing.
But a prolonged stay in any one place only makes me
write more than ever. It has been much better for me to
learn a little by doing without Anders and other such comforts, which were perhaps too conducive to work.

But the financial question in these troubled times has
certainly weighed upon me. However, it was undoubtedly
a good thing that my attention was drawn to it in time.
It also helps to consume such selfishness as there is in me
and in my work; for my position as an author will certainly
become serious enough.

It is terrible when I think, even for a single moment,
over the dark background which, from the very earliest
time, was part of my life. The dread with which my father
filled my soul, his own frightful melancholy, and all the
things in this connection which I do not even note down.
I felt a dread of Christianity and yet felt myself so strongly
drawn towards it.

And later on what I suffered through Peter, when he
became morbidly religious.

As I have said, it is terrible to think, at moments, of
the life I led in the hidden centre of my heart, of course
literally never a word breathed to anyone, not even daring
to note down the least thing about it—and that I was able
to clothe that life with an outwardly lively and cheerful
existence.

How true are the words I have so often said of myself,
that as Scheherazade saved her life by telling fairy stories
I save my life, or keep myself alive by writing.

Severity first, that is to say the severity of the ideal, and
then gentleness. I myself have as much need as anybody

of being spoken to gently, my soul is much disposed to speak gently—but in a time of confused thinking the first must be put first, lest gentleness be an occasion for slothful indulgence.

Fundamentally a reformation which did away with the Bible would now be just as valid as Luther's doing away with the Pope. All that about the Bible has developed a religion of learning and law, a mere distraction. A little of that knowledge has gradually percolated to the simplest classes so that no one any longer reads the Bible humanly. As a result it does immeasurable harm; where life is concerned its existence is a fortification of excuses and escapes; for there is always something one has to look into first of all, and it always seems as though one had first of all to have the doctrine in perfect form before one could begin to live—that is to say, one never begins.

The Bible Societies, those vapid caricatures of missions, societies which like all companies only work with money and are just as mundanely interested in spreading the Bible as other companies in their enterprises : the Bible Societies have done immeasurable harm. Christendom has long been in need of a hero who, in fear and trembling before God, had the courage to forbid people to read the Bible. That is something quite as necessary as preaching *against* Christianity.

The only person of whom I can say that I am envious is the person, when he comes, whom I call my reader, who in peace and quiet will be able to sit down and purely intellectually enjoy the drama of infinite comedy which I, by living here, have allowed Copenhagen to play. To be sure, I perceive the value of the drama better than he; but I have felt the misery and bitterness of every day, as well as the new misunderstanding of people not even daring to laugh with me, because they were suspicious and unable to conceive that in the midst of all that nonsense I still had an eye for the comic. Poetically it is of no interest that the drama was played every day year after year, poetically it is too absurd; poetically it must be shortened. And so it will be, for my reader. But in and through the daily repetition begins religion and that is how I understand my life : to me that infinitely comic drama was a martyrdom. And yet if I were not conscious of being absolutely religiously bound, I should feel like going to some lonely place to laugh and laugh—though I should still suffer at the thought that this Gotham, the beloved country of my birth, is the prostituted residence of the bourgeoisie, my beloved Copenhagen.

. . . The first form of rulers in the world were the "tyrants," the last will be the "martyrs"; in the history of the world this development is an ever-increasing worldliness; for worldliness is at its greatest, must have the upper hand in the most frightful way, when only martyrs can be rulers. When one man is the tyrant "the masses" are not entirely worldly; but when "the masses" want to be the tyrant, then worldliness has become quite universal, and then only the martyr can be the ruler. Between a tyrant and a martyr there is of course an enormous difference, although they both have one thing in common : the power to compel. The tyrant, himself ambitious to dominate, compels people through his power; the martyr, himself unconditionally obedient to God, compels others through his suffering. The tyrant dies and his rule is over; the martyr dies and his rule begins. The tyrant was egoistically the individual who inhumanly made the others into "the masses," and ruled over the masses; the martyr is the suffering individual who educates others through his Christian love of mankind, translating the masses into individuals—and there is joy in heaven over every individual whom he thus saves out of the masses. And on this whole books could be written, even by me a sort of poet and thinker, not to speak of him when he comes : the thinker-poet or the poet-thinker who, moreover, will have seen at close quarters what I dimly suspect, who will have seen what I only dimly imagine will be done one day in the distant future.

There *really* only exist two parties; to choose between them is an Either-Or! It goes without saying that in the activity of the world there are many parties—but it is not really so, it is only figuratively that one can speak in this case of making a choice, because it does not matter and is equally wrong whatever one chooses. In the profoundest sense, really, there are only two parties between which to choose, and there lies the category " the individual " : *either* obedient to God, fearing and loving him, to cling to God against men, so that one loves men in God; *or* to cling to men against God, so that one distorts and humanises God and " savours not the things of God but those that be of men." For between God and man there is a struggle, a struggle for life and death; was the God-Man not put to death!—And so on this alone, which is solemn; and about " the individual "; what demonia is : whether the demoniacal is good or evil; about silence in regard to evil and in regard to good; on " deceiving into truth "; on indirect communication, how far it is a betrayal of the human, an importunity towards God; what one learns about the demoniacal through consideration of the God-Man—on that alone whole books could be written even by me, a sort of thinker, not to say by him, when he comes : " the thinker " who will have seen " the missionary of Christendom," and will know at first hand about all that I have only little by little learnt to understand a little.

It is high time that Christianity was taken away again from men in order to teach them to appreciate it a little.

What does being a poet mean? It means having one's own personal life, one's reality in quite different categories from those of one's poetic work, it means being related to the ideal in imagination only, so that one's own personal life is more or less a satire on poetry and on oneself. In that sense all modern thinkers, even those of standing (I mean the Germans, there are no Danish ones at all), are poets. And altogether that is the maximum which life shows. The majority of people live entirely without ideas; then there are the few who have a poetic relation to the ideal, but deny it in their personal lives. And so the parsons too are poets, and because they are parsons they are " deceivers " in a far deeper sense than the sense in which Socrates long ago called the poets.

The second time I talked to Christian VIII was at Sorgenfrie many months later. Moreover his conversations were in a certain sense not very important to me, for he wished me to talk. But it was stimulating to talk with him and I have never seen an oldish man so animated, in a fever of excitement, almost like a woman. He was a sort of spiritual and intellectual voluptuary. I saw at once that here was danger, and I was therefore very careful to keep as far from him as possible. In the presence of a king I found it unsuitable to make my eccentricity into a pretext for not visiting him and so used different tactics, saying I was unwell.

Christian VIII was brilliantly gifted but ran to seed,

lacking a moral background of corresponding proportions. If he had lived in a southern country, I can imagine that Christian VIII would have been the certain prey of a cunning priest. No woman would ever really have got power over him, not even the most gifted, partly because he was too intelligent and partly because he shared a little the manly superstition that man is more intelligent than woman.

But a Jesuit—he could have turned and twisted Christian VIII any way he liked, but the Jesuit would have had to have complete command of *the interesting,* for that was what he was really panting for. But without a doubt he was captivating, extraordinarily subtle, and had an unusual eye for whatever could please or satisfy the individual, just that particular individual.

And so I went in. He said: "It is a long time since I have seen you here." To that I answered, still at the door: "Your majesty will perhaps first of all let me explain myself. I must ask your majesty to rest assured how much I appreciate the graces and favours which you show me; but I am poor in health and that is why I come so seldom, I cannot endure waiting in an antechamber, it exhausts me." He answered that I need not wait, but that in any case I could write to him. I thanked him for that. Thereupon we began talking, walking about part of the time. He always preferred to talk about the government's affairs, or general remarks about some political theme or other. That day he led the conversation to communism of which he was plainly enough anxious and afraid. I explained to him that as I understood it the whole movement which was impending was a movement which did not come in contact with kings. It would be a fight between classes, but the fighting parties would always find it in their interest to be on good terms with the King. It was a return to the problems of antiquity and it was therefore easy to see that in a sense the king would stand outside them. It

would be like the fights in a house between the cellar and
the ground-floor, and between these and the first floor,
but the landlord would not be attacked. I talked next of
how to fight with "the masses": simply remain quite quiet;
that "the masses" were like a woman with whom one
never fought directly but indirectly, and helped them to
put their foot in it, and since they were wanting in intelligence they would always lose in the end—but simply stand
fast. Here he said: "yes, of all people a king should do
that." To that I answered nothing. And so I said that
what the whole age needed was education, and that what
became violence in a large country, in Denmark became
rudeness. Then he said some complimentary things to me
about my mind etc. I made use of the situation and said:
Your Majesty sees best of all from me that what I say is
true, for where I am concerned everything really turns
upon the fact that I am well brought up, and therefore
really upon my father. And so we talked about Guizot,
an attack which had just been made upon him. I explained how ambiguous the position was in modern states,
where scandal has really been given an official position,
and the right tactics were, consequently, to ignore it, but
that they suddenly took it into their heads one day to take
such an attack seriously. "I imagine Guizot reading the
attack, and then at the most, perhaps, looking in the glass
to see that his smile and appearance were the same as
usual—and then, then people hit upon the idea of taking
it seriously; and if on the other hand he had taken such
an attack seriously he would have been laughed out of
court as a country bumpkin who was not used to life in a
big city."

Then he talked a little about Sorø, gave a sort of lecture
on it, and questioned me: I answered that I had never
thought about Sorø. He asked me whether I would not
like to have a position there. Now I knew that he had
been out fishing that very morning and so my answer con-

tained an allusion to it. That in addition to the real line
fishermen had a special little line on which they sometimes caught the best fish—and I was a little line of that
kind.

Then he thanked me for the book I had lately brought
him, he had read in it, "it was very profound but above
him," I answered: "Your majesty naturally has not got time
to read books and what I write is not intended for you. On
the other hand you have recently had the natural scientists
with you, that is something for you, something which satisfies your sense of beauty at the same time." At that he was
obviously a little vexed and said: yes, yes, the other can
also be good.

I had several times made as though to depart and said
I would not keep him longer. Each time he answered:
yes, yes, I have plenty of time. When it happened the
third time I said: yes, your majesty will understand that
I have enough time, I was afraid your majesty might not
have time. Afterwards I learnt from a more experienced
man, to whom I related it, that I had behaved like a
bungler, that by trying to be polite in that way to a king
one is being impolite, since one has only to wait till he
bows.

In the end I got away. He said that it would be a great
pleasure for him to see me. Thereupon he made a movement with his hand meaning, as I knew from the last
time, that he wished to give me his hand; but as the same
man told me it was the custom, when the king offered one
his hand, to kiss his hand, and as I could not bring myself
to do it, I behaved as though I did not understand and
bowed.

In the meanwhile I resolved to visit him as rarely as
possible.

The third time I visited him was at Sorgenfrie, I gave
him a copy of *Works of Love*. Parson Ibsen had told me

that he had once and for all got it into his head that he could not understand me, and I was unable to get that idea out again. That was what I had in mind. I came in, handed him the book, he looked at it a little, noticed the arrangement of the first part (Thou *shalt* love, thou shalt love thy *neighbour, thou* shalt love thy neighbour) and understood it immediately; he was really very gifted. Thereupon I took the book back from him and asked him whether I might read him a passage, choosing part one (p. 150). It moved him, moreover he was always easily moved.

Then he walked over to the window and so I followed him. He began to talk about his government. I said that I could naturally tell him one or two things which perhaps he would not otherwise get to know, for I could tell him what he looked like from the street. "But am I to speak, or am I not to speak; for if I am to speak I shall speak quite straight out." He answered: "Go on then." And so I told him that he allowed himself to be seduced by his personal gifts and that a king should in this respect be like a woman, who ought to hide her personal talents and simply be the woman of the house—and he simply a king. "I have often pondered over what a king should be. In the first place he can perfectly well be ugly; then he ought to be deaf and blind, or at least pretend to be so, for that gets over many difficulties, a tactless or stupid remark which being addressed to a king has a certain importance is best put off by a: "I beg your pardon"—*i.e.* that the king has not heard it. Finally the king ought not to say much but have some expression or other which he can use on every occasion, and which is consequently meaningless. He laughed and said: a charming portrait of a king. So I said: "yes, it is true, one thing more: the king must take care to be ill every now and then, so as to arouse sympathy." Then he broke in, with a peculiar expression which was almost one of joy and delight: "Oh, that is why you go talking about being ill, you want to make yourself interesting."

It was really like talking to a woman, he could get so animated. Then I showed him that he had done harm to himself by his audiences, that he was too familiar with Tom, Dick, and Harry, that by doing so he alienates the upper official class in particular, who are impatient at the fortuitous kind of influence of unauthorised people, that he would have to admit that it was impossible to rule by talking with all his subjects in that way. He did not perhaps realise that everyone he spoke to went away and gossiped. That the mistake must be apparent at this very moment as I stood here talking with him, though I was certainly an exception because I considered myself religiously bound not to divulge a single word. (That is moreover true, as long as he lived I never said a word about it to anyone, and afterwards only to one and then only partially.) He answered: that I must not think that it was only due to his possible gifts, but that when he came to the throne he was of the opinion that to be a king no longer meant prestige, but little by little he had changed his mind.

I had said that I had had occasion to make some of these observations the very first day he came to the throne. To which he said: yes, wasn't that the time when there was a general meeting[1] of which you were president.— He certainly had a good memory.—At that moment a side door opened, but was immediately closed again. I stepped back a yard. He went to the door, but as he went he said it was sure to be the Queen: she very much wishes to see you, now I will fetch her. So he came leading the Queen by the hand—and I bowed. That was really not polite to the Queen, who did not get a chance of making

[1] Of the university students.

a proper entry, she even looked rather insignificant—but
what else can happen if a queen suddenly has to appear
like that.

The King showed the Queen the copy of my new book,
to which I answered : Your majesty makes me feel embarrassed at not having brought a copy for the Queen. He
answered : Oh, we can share one.

The Queen said she already knew me, she had seen me
once on the ramparts (where I ran away and left Tryde
in the lurch), that she had read part of " your *Either and
Or*, but could not understand it." To which I answered :
your majesty will easily understand that that is all the
worse for me. But there was something even more notable
about the situation. Christian VIII immediately heard
the mistake " Either *and* Or " and I certainly did; I was
surprised to hear the Queen saying exactly what servant
girls say. I caught the King's eye; I looked away. After
we had spoken a few words the King said to the Queen :
is Juliana alone in your room? She answered " yes "—
and went away.

I went on talking with the King. He asked me whether
I was going away this year. I answered that if I did it
would only be for a very short time, to Berlin. " You
are sure to know a lot of interesting people there." " No,
your majesty, in Berlin I live completely isolated and work
harder than ever." " But then you might just as well go
to Smørum-Ovre " (and then he laughed at his own joke).
" No, your majesty, whether I go to Smørum-Ovre or to
Smørum-Nedre I do not find an incognito, a hiding-place
of 400,000 people." Now that was a little pointed, he
answered : yes, that is perfectly true.

Then he asked me about Schelling. I tried to give him
a rough impression. He asked me about Schelling's personal attitude towards the court and his reputation at the
university. I said that Schelling was like the Rhine at its

mouth where it became stagnant water—Schelling was de-
generating into a Prussian "Excellency." I talked a little
more to him about Hegelian philosophy having been the
government philosophy, and that now it was supposed to
be Schelling.

This last visit was an example of Christian VIII's
delicacy in showing exactly the right attentions to people,
it was as flattering as could be to have made it into a
sort of family visit.

I did not speak to him again. I had resolved to visit him
as little as possible, preferably when I had a book to give
him. But I did not regret having been to see him; it is
a very pleasant memory. If he had lived longer it would
have been awkward for me, for he could not bear anyone
being a private individual, he thought it was part of the
king's right to show everyone exactly what they had to
do. And so it was when I first began to think of taking
an official position that I went to see him.

The whole episode is a charming memory, he never had
occasion to receive anything but an impression of anima-
tion, and I only saw him as charm and liveliness itself.

Moreover in one sense I owe much to Christian VIII,
namely the pleasant and comfortable impression of life
which he taught me. I have always had far too great a
tendency not to bother about worldly things; and if my
expeditions to see the King had taken an unpleasant turn
it would certainly have made me even more indolent. The
very reverse happened. And then the relationship was
useful to me in another connection. Surrounded by vulgarity and petty envy and without the assistance of even
the smallest illusion, since I was nothing but a private
individual, and having become an eccentric in the eyes of
the masses through that which is best in me, as a result
of the wretched conditions in Denmark and because they

could not understand me. It was to that extent a good thing that the envious superior classes, who always made underhand use of all that vulgarity against me, should have something to bite on to, and so my life had to be thrown into relief. That is where my relations with the King come in. In a sense it was just the thing for me : only one man, an absolute King and what is more Christian VIII. I quickly perceived that the situation might become dangerous, that Christian VIII might appreciate me too much; I therefore took the greatest care, as everyone would admit who knew how much he made up to me. But on the other hand the relationship was so clearly marked that I could at any moment, had it become necessary, have emphasised it.

Christian VIII was only intelligent up to a point and, having an almost superstitious belief in his own sagacity, he became almost fantastic if he was impressed by a superior intelligence, and was easily alarmed. His nerves were not strong, his life had left its mark on his intellectual constitution, he had no moral attitude, religion only touched him æsthetically—and so he was clever. It is obvious that such a constitution was lacking in proportion and would inevitably be the prey to fraud, though, be it noted, in the most comfortable and pleasant way possible. He was afraid of real character. Fundamentally he was very domineering. The fact that he preferred to use other than official roads was an artifice of his sagacity. He was afraid of real character. If such a person were so powerfully built that the muscular development was, so to speak, visible, he kept him at a distance. But his limit was an unshakable character, concealed by the flexibility of intelligence and imagination. He could not solve that X, and as though by a law of nature he would have been in the power of such a man.

Altogether Christian VIII enriched me with a number of psychological observations. Perhaps psychologists ought to take notice of kings and particularly absolute kings, for the more free a man is, the less he is bound by the cares of every day, the better one can know him.

Feb. 9. The end of Luther's sermon on 1 Cor. xiii, where he concludes that faith is more than love, is sophistry. Luther always wants to explain love as love of one's neighbour, as though it were not also a duty to love God. Luther really put faith in the place of love of God, and then called love, love of one's neighbour.

This is what happens. I set the problem, the problem which faces the whole age : equality between man and man. I put it into practice in Copenhagen. That is something more than writing a few words on the subject : I expressed it approximately with my life. I have levelled in a Christian sense, not in rebellion against power and worth which I have upheld with all my strength.

But people do not know what they are talking about— and I am sacrificed, guilty of pride; I, who with every sacrifice, have fought for equality.

And the result. Well, the result is quite simply that had I not been so thoroughly influenced by religion I would have been forced to withdraw and associate—with the upper classes : *i.e.* I should have become proud.

Oh, you fools !

I drew Rasmus Nielsen into my intimacy because I looked upon it as my religious duty; so that there should be *at least one man,* so that it could not be said that I had overlooked the human factor.

He cannot of course be very much use to me; he is too heavy, too thick-skinned, too corrupted by the age of Christian VIII. If I were to become worldly he would of course be useful.

I have had to make him keep his distance, otherwise he

gossips about my matter in a friendly sort of way, and it must either be strung to a high pitch or hidden in complete silence.

It is as though a man possessed a great treasure and kept it so safely hidden that he threw away the key. The thought that troubles me is whether I have a right to do that, whether this silence is permissible in relation to God, whether it is permissible, with respect to a work which is so infinitely indebted to Him for its acuteness, to let it remain an enigma and for many a mere curiosity. And why? Partly because the author thinks it is self-denial, partly because he thinks he is unable to take over all the misunderstandings in reality consequent upon giving the explanation.

(The fact that I exposed myself of my own free will to becoming a laughing-stock.)

. . . There is one thing, in this connection, which fills me with sadness; for no one in Copenhagen has loved or does love what are called the simple classes, the ordinary man, with so unselfish and Christian a love as I do. But here as everywhere there are plenty of those who in the capacity of journalists wish to take his hard-earned money —by teaching him false ideas which only make him unhappy and help to embitter the relations between the classes; plenty of those who, in the capacity of agitators and what not use his number in order to help him to be shot down by taking a false view from above and saying : the simple classes are demoralised, they must be shot down. No, no, no, the misfortune is the bourgeoisie and if there is any suggestion of shooting people down, then let it be the journalists for the way in which they have used and profited by the simple classes. God knows that I am not bloodthirsty and I think I have in a terrible degree a sense of my responsibility to God; but nevertheless, I should be ready to take the responsibility upon me, in God's name, of giving the order to fire if I could first of all make absolutely and conscientiously sure that there was not a single man standing in front of the rifles, not a single creature, who was not—a journalist. That is said of the class as a whole.

The Middle Ages went further and further astray in stressing the aspect that Christ was the model—then came Luther and stressed the other aspect, that Christ is a gift which must be received through faith.

As for the rest, the closer I examine Luther the more convinced do I become that he was muddle-headed. It is a comfortable kind of reforming which consists in throwing off burdens and making life easier—that is an easy way of getting one's friends to help. True reforming always means to make life more difficult, to lay on burdens; and the true reformer is therefore always put to death as though he were the enemy of mankind.

Luther's "Hear me, thou Pope" not to mention anything else, sounds to me almost disgustingly worldly. Is that the sacred earnestness of a reformer concerned only with his own responsibility, who knows that true reformation consists in becoming more inward. Such an expression is just like a journalist's slogan. That unholy political attitude, that desire to overthrow the Pope is what is so confusing about Luther.

But in our times it is obvious that the aspect of Christ which must be stressed is that he is the model. The only point being to avoid the confusion of the Middle Ages. But that is the side that must be stressed, for in Lutheranism faith has simply become a fig-leaf behind which people skulk in the most unchristian way.

NB   NB

On each of the later works there is, on the title page :
Poetic, in order to show that I do not proclaim myself
to be an exceptional Christian, or to be what I describe.
Without authority, in order to denote that I do not lay
others under an obligation, or judge them.
A spiritual revival, in order to show that I have nothing
to do with outward changes, or that kind of reformation.

One man alone cannot help or save the age in which he
lives, he can only express the fact that it will perish.

NB   *NB*

Oh, what are the dangers to which one could possibly
expose oneself ! Danger is my very element.
But there is one danger, or rather there is something
which is in such complete contradiction with the whole
structure of my personality that it is really a revolution :
and that is to have to speak of my inwardness, of my relation to God. In that connection I would pray that it
might be taken from me, it seems as though it would make
my spirit heavy. I have been willing to expose myself to
everything and I still am so, but that is something quite
different, that is not polemic but resignation.
And that is why the publication of my last books costs me
so much suffering.
In the meanwhile it may be my duty to God. To have
to say how I spend my time in prayer, how it is that I
really live with God like father and son : that baring of
myself, if I may so describe it, I find so difficult, so difficult;
my inwardness is too true for me to be able to talk about it.
And yet perhaps it is my duty to God, and my hidden in-

wardness something which God countenanced my having until I had grown strong enough to talk about it. My unhappy childhood, my boundless melancholy, my miserable personal life until I became an author, all that helped to develop in me a hidden inwardness. . . .

Job endured everything—until his friends came to comfort him, then he grew impatient.

As far as I know no one has ever thought of writing a comedy:

A play in $5\frac{1}{2}$ or almost 6 Acts.

Just try to imagine quite clearly to yourself that the model is called a "Lamb," that alone is a scandal to natural man, no one has any desire to be a lamb.

The misfortune of Christianity is clearly that the dialectical factor has been taken from Luther's doctrine of faith so that it has become a hiding-place for sheer paganism and epicureanism; people forget entirely that Luther was urging the claims of faith against a fantastically exaggerated asceticism.

Should my journals be published after my death it might be done under the title:

The Book of the Judge.

NB   NB   NB   NB

How wonderfully melancholy and religion can blend together, and how dangerous it is to have such tremendous powers as have been granted me—and then to have to live in such restricted circumstances.

I have considered the possibility of taking another step forward and steering systematically on, with the possibility of being put to death always before my eyes. The aim and everything was right—oh, and in this I recognise myself again : in being able to review all the circumstances just as easily as though it were a love affair—the conflict was right—succumbing before the rabble urged on by the envy of the upper classes. It would certainly have happened the moment I came forward decisively, in character, with the proper incentive for all the clique, and gave the signal : that there was no Christianity in the land, and that it was necessary to introduce it. The clergy would have raved, and would have been pleased that I was already in such a scuffle with the rabble—and would have used it.

I do not doubt for a second that Christendom needs to be made aware in that sense, or rather I am absolutely certain. I am also convinced that I should have succeeded. I know that, humanly speaking, more could not have been expected of my life.

But now we come to what is melancholy and untrue. That it was important for me to succumb. I had reckoned upon having enough fortune to last for a few years longer, and the catastrophe of 1848 helped me quite extraordinarily : otherwise I should have avoided the question of my livelihood. Furthermore I fought with men and perhaps it pleased my pride to let them imagine that they had fought with me; for I have studied the passive way of fighting as much as any general has studied the active, and the passive way is the religious and profound way.

It must be said in my defence that what makes my position in a little hole like Copenhagen so difficult, so long as I am to be a public personality, is that I must always have the idea with me. The nonsense men talk can, when it is brought up against the ideal, become something very serious; and that was really my thought. That my life should take the turning it has taken, not to say end in a martyrdom, is something which has never occurred to a single one of my contemporaries. It is I who secretly direct the intrigue—and according to my tactics my contemporaries were not to have their eyes opened before it happened—and by themselves : look, here I come again.

But in this there is also an injustice towards men. Men are really only children and so it is unjust towards them, just as it is wrong towards oneself, to allow them to be guilty on that scale.

That is how I take the final view of my life. I now turn away, faithful to my original self : I am essentially a poet and shall be obliged to give up being an author in any real sense as soon as I have no more money.

And so I draw away. The problem is then quite a different one; I am no longer in the rôle of being that which is depicted.

But I shall never be able to thank providence enough for all it has done for me and the way in which it helps me. And as regards my really having thought of taking that step seriously, of being put to death : I must certainly regret it. But for one thing it never got further than my thoughts, and for another as soon as I was aware (or God helped me to become aware) of where it was leading me, and as soon as I felt my genius rebel against it I also opposed it. And providence, which is infinite love, has also bequeathed me this marvellous fund of profundities which I have understood, a present which I can dispose of poetically, and can also put to good use by communicating it in the proper way : *poetically*.

How shall I ever be able to thank God sufficiently.

And so now I am enriched by a loving providence with

an eminent understanding of truth, such as has seldom
been given to a man, and moreover armed by the same
loving providence with outstanding gifts with which to
set forth what I have understood. In that respect I only
have to humble myself beneath one thing : the fact that
I have not the strength myself *to be* that which is understood. Had I not been in financial difficulties and yet
understood what I have understood, that would not
perhaps have been clear to me. But providence knew how
to humble me. Nevertheless it has at the same time done
so indescribably much more than ever I expected.

. . . Sometimes I am almost afraid for the man when
I think of Bishop Mynster. He is now 72 and soon he will
go to his judgment. And what has he not done to harm
Christianity by conjuring up a lying picture—so that he
could sit back and rule. His sermons are quite good—but
in eternity he will not have to preach—but be judged.

The truth that is troubled

is the truth which while itself eternally certain of being
the truth, is essentially concerned with communicating it to
others, concerned that they should accept it for their own
good in spite of the fact that the truth does not force itself
upon them.

This is the dialectical point. Mere dabblers, half-men,
desire to communicate simply in order to reassure themselves. The purely intellectual effort is only concerned
with discovering the truth. The " troubled " truth is certain enough of being the truth but is concerned, or
" troubled," to communicate it. That is Christianity. . . .

The idea of attaining the peak of one's development—
and then of breaking off absolutely, and abiding by my

achievement, of attaining to my peak as an author and then stopping completely and never again setting pen to paper (an idea which came to me very early and pursued me), that thought (even if I could realise it) is not religious but proud and worldly.

. . . Like the Guadalquivir which somewhere rushes below ground and later on appears again, I must now sink myself behind pseudonyms, but now I understand where I shall reappear again with my name.

The thoughtlessness, carelessness, and cocksureness with which children are brought up is frightful to see : and yet everyone is essentially what they are to be when they are ten years old; and yet one would find that almost everyone bears with them a defect from their childhood, which they do not overcome even in their seventieth year; together with the fact that all unhappy individualities are related to a false impression received in childhood.

Oh, piteous satire upon mankind; that providence should have endowed almost every child so richly because it knew in advance what was to befall it : to be brought up by "parents," *i.e.* to be made a mess of in every possible way.

My misfortune, or the thing that made my life so difficult, is that I am strung a whole tone higher than other men, and where I am and what I am about does not have to do with the particular, but always also with a principle and an idea. At the best, most people think which girl they ought to marry; I had to think about marriage. And so in everything.

Now the same thing is happening to me. At the best, most people consider what occupation they are to take up, now I am in the midst of the stream, of the struggle with ideas and questions of principle whether, from a Christian point of view, there should be official Christian offices.

What makes me unpopular is not so much the difficulty of my works as my own personal life, the fact that in spite of all my endeavours I do not achieve anything (the finite teleology), do not make money, do not get a position, am not decorated, but achieve nothing all along the line and am despised into the bargain. Now in my opinion that is what is great about me, if indeed there is greatness. But it costs me many a struggle and great efforts, for I too am flesh and blood—and yet that is exactly why I am misunderstood and ill-treated.

. . . Frederica Bremer has been pleased to favour Denmark with a criticism. It is naturally an echo of what the people in question have told her. That can best be seen from Martensen who has been in close touch with her. [*In the margin* : She has lived here for a long time and has had sexual intercourse with the notables; she also wanted to have sexual intercourse with me; but I was virtuous.] She was sweet enough to invite me, in a most obliging *billet,* to a *conversazione.* I almost regret now that I did not answer, as I first intended : no, many thanks, I don't dance. But in any case I refused her invitation and did not go. And then one discovers in print that one is "unapproachable." It is presumably owing to Martensen's influence that Frederica has made me into a psychologist and nothing else, and has given me a wide public among women readers. That is really funny, how in all the world can I be looked upon as a ladies' author? But that is Martensen's fault. He sees right enough that his star is declining in the university. It would be quite amusing to read to Rasmus Nielsen and the younger generation : that I am a ladies' author.

Sept. Nowadays one does not become an author as a result of originality and inspiration but—by reading. One becomes a man by imitating others. One does not

know instinctively that one is a man, but as a result of a
deduction : one is like others—*ergo* one is a man. God
knows whether any of us really are men!

The majority of men in every generation, even those
who, as it is described, devote themselves to thinking (dons
and the like), live and die under the impression that life
is simply a matter of understanding more and more, and
that if it were granted to them to live longer, that life
would continue to be one long continuous growth in understanding. How many of them ever experience the maturity
of discovering that there comes a critical moment where
everything is reversed, after which the point becomes to
understand more and more that there is something which
cannot be understood.

That is Socratic ignorance, and that is what the philosophy of our times requires as a corrective.

As Johannes Climacus truly observes, the majority of
men turn aside precisely where the higher life should begin for them, turn aside and become practical, "Man,
father and champion bowler"; and, as Anti-Climacus truly
remarks, the majority of men never experience the spiritual
life; they never experience that qualitative encounter with
the divine. To them the divine is simply a rhetorically
meaningless hiatic superlative of the human : which explains their satisfaction with the idea of being able to
form ever clearer conceptions of it, so that if they only
had time, did not have to go to the office or their club or
talk to their wives, if they only had time enough they
would manage to understand the divine perfectly.

Socratic ignorance, but *nota bene* modified by the Christian spirit, is maturity, is intellectually speaking what conversion is morally and religiously, is what it means to become a child again.

It is quite literally true that the law is : increasing profundity in understanding more and more that one cannot

understand. And there once again comes in "being like a child," but raised to the second power. The man who is mature in that sense is naïve, simple, and he marvels, but he is all that essentially humorously, and yet not in such a way that it is humour.

And that this life is happy, is blessed as it is blessed to adore, more blessed even than for a woman to be in love, well, as to that, those who are made happy by their conceits have no conception what it means. They never feel the pressure of quality but deceive themselves more and more.

It is the tolerance of the orthodox which best shows how completely Christianity is lost. Their solution is : if only we may keep our faith to ourselves, the world can take care of itself. Merciful God, and that is supposed to be Christianity. That is the power which once broke upon the world and through readiness to suffer forced Christianity on the world, compelled it more forcefully than any tyrant.

The orthodox do not even suspect that this, their tolerance, is the effect of sheer worldliness, because they have not really either understanding, respect or courage for martyrdom or a true belief in eternity, but really desire to have a good time in this world.

And now, what makes the position more terrible is that this "tolerance" is willing to allow the tremendous falsehood to continue, namely for the whole world to call itself Christian—when the private belief of the orthodox is, nevertheless, that the world is pagan.

How low has Christianity sunk, how powerless and miserable it has become! It is reason that has conquered : reason that has tyrannised enthusiasm and the like, making it ridiculous. That is why people dare not be enthusiastic, do not acknowledge that martyrdom is a glory beyond all comparison, they are afraid of being laughed at instead of put to death—and so people come to an agreement; they wrap themselves up in their donkey-skin only asking to be allowed to be Christians themselves, call that tolerance and flatter themselves that they are true Christians.

Christianity's position in possibility—and in reality

The moment I take Christianity as a doctrine and so indulge my cleverness or profundity or my eloquence or my imaginative powers in depicting it: people are very pleased; I am looked upon as a serious Christian.

The moment I begin to express existentially what I say, and consequently to bring Christianity into reality: it is just as though I had exploded existence—the *scandal* is there at once.

On "the voluntary"

I now understand perfectly why Christianity clings to the idea "voluntary." The existential *authority* to teach corresponds to "the voluntary." Who is to teach poverty? The person who is himself struggling for money or has it can talk about it, but without authority; only the "voluntary" poor, the person who has freely given up riches and is poor, has authority.

It may truly be said that there is something socratic about me.

Indirect communication was my natural qualification. As a result of all I experienced, all I went through and thought out last summer on the subject of direct communication, I have made a direct communication (the thing about my literary work with its category: the whole thing is my education) and at the same time acquired a deeper understanding of indirect communication, the new pseudonymity.

To me there is something so inexplicably happy in the antithesis Climacus—Anti-Climacus, I recognise myself, and my nature so entirely in it that if someone else had discovered it I should have thought he had spied upon me. —The merit is not mine, for I did not originally think of it.

The *category* of my work is : *to make men aware* of Christianity, and consequently I always say : I am not an example, for otherwise all would be confusion. My task is to deceive people, in a true sense, into entering the sphere of religious obligation which they have done away with; but I am without authority. Instead of authority I make use of the very reverse, I say : the whole thing is my own education. That, once again, is a truly socratic discovery. Just as he was ignorant, in my case it is : instead of being the teacher, being the one who is educated.

People must have lived ever so much more simply in the days when they believed that God made his will known in dreams. Even from the point of view of diet they must have lived more simply. The idyllic life of a shepherd and living partly on vegetables—then it is possible. Think of life in big cities and the manner of life : no wonder people attribute their dreams to devils and demons.— Moreover the poor opinion in which dreams are held nowadays is also connected with the intellectualism which really only values the conscious, while in simpler ages people piously believed that the unconscious life in man was the more important as well as the profounder.

About Peter

I have been an author all this time, and Peter found no occasion to speak his mind. But hardly does it begin to seem as though I were to be singled out on an important

scale before he is busy unburdening himself, presumably
in order to bid for me on behalf of the party, and assuredly
led on by the excellent opportunity of attacking R.N.[1] (a
very profitable task at the moment) and making an example
of him for being a disciple—he who has been the imitator
and follower of Grundtvig to the point of ridiculous affectation.

The whole thing has hurt me very much. Peter was so
entirely unsympathetic all the time I endured the persecution of the mob, literally never a word either written or
spoken on the subject; we were never very close to one
another, but from that time on he withdrew. He knows
that I am worried about my financial position—never a
word about it. He knows that I suffer from being out of
proportion to this little country—never a word about it.

In the end he sees his opportunity. He takes up an
attitude superior to the two directions: Martensen—and
S.K. He hits out in the popular and careless jargon of
the day, which is quite capable of dismissing in half an
hour the work of seven years; he movingly proclaims the
supremacy of the country parson and the sovereignty of
mediocrity, carefully shielding himself behind the excuse
that it was only a hurried piece of work; he profits by the
deceit: I, as the author's elder brother, must know about
the whole thing (which is the most frightful untruth, so
much so that he ought, for that very reason, to have emphasised it); he has tied my hands, for I cannot make a
single move without everyone shouting "Shame;" and
remain affectionate, for it is after all a favourable discussion of me, which once again I shall have to put up
with, for people will say that it is prejudice; he complicates
my relations with R.N. who may think that I am behind
the attack upon him, and then if R.N. attacks Peter he
will certainly believe that I am behind R.N. I do not mean
that all this was clear to Peter, but part of it should have

[1] Professor Rasmus Nielson an opponent of Martenson.

been clear to him, and moreover would have been
clear to him if he had not grown self-complacent
among the parsons and Conventions, so complacent that he
perhaps even thought in some kind of stupid *gemütlich*
way that he was doing me a kindness, in spite of the fact
that he should understand that in order to do so he would
have to show up the real proportions of my work, and least
of all connive at the numerical evaluation of men and the
whole deceit.

About Peter

Peter came down here in the month of December. He
told me that he had given a lecture at the last Assembly
in which he spoke about Martensen and me, and was
surprised I had not heard of it. He went on to say that
in the same lecture he had spoken against R. Nielsen and
a certain H.H. Thereupon I said to him : H.H. is me.
He was rather put out by that; for he had presumably not
read the little book carefully, quite convinced that it was
not by me. So we spoke about it a little. Then Peter
said : yes, now there is no point in our talking about it any
further; for I have still to write the lecture. So he wrote
the lecture. He was very brief in what he said about H.H.
and remarked at the same time : that it bore a striking
resemblance to S.K. God knows what he really said at
the Assembly. . . .

In all that is usually said about Johannes Climacus being
purely subjective and so on, people have forgotten, in
addition to everything else concrete about him, that in
one of the last sections he shows that the curious thing is :
that there is a " how " which has this quality, that if *it*
is truly given, then the " what " is also given; and that it
is the " how " of " faith." Here, quite certainly, we have

inwardness at its maximum proving to be objectivity once
again. And this is an aspect of the principle of subjectivity
which, so far as I know, has never before been presented
or worked out.

There is yet another reason, too, why Christianity should
be delineated by an unmarried man. In the end the whole
of Christendom's little crumb of Christianity ends in:
Christmas and Christmas pudding. The little child Jesus,
that is the sort of Christianity which is furthest from em-
phasising the idea of: imitation. The point is not even to
become a child—no, the Saviour himself is neither more nor
less than a child, and it stops short at that; and father and
mother both look upon little Sophie as a little God-child.
What twaddle! Altogether that absolute emphasis upon
Christmas, to the exclusion of all else, turns Christianity
all topsy-turvy. Moreover Christmas only appeared in the
IVth century; but in that respect orthodoxy does not cling
zealously to the first three centuries.

Luther

Here one sees the result of not being dialectical. In a
sermon Luther inveighs most violently against the faith
which clings to the person instead of to the word; true
faith clings to the word no matter who the person is.

Well, that is all very well among men. But as for the
rest this theory does away with Christianity. We thus receive a doctrine in the ordinary sense, where the doctrine
is more than the teacher, instead of which Christianity is
this paradox, that the person is all important. Why does
St. Paul inculcate so clearly that he is an apostle ουκ απ
ανθρωπων ουδε δι ανθρωπου[1] except to show the difference
in kind, which again is authority. In another connection

[1] Gal. i. 1, not of men, neither by man.

St. Paul can, quite consistently, do away with that his
difference, when it is a matter of bringing in Christ in
person, as for example when he inveighs against some for
saying " I am of Paul," others of Apollos, others of Cephas
instead of all being of Christ.[1]

And once again Christianity's paradoxical difference
from every other doctrine, from a scientific point of view,
is that it posits : authority. A philosopher with authority
makes nonsense. For a philosopher goes no further than
his doctrine; if I can show that his doctrine is self-con-
tradictory, incorrect etc. he has nothing to reply. The paradox is that the personality is above the doctrine. It is therefore also nonsensical of a philosopher to demand faith.

[1] I. Cor. i. 12.

A true sentence of Hugo de St. Victor (Helfferich: *Mystik,* Vol. I, 368).

"In things which are above reason faith is not really supported by reason, because reason cannot grasp what faith believes; but there is also a something here as a result of which reason is determined, or which determines reason to honour faith which it cannot perfectly understand."

That is what I explained (*e.g.* in the *Final Postscript*); not every absurdity is "the absurd" or the paradox. The effect of reason is in fact to know the paradox negatively —but not more.

Victor Hugo indeed! Accustomed of course for years past to the kind of debauchery indulged in by novel writers who are always "carrying on" poetically with feelings which are the very reverse of what their lives express; and now he attacks the clerical party in a "brilliant speech."

One can imagine the voluptuous pleasure he got from the situation, thinking of himself as a "witness to the truth" and being praised, honoured, and admired.

I am beholden to the clerical party—its cause is in the minority; and the natural sciences much admired. And now he turns up. Nobody denies that natural science had its martyrs; but Victor Hugo seems to have forgotten entirely that latterly that is as far as possible from being the case since, on the contrary, it is science which is everywhere triumphant.

And which tyrant, which idol is it that he serves with that speech of his? It is "the masses," "votes for all" and the rest of it. And has it called for no martyrs? It called for Christ and Socrates and the "host of martyrs."

As for the examples of what true religiousness is? The

fool, for wanting to talk about things he knows nothing about. The examples he gives are ordinary great and good actions, in no sense specifically religious, not to say specifically Christian; paganism has just the same examples. Those great and good actions are honoured in the world—but Christ and his followers were, if it comes to that, just as practised in noble actions, but they were persecuted and put to death for them.

If I had my way, Victor Hugo would be put to read about Christianity for six months!

But what a chance for a "poet"! One can imagine the other poets being quite envious of him, not being members of the Chamber. Just think of Eugène Sue, who has written himself into a millionaire—by describing poverty and misery: Yes, he was capable of giving Rd. 50 to the poor for having been the fortunate man to whom the envious opportunity was given—of playing the hero, the witness to the truth, with applause and laurel-leaves.

Real self-reduplication without a third factor, which is eternal and compels one, is an impossibility and makes any such existence into an illusion or an experiment.

Kant held that man was his own law (autonomy), *i.e.* bound himself under the law which he gave himself. In a deeper sense that means to say: lawlessness or experimentation. It is no harder than the thwacks which Sancho Panza applied to his own bottom. I can no more be really stricter in A than I am, or than I wish myself to be in B. There must be some compulsion, if it is to be a serious matter. If I am not bound by anything higher than myself, and if I am to bind myself, where am I to acquire the severity as A by which, as B, I am to be bound, so long as A and B are the same.

This can be seen best of all in religious matters. The transformation which really lies in changing from immediacy to spirituality, that mortification is not serious, becomes in fact an illusion, a form of experimentation if there is not some third and compelling factor, which is not the individual himself.

That too is why all outstanding individualities, the real " instruments," are compelled.

Not only is the law which I give myself as maximum not a law; but there is a law which is given to me by one higher than I. And not only that; but that lawgiver takes the liberty of joining in at the same time in the character of educator, and applies the compulsion.

Now if during the whole course of his life a man never acts in so decisive a way that the educator can get a hold on him : well, then the man is certainly allowed to live on complacently in a state of illusion, imagination, experimentation—but that also connotes : the greatest lack of grace.

A man may be so severe with himself that he understands : all my severity is nothing, I must have another to help me, who can be severity itself, even though he is gentleness itself.

But to enter into relations with this other does not mean to make assurances, and assurances and more assurances; it means : to act.

Once a man acts in a decisive sense and comes out into reality, existence can get a grip on him and providence educate him.

It is perfectly true that. however much a man may protect himself it may all the same occur to providence to put him to school. But it does not like that, that is almost anger. It wishes a man to believe, and believe in it. Providence is no friend of that effeminate attitude whereby a man wishes to play at being autodidact, when there lives at the same time a teacher so outstanding as Our Lord, to whom he can turn.

But as a rule in human affairs to be put to school and to try to go to school means that I go wherever the teacher

lives. Spiritually it means that I act decisively : there, at
once, is the teacher. For what is it that I desire, I desire
to be educated spiritually—and yet I do not desire to act
decisively? Nonsense.

In this respect, too, I have not been understood at all.
All the profounder thinkers (Hegel, Daub—and to name
one less famous but most worthy of respect : Julius Müller)
are agreed in placing evil in isolated subjectivity—objectivity being the saving factor.

Now that is already a platitude; and every student knows
that I am an isolated individuality—*ergo* I am all but
evil, " pure negativity, not serious, etc."

Oh, depths of confusion. No, the whole concept of objectivity, which has been made into our salvation, is merely the
food of sickness, and the fact that it is admired as the cure
simply proves how fundamentally irreligious our age is,
for that saving factor is really a return to paganism.

No, in order to put an end to subjectivity, in so far as
it is untruth we must, on the contrary, go right through
to " the individual "—before God.

But people do not know what religion is. They do not
even suspect that Christ and all the heroes of the faith
were in a sense isolated individualities—and they belonged
absolutely to God.

Take Socrates for instance ! In those days one sophist
after another came forward and showed that the misfortune was the lack of sufficient knowledge, more and more
research was necessary, the evil was ignorance—and then
along came old father Socrates saying : no, it is precisely
ignorance which is our salvation.

Now exactly the same thing happened to Socrates in his
day as has happened to me. He was looked upon as representing evil; for, in the eyes of that age, ignorance was
evil—and yet Socrates was indeed the doctor.

It requires a fortunate genius (or an infinite profundity

and a perfect ear, in order that all the demoniacal phenomena should, always understood *à rebours*, themselves proclaim what they need) in order not to make a mistake in
those spheres. I do not praise myself for anything.

It is perfectly true, isolated subjectivity is, in the opinion
of the age, evil; but "objectivity" as a cure is not one
whit better.

The only salvation is subjectivity, *i.e.* God, as infinite
compelling subjectivity.

The dialectic of becoming a Christian

Socrates did not first of all get together some proofs of the
immortality of the soul in order then to live in that belief,
on the strength of the proofs. The very reverse is the case;
he said : the possibility of there being an immortality
occupies me to such a degree that I unquestionably stake
my whole life upon it as though it were the most certain
of all things. And so he lived—and his life is a proof of
the immortality of the soul. He did not believe merely
on the strength of the proofs and then live : no, his life
is the proof, and only with his martyr's death is the proof
complete.—That, you see, is spirit; it is a little awkward
for those who repeat him and for all those who live second-
hand, or tenth-hand lives, and those who chase after results,
and for cowardly, effeminate natures.

Carefully used that may be adapted to the problem of
becoming a Christian.

First of all there is, quite rightly, the doubt (Lessing's)
whether one can base eternal happiness upon something
historical.

And consequently here is something historical, the story
of Jesus Christ.

But now is the historical fact quite certain? To this one
must answer : even though it were the most certain of all
historical facts it would be of no help, there cannot be

any *direct* transition from an historical fact to the foundation upon it of an eternal happiness. That is something qualitatively new.

How then do we proceed? Thus. A man says to himself, à la Socrates : here is an historical fact which teaches me that in regard to my eternal happiness I must have recourse to Jesus Christ. Now I must certainly preserve myself from taking the wrong turning into scientific enquiry and research, as to whether it is quite certainly historical; for it is historical right enough : and if it were ten times as certain in all its details it would still be no help : for *directly* I cannot be helped.

And so I say to myself : I choose; that historical fact means so much to me that I decide to stake my whole life upon that if.* Then he lives; lives entirely full of the idea, risking his life for it : and his life is the proof that he believes. He did not have a few proofs, and so believed and then began to live. No, the very reverse.

That is called risking; and without risk faith is an impossibility. *To be related to spirit means to undergo a test;*†

*in the margin.** That occurs, too, in Christ's words[1] : if anyone will follow my teaching, *i.e.* live according to it, *i.e.* act according to it, he shall see etc. That means to say, there are no proofs beforehand—nor is he satisfied that the acceptance of his teaching should mean : I assure you.

in the margin.† That is because man is a synthesis of body-soul and spirit. But "spirit" sows dissension—whereas effeminate men always want to include what is lower in every relationship, and to have its consent. Hence the dread of "risking." The unspiritual man always desires "probability." But "spirit" will never grant it, for "spirit" is the test : do you wish to avoid probability, do you wish to deny yourself, give up the world etc.

[1]Mat. 7. 24, Luke 6. 47, John 8. 31 f.

to believe, to wish to believe, is to change one's life into a trial; daily test is the trial of faith.—Yet one can preach on that score till doomsday to cowardly, effeminate unspiritual natures, they do not understand it, they do not really want to understand it. It seems to them that it is good enough if someone else takes the risk, and then they follow him—giving their assurance. But take the risk themselves—no thank you.

But where becoming a Christian is concerned there is, as compared with Socrates, a dialectical difference which must be remembered. Namely, where immortality is concerned man is only related to himself and to the idea, no further. But when a man chooses all at once to believe in Christ, *i.e.* chooses to stake his life upon him, he is allowed to have immediate (direct) recourse to Christ in prayer. Thus the historical is the cause, yet the object of faith.

But all unspiritual natures turn the question round. They say: to stake everything upon an if, that is a sort of scepticism, it is quite fantastic, not positive. That is because they will not take the "risk." And that is the crumb of unspirituality which Christianity has carried along with it and which has, in the end, done away with Christianity.

About myself

Nevertheless it is fortunate, indeed it is an inestimable blessing to have been melancholy as I was. Had I been a happy nature—and had then experienced what I did experience as an author; I believe it would have sent a man mad. But within me, where I really suffered I knew more frightful tortures still.

And so what happened? Oh, the marvel, even though it has not yet quite happened, nevertheless it has happened to a certain degree and, as I believe, will continue to happen more and more: this marvel: that those outward spectacles have lured my melancholy from its hiding place, and to a certain extent have already saved me from it; which will continue to happen still more completely!

O depths of the riches of God, O, how unsearchable are Thy ways O God,[1] but in all things fatherly and grace-giving.

How often have I shown that fundamentally Hegel makes men into heathens, *into a race of animals gifted with reason.* For in the animal world "the individual" is always less important than the race. But it is the peculiarity of the human race that just because the individual is created in the image of God "the individual" is above the race.

This can be wrongly understood and terribly misused: *concedo.* But that is Christianity. And *that* is where the battle must be fought.

What a curious, yet profound turn of phrase which makes it possible to say: in this case there is no question of a *choice*—I choose this and this. To continue: Christianity says to a man: you shall choose the one essential thing but in such a way that there is no question of a choice—if you drivel on any longer then you do not in fact choose the one essential thing; like the Kingdom of God it must be chosen *first.*

So there is consequently something in regard to which there may not be, and in thought cannot be a choice, and nevertheless it is a choice. Consequently, the very fact that in this case there is no *choice* expresses the tremendous passion or intensity with which it must be *chosen.* Could there be a clearer expression of the fact that the liberty of choice is only a qualified form of freedom? . . . However astonishing it may seem, one is therefore obliged to say that only "fear and trembling," only constraint, can

[1] Rom. 11. 33.

help a man to freedom. Because "fear and trembling" and compulsion can master him in such a way that there is no longer any question of choice—and then one chooses the right thing. At the hour of death most people choose the right thing.

Now how are the sciences to help? Simply not at all, in no way whatsoever. They reduce everything to calm and objective observation—with the result that freedom is an inexplicable something. Scientifically Spinoza is the only one who is consistent.

The problem is the same as with belief and speculation, and as Johannes Climacus has said, it is like sawing : in one case it means making oneself objectively light, in the other case making oneself subjectively heavy—and people want to saw in and out at the same time. Freedom really only *exists* because the same instant it (freedom of choice) exists it rushes with infinite speed to bind itself unconditionally by choosing resignation, the choice of which it is true that in it there is no question of a choice.

The inconceivable marvel of the omnipotence of love is that God can really grant so much to man, that almost like a lover[1] he can say of himself : " will you have me or not," and so wait one second for the answer.

But alas, man is not so purely spirit. It seems to him that since the choice is left to him he can take time and *first of all* think the matter over *seriously*. What a miserable anti-climax. "Seriousness" simply means to choose God at once and "first." In that way man is left juggling with a phantom : freedom of choice—with the question whether he does or does not possess it etc. And it even becomes scientific. He does not notice that he has thus suffered the loss of his freedom. For a time perhaps he delights in the thought of freedom until it changes again, and he becomes

[1]S. K. is playing on the two words " at fri " and " at frie," to woo and to make free.

doubtful whether he is free or not. Then he loses his freedom of choice. He confuses everything by his faulty tactics (militarily speaking). By directing his mind towards
"freedom of choice" instead of choosing he loses both
freedom and freedom of choice. Nor can he ever recover
it by the use of thought alone. If he is to recover his freedom it can only be through an intensified "fear and
trembling" brought forth by the thought of having lost
it.

The most tremendous thing which has been granted to
man is: the choice, freedom. And if you desire to save it
and preserve it there is only one way: in the very same
second unconditionally and in complete resignation to give
it back to God, and yourself with it. If the sight of what
is granted to you tempts you, and if you give way to the
temptation and look with egoistic desire upon the freedom
of choice, then you lose your freedom. And your punishment is: to go on in a kind of confusion priding yourself
on having—freedom of choice, but woe upon you, that is
your judgment: You have freedom of choice, you say,
and still you have not chosen God. Then you will grow
ill, freedom of choice will become your *idée fixe,* till at last
you will be like the rich man who imagines that he is poor,
and will die of want: you sigh that you have lost your
freedom of choice—and your fault is only that you do not
grieve deeply enough or you would find it again.

Christianity begins more or less where Hegel leaves off:
the misunderstanding is simply that that is the point at
which Hegel thought he had finished with Christianity,
and even thought he had gone beyond it.

I simply cannot help laughing when I think of Hegel's
conception of Christianity, it is so utterly inconceivable.
And what I have always maintained is true: Hegel was a
don, a professor of philosophy, not a thinker; and more-

over he must have been very insignificant as a person, making no real impression—but as a professor quite exceptional, that I do not deny.

The day will certainly come when the idea "Don" will stand for a comic person. Only think of Christianity! How altered since the times when it had inflexible confessors—and now that it has only got professors who are willing to agree in all *casibus*.

Which is harder : to be executed, or to suffer that prolonged agony which consists in being trampled to death by geese.

The greatest danger for a child, where religion is concerned.

The greatest danger is not that his father or tutor should be a free-thinker, not even his being a hypocrite. No, the danger lies in his being a pious, God-fearing man, and in the child being convinced thereof, but that he should nevertheless notice that deep in his soul there lies hidden an unrest which, consequently, not even the fear of God and piety could calm. The danger is that the child in that situation is almost provoked to draw a conclusion about God, that God is not infinite love.

What and—How

What makes the difference in life is not what is said, but how it is said. As for the "what," the same thing has already been said perhaps many times before—and so the old saying is true : there is nothing new under the sun, the old saying which is always new. . . .

In contradistinction to the Middle Ages and those periods

with all their discussion of possession, of particular men giving themselves to evil, I should like to write a book :

On diabolic possession in modern times

and show how mankind *en masse* gives itself up to evil, how nowadays it happens *en masse*. That is why people flock together, in order that natural and animal hysteria should get hold of them, in order to feel themselves stimulated, inflamed and *ausser sich*. The scenes on the Blocksberg are the absolute pendants to this demoniacal pleasure, where the pleasure consists in losing oneself in order to be volatilised into a higher potency, where being outside oneself one hardly knows what one is doing or saying, or who or what is speaking through one, while the blood courses faster, the eyes are bright and staring, the passions and lust seething.

O, depths of confusion and depravity, when it is at the same time valued as the seriousness of life, warm-heartedness, love, yes even—Christianity.

The railway mania is in every sense a second Babel. It belongs to the end of a period of culture, it is the final spurt. Unfortunately the new one began more or less at the same time, 1848. The railways are related as a heightened potency to the idea of centralisation. And the new period is related to dispersion into *disjecta membra*.

Centralisation will probably also be the financial ruin of Europe.

The difference between "popular" and "philosophical" is the amount of time a thing takes. Ask a man : do you know this, or do you not know it—if he answers immediately then the answer is popular, he is an undergraduate. If it takes ten years for the answer to come, and if it comes in the form of a system, if it is not quite clear whether he knows it or not : then it is a philosophical answer and the man a professor of philosophy—at least that is what he ought to be.

During the first period of a man's life the greatest danger is : *not to take the risk*. When once the risk has been really taken then the greatest danger is to risk too much. By not risking at first one turns aside and serves trivialities; in the second case, by risking too much, one turns aside to the fantastic, and perhaps to presumption.

May 19. To-day, Whitsunday, Mynster preached against monks and hermits—Good God, to want to play that tune in the 19th century, in order to be rewarded with applause. He did not attack a single one of the forms of evil prevalent in our day—ugh, God forbid, that might easily have become all too serious, no, he preached against—the monasteries.

Perfect Love

Perfect love means to love the one through whom one became unhappy. But no man has the right to demand to be thus loved.

God can demand it; that is infinite majesty. And it is true of the man of religion, in the strictest sense of the word, that in loving God he is loving him through whom he became unhappy, humanly speaking, for this life— although blessed.

I have not got the strength to understand it in that way; at the same time I am very afraid of being caught in the most dangerous of all snares : of becoming meritorious in my own eyes. In the meanwhile that danger is one which a truly religious man has already overcome.

"The Fatherland"

Everyone who knew anything about the state of affairs, knew how *The Fatherland* suffered from the vulgar press, which quite took the wind out of its sails.

I acted: Gjødwad stood impatiently at my side waiting for the article in which I demanded to be abused.[1]

One of two things: *either* they had to maintain that the paper should be ignored—and so not have accepted my article, even though I begged them to; *or* (and this would have been right) have recognised that their position was so desperate and the state of affairs so topsy-turvy that something had to be done—in which case they ought to have supported my action, which only required a few words of acknowledgment.

They did nothing, they betrayed me. At last they gave up taking *The Corsair,* as though that were something. In the course of conversation, where they seemed to be asking me whether they ought to do anything (without the question ever coming out directly) I always said: do nothing at all. Indeed, if people do not feel more than that for a just cause, I am not the one to beg them.

The Fatherland is perhaps more guilty, where I am concerned, than Goldschmidt. And in any case they are guilty of never having tried to point the way, even in a few words. To tell me privately that my actions are so exceptional that no one can take upon himself to write them up is merely a joke. They could of course, have said that publicly—and not kept silence while the mob alone spoke.

I note all this down for the following reason in par-

[1] Gjødwad was the editor of *The Fatherland* in which S. K. published his articles against P. L. Moller and subsequently against Martensen.

J.   G ticular. My time will come. Then it will suit *The Father-land* to throw some guilt on Heiberg,* and particularly upon Mynster for not having borne witness in my favour—and *The Fatherland* will in that way make itself appear quite innocent. But I will not tolerate that.

Personally I call Gjødwad my friend, and in the last three or four years have spoken with him every mortal afternoon and found him to be, what I knew, a lovable man. If he had not been a journalist I should have found in him the person whom I could most nearly have made a real friend. But *The Fatherland* is another question. I readily admit that at the time it was a difficult situation in which to act; but then that is the real test.

There was some truth in what Goldschmidt said to me (which I recognised at the time, but I had other reasons which determined me) when, immediately after the first article had appeared, and so even before he had begun the attack, when he said: that he could not understand why I insisted on doing so much for *The Fatherland,* for Plough, after all, was no better than he was. He said the same thing about Gjødwad; but I dismissed that with the words: Gjødwad is my friend. . . .

. . . Thus it is really terrible to have anything to do with God who neither can nor will give one direct certainty or a legal relationship—and yet it is blessed; blessed to be, as it were, nothing in his hand, who is and ever will be love, however things may go. This is all I have known for certain, that God is love. Even if I have been mistaken on this or that point: God is nevertheless love, that I

*He too thanked me in the strongest terms *privately* for the articles against P. L. Møller and added: I ought to have done that long ago. And consequently he spoke like that *in private,* but *publicly* he was silent.

believe, and whoever believes that is not mistaken. If I
have made a mistake it will be plain enough; so I repent
—and God *is* love. He *is* love, not he *was* love, nor : he
will be love, oh no, even that future was too slow for me,
he *is* love. Oh, how wonderful. Sometimes, perhaps, my
repentance does not come at once, and so there is a future
—But God keeps no man waiting, he is love. Like spring-
water which keeps the same temperature summer and
winter—so is God's love. But sometimes a spring runs dry
—no, no, how shall I praise him, there is no other praise
than the expression which perfectly fits him whom we speak
of, "God be praised!"—and so, God be praised, God's
love is not of such a kind. His love is a spring which never
runs dry.

My home

If one lives alone as I do one is thrown back much more
on one's home and all one's little comforts.

And what is it like now! I suffered unspeakably from
the smells last summer in the tanner's house. I dared not
risk remaining there another summer, and then it was too
expensive. Where I am living now I suffer so much from
the reflection of the sun in the afternoon that at first I
was afraid of going blind.

On top of everything there is trouble with Strube. That
the man whom I depend upon more than any one, whom
I inherited from father, have known for twenty years,
whom I looked upon as one of those strong, healthy, tireless
workers—that he should become eccentric, have to go to
the hospital, want to reform the whole world, that all this
should happen just when he is with me. If one does intellectual work on the scale I work on one wants someone about
of the sort I had imagined Strube to be. And now all the
worry with him, the feeling that he is suffering, although

they have succeeded in calming him somewhat; the thought that it may return again, and then, because it all happens in my house, become an important event which will be discussed in the papers, while on the other hand I fear that if I were to try to get rid of him now it would react too violently upon him, and God knows he is still the best natured fellow I have ever known, or one of the best, and where I am concerned, care itself; but I saw, at the time, how vehement he could be and how obstinate.

And then from another point of view. Not long ago (while I was still living at the tanner's), once on returning home I found that somebody must have been at my desk, and at my only chest, the mahogany one. Possibly I forgot to lock up when I went out, although that is almost unthinkable, but all the same most uncomfortable. Things like that can make one's home most uncomfortable, even if one has, as I have, the most faithful household. It made me feel very uncomfortable for Anders' sake.

And when one comes home so tired to it all, often made so uncomfortable by the rudeness to which I am exposed every day: oh, to proclaim Christianity in that way is very different from being a parson.

And then not to be able to produce any new books; for when I am working I forget everything.

R. Nielsen and I

I am certainly no Socrates and Nielsen no Plato but the relation has nevertheless some analogy.

Now take Plato! There is undoubtedly a quite paramount number of thoughts which belong to Plato himself; but he never minded attributing them to Socrates in order to preserve the purity of the source, he was never afraid of people growing tired of it always being Socrates, Socrates.

Oh, but Nielsen took the thoughts, and concealed the
source; finally he gave his source, but concealed the scale
on which he had used it, *item* that I had privately done
an unusual amount to initiate him into my matter.

I have done nothing, but left everything in the hands of
providence.

About myself

Christianity is as good as done away with. But first a
poet's heart must break, or a poet must be torn in two in
such a way as to close the way to all deceptions.

That is the check; and in our limited sphere that is my
task.

June 9. What infinite confidence there is in Martensen!
He always speaks on such a vast scale, about the whole
church, the Apostolic age, the doctrine of the first three
centuries, mediæval doctrine, the doctrine of the Reformation period, the whole chain of doctors of the Church—
and Christ says : will there be faith on earth at my second
coming.

Such things do not bother Martensen; he is objective.

Humour

If it were not in one sense madness it would be a good
example of humour if a man were to say to God : although
I was strictly brought up as a Christian I was, as you
know, born in the 19th century and so have my share of
the universal superstitious belief in reason etc. The humour
lies in the " as you know."

An excellent saying of Stilipo's

A man asked Stilipo whether the gods were pleased with our adoration and our offerings. Stilipo answered: "You are very hasty about it: let us go to one side if you want to talk about it."

I remember having given the situation a similar turn myself. It was up at Gjødwad's. There were several people there and among others Martin Hammerich who spoke in that free and easy way about Christianity. I answered: "What you are saying sounds all very well here where we are all together; if there were a few more people it would sound even better—but if, on the contrary, you will go into the room next door, where we should be alone, you will find that it will sound pretty poor."

As for the rest Stilipo's intention was rather different.

. . . Mynster bears a certain resemblance to Louis Philippe: he is without inspiration or pathos, but makes a clever use of little means and understands that what really rules the world is the question of a living, and that the person who has livings in his gift rules quite securely.

Nullum unquam exstitit magnum ingenium sine aliqua dementia

The explanation is perfectly simple. In order really to be a great genius a man must be the exception. But in order that his being exceptional should be a serious matter he himself must be unfree, forced into the position. There lies the importance of his dementia. There is a definite point at which he suffers; it is impossible for him to run with the herd. That is his torture. Perhaps his dementia has nothing whatsoever to do with his real genius, but it is the pain by which he is nailed out in isolation—and he must be isolated if he is to be great; and no man can freely isolate himself; he must be compelled if it is to be a serious matter.

Concerning bashfulness in relation to sex

Montaigne says somewhere that it is extraordinary that what we all owe our existence to should be something despised. He means that bashfulness, in this case, is really prudery. And indeed many great minds have held the same view.

But to this it should be replied. It is only true in one respect that man owes his existence to the act of procreation; there is also an act of creation to be included which must be attributed to God. It is not true of the human race, as of animals, that every individual is only an example. The man who really becomes spirit, for which he was intended, takes over his whole being (by choosing himself, as it is put in *Either-Or*) and reduces propagation to nothing but the lowest side of human nature.

What wonder then that there is bashfulness in relation to sex! Procreation only represents the lower side, just as in the act of procreation man is qualified by the lower part of his nature, or at the extreme end of the synthesis in the direction away from spirit. It is the very fact of the direction being away from spirit which is bashfulness, spirit is bashfulness, or the fact that a man is defined as spirit is bashfulness. Animals have no bashfulness, neither has bestiality, and the less spirit the less bashfulness.

A disingenuous turn which may perhaps be given to my matter

People will make it appear that I wanted to introduce pietism, little, pusillanimous self-abnegations in matters of no consequence.

No thank you, I never wanted that in the very slightest degree. What I want is to spur people on to becoming moral characters, witnesses to the truth, to be willing to suffer for the truth, and ready to give up worldly wisdom.

Mynster's importance for my whole work as an author

My task has been to bring a corrective where the establishment is concerned, not to bring anything new which might subvert or supersede it.

Now, had I overlooked that from the beginning and had Mynster not existed, then I should have had to create someone or other to represent the establishment and then buttress him up.

But I did not understand my task so clearly from the beginning; that would certainly have escaped my notice and everything would have been difficult and perhaps unsuccessful.

But Mynster stood there as the representative of the establishment. It followed quite naturally that I venerated Mynster and did everything to express the fact.

In that way I was given my correct position. Here is another example of my good fortune! From a purely personal point of view my veneration for Mynster was essential to me—but it is only long after that I see how very important it was for my task, and so that I should be quite correctly situated.

Faith

It is clear that in my writings I have given a further definition of the concept faith, which did not exist until now.

A remark of Abelard's

. . . Abelard . . . considered it a proof of the decline of faith and the secularisation of Christianity that no more miracles occurred. "And," he adds, "at the present time miracles are really even more necessary than at the doctrine's first appearance, now that a dead faith dominates everywhere."

To this Neander cannot forbear saying that it is easy to see that Abelard is merely looking for arguments against his opponents, since it is quite a different thing to require miracles at the first appearance of the doctrine, and that moreover a dead faith holds most of all to miracles.

Oh no, oh no, Abelard is right. Of course it requires even more miracles to drag a people out of the deception that they have the faith; for the terms of the fight and the task are far more difficult than when Christianity has to deal with paganism. And further, as to a dead faith clinging most of all to miracles, that is only true of miracles at an historical distance. A dead faith dares not have anything to do with contemporary miracles.

Nov. 13. . . . No, instead of wishing, like the young man, to tear away the veil from divinity, I wish to tear the veil from human twaddle and from the conceited self-complacency with which men try to convince themselves and others that man really wants to know the truth. No, every man is more or less afraid of the truth; and that is what is human, for truth is related to being "spirit"— and that is very hard for flesh and blood and the physical lust for knowledge to bear. Between man and truth lies mortification—you see why we are all more or less afraid.

Epictetus

The thing I hold most against him is that one sees at once that he was a slave. The frightful thought of knowing oneself to be a slave, and the question thus decided for ever, put such a weight of despair upon him that he discovered the pride of Stoicism.

But we were not brought up like that, we did not begin with such terrors.

It is perfectly true that only terror to the point of despair develops a man to his utmost—though of course many succumb during the cure; but it is also useful for a man to be handled as roughly as all that.

Even in the very first words of Epictetus: some things are in our power, others are not in our power—even there I can already hear the slave; and thus understood those cold words conceal a frightful passion; one hears the slave sighing in chains, or one hears the sigh from the time when, as a slave, he learnt that, learnt to make that distinction.

The distinction is correct, but the passion with which it is made quite another matter.

There is no doubt that nowadays we are a lot of old women compared with antiquity, and the misfortune no doubt lies, to a great extent, in our not being effectually unhappy—the pressure from outside is so gentle and we have not got character enough to make ourselves unhappy —but nevertheless character too can be bought too dear; character can, in one sense, be bought at the cost of character.

. . . Le Moine's book: *La dévotion aisée,* comfortable
piety, Paris, 1652, a Jesuit. Here sophistry and indulgence
are reduced to a system, and mediocrity is legitimised.

The whole book deserves to be quoted, for it is exactly
like the sermons now in use. And if one were to do so
without giving the title or saying that its author was a
Jesuit, the average run of parson would find it was true
Christianity.

. . . I too have a heart and I have tried to preserve it,
and therefore made every effort to keep it in the proper
place, so as not to have it on my lips at one moment, and
on my sleeve at the next, and never in the proper place,
and not to confuse having a heart with sentimental twaddle.

Has a man the right to talk to any other man on the highest matters?

That one may talk to him about the weather I know
quite well.

But the other thought has occupied me my whole life
long, and to such an extent that I do not know whether
I ought to say: has a man the right etc. for at the same
moment I should really have broken that relation to God
which is silence.

There is a God; his will is made known to me in Holy
Scripture and in my conscience. This God wishes to inter-
vene in the world. But how is he to do so except with the
help of, *i.e. per* man? Now one can say, we can all say:
yes, that is of course what he does, but not *per* me: no
one of us wishes to be that individual; for if God is to inter-
vene in the world it must be through the individual.

And how does a man become that individual? Well,
unless he has to do with God alone, where the highest
matters are concerned, and says: now I weigh the matter

as best I can, act upon it that you, O God, may be able to seize hold of me, and I therefore speak to nobody at all, I dare not do so—unless he does that he cannot become the individual. The moment I talk to another man about my highest concerns, of what God wills for me, in that very moment God has less power over me. How many are there who are able to grasp God's priority of claim on a man, so that the permission to talk to another man about one's highest concerns is an indulgence, a concession which one must pray for, because no mere man can endure being the individual absolutely.

Religion—Politics

Everything depends upon "how" a thing is put into practice, on the reduplication of the proposition in working form in relation to the proposition: of that I am ever more certain.

In fact one may say, in two words, that the difference between politics and religion is that no politics wishes to have anything to do with reduplication, for that it is too busy, too earthly, too worldly.

For reduplication is the longest operation of all, is really that of eternity.

When Luther introduced the idea of the Reformation, what happened? Even he, the great reformer, became impatient, he did not reduplicate strongly enough—he accepted the help of the princes, *i.e.* he really became a politician, to whom victory is more important than "how" one is victorious; for religiously the one important thing is the "how," just because the religious person is infinitely certain that he or his matter will be victorious, indeed that it has already won—he has therefore only to watch out for the "how," *i.e.* to reduplicate.

The Abolition of Confession

the joint action of priest and congregation. The congregation were afraid of going to confession, the confessional-box made it all too real. The priests were afraid of hearing confession, it became much too serious a matter.

A change in the preaching of Christianity answering to the position of the clergy

As long as the clergy were exalted, sacrosanct in the eyes of men, Christianity continued to be preached in all its severity. For even if the clergy did not take it too strictly, people dared not argue with the clergy, and they could quite well lay on the burden and dare to be severe.

But gradually, as the nimbus faded away, the clergy got into the position of themselves being controlled. So there was nothing to do but to water down Christianity. And so they continued to water it down till in the end they achieved perfect conformity with an ordinary worldly run of ideas—which were proclaimed as Christianity. That is more or less Protestantism as it is now.

The good thing is that it is no longer possible to be severe to others if one is not so towards oneself. Only someone who is really strict with himself can dare nowadays to proclaim Christianity in its severity, and even then things may go badly for him.

. . . Christianity, then, did not so much come in order to develop heroic virtues in the individual as to take away egoism, and put love in its place, " let us love one another." Time and energy are used not in perfecting oneself up to a certain maximum—which can too easily become egoism —but in working for others.

. . . I have therefore always urged that Christianity is really for the poor, who perhaps toil and moil the whole day long and hardly get a living. The more advantages the more difficult it is to become a Christian, for reflection can so easily take a wrong turn.

It was always my wish to preach to the common man. But when the vulgar press did everything in order to make me seem mad in the eyes of the common man I was obliged for a time to give up that wish, but I shall come back to it again.

The meaning of my existence in the present time

Neither church, nor doctrine is to be reformed. If anything is to be done—then it is the reformation of us all. That is what my existence expresses.

I am, humanly speaking, the most advanced existence we have. And what have I learnt? That I hardly dare call myself a Christian—so how should I dare to wish to reform the Church or concern myself with such things.

In the same way that other young men travel abroad and then bring home news of the habits and customs of foreign countries—I too have lived abroad for many years, in the company of ideals where it is such happiness to be, where everything is gentle and mild, if only one is unassuming and humble.

... The doctrine of the established Church, its organisation, are both very good. Oh, but our lives—believe me, they are indeed wretched. ...

Just as one talks of being elf-shot so I should like to say : wounded by ideas.

Grundtvig—and I

Grundtvig came before the world with his probational sermon : Why is the word of God gone from the House of God?

I could never say a thing like that. I should have to say : why has the power gone from the preaching of the word of God?

For in my opinion it is the word of God which is heard about the country—the misfortune simply is that we do not follow it. Very little satisfies me, a few words from the Bible is enough—and I immediately ask myself : have you done that?

That is why I can listen to any parson or lay preacher. Almost from the beginning Grundtvig was reduced to listening to nobody but himself. And that continual dwelling upon Christianity as a doctrine, dogmas—and then that " universal history."

The proper tactics against tribulation

James iv, 7 : Resist the devil, and he will flee from you. These are therefore the tactics. Not the reverse, not to fly the devil; that can only be the tactics in temptation.

From which it may also be learnt that tribulation is a whole quality above temptation. Humanly speaking it is always a relief to know that there is the possibility of salvation in flying from danger. But where tribulation is concerned that is not so. That is precisely what, for a time, gives birth to new tribulation, because it will seem to the one who is thus spiritually tried as though he had been too sure of himself, as though he ought to have looked about for a way of escape. This again is tribulation. Spiritual tribulation can only be fought with the foolhardiness of faith, which attacks directly. But in his weak moments the believer grows afraid of the foolhardiness of faith itself, as though perhaps it were to tempt God, which once again is tribulation.

Rousseau

The fourth volume of his *Confessions* (*Les promenades*) is admirable, the fifth promenade æsthetically unequalled.

As for the rest, here is an example of what it means not to be well read in Christianity.

There are analogies in Rousseau's life with the truly Christian conflicts (to do good and suffer for it, to do good and thereby make oneself and others unhappy). That is what he cannot endure; he complains that it paralyses him so terribly. How it would have strengthened him had it been really clear to him that such is the properly Christian conflict.

But as he is completely ignorant of Christianity he is paralysed on the one hand, and on the other falls into the conceit that he is the only man who has ever suffered in this way.

The establishment—and me

If I come into conflict with the establishment it will be entirely Mynster's fault. My whole endeavour is a defence

of the established order, the only one that can honestly
be made. Everything has been done to make things as
gentle as possible for Mynster. But if he ends by obstinately
maintaining that all his questionable preaching of Christianity, which has made Christianity into a theatrical
amusement, is wisdom and Christianity, then it is he who
made my attitude into something different.

Religion—Doubt

Official preaching has falsely represented religion,
Christianity, as nothing but consolation, happiness etc.
And consequently doubt has the advantage of being able
to say in a *superior* way : I do not wish to be made happy
by an illusion.

If Christianity were truthfully presented as suffering,
ever greater as one advances further in it : doubt would
have been disarmed, and in any case there would have
been no opportunity for being superior—where it was a
matter of avoiding—pain.

Humanism

It is incredible how impertinently many people nowadays
urge the purely human as opposed to Christianity.

And what is it we now call "Humanism"? It is a
vaporised Christianity, a culture-consciousness, the dregs
of Christianity. . . . One ought to say to the humanists :
produce "undiluted humanism"—for the humanism we
now have is really Christianity's, though it will not own it;
but you cannot, with justice, call it yours in opposition to
Christianity.

Mynster—and I

Imagine for a moment a knot. Some people wish to untie it. That is what Mynster desires least of all. Then along I come and say : just let me pull the knot a little tighter. But no, he is also afraid of that, nobody must touch it, and that in spite of the fact that it is so loose that it cannot hold together unless it is tightened.

Socrates's way of life

. . . Now if Socrates had had to live the life of an ascetic, alone in the country, it is doubtful whether he could have endured it.

Precisely because he stopped at the infinite negative— he had to be among crowds, needed men, for ever new men, like a fisherman fish, in order to make his experiments on them.

That filled his life, perfectly true, but one might also ask whether he did not use it in order to fill his life.

I began with the socratic method; but I nevertheless recognised my inferiority profoundly, for I had means and, to that extent, a great help towards independence from others. In so far as I now strive to attract people more directly towards me or towards the Idea, I look upon it as an abatement, in a sense an accommodation, but also as a movement in the direction of Christianity. In the meantime I do not talk nonsense and say that my method is superior to the socratic. No, no; besides, it does not tend towards the socratic method but towards proclaiming grace, though of course infinitely lower than the apostolic.

1852

"The Don"

Jan. In the early days of antiquity the philosopher was a power, moral power, character—the empire safeguarded itself by recompensing them, by making them into " dons." The same thing is true of Christianity.

The don is the eunuch; but he has not emasculated himself for the sake of the Kingdom of Heaven, but on the contrary, in order to fit better into this characterless world.

The Annunciation

Theme : That the Angel chose the right person—because Mary chose rightly.

Certainly, she was the chosen one, and so decidedly so that she was chosen. But there is also another factor, freedom and the moment of choice, where we see that such a one is the right one. Had the angel not found her as he did find her, she would not have been the right one.

She said : Behold, the handmaid of the Lord, be it done to me according to thy word.

We are so accustomed to hear this that we easily overlook its meaning, and even imagine that we should have made the same answer under similar circumstances.

Let us consider what she might—oh, much more naturally—have replied. It is profitable for us to consider this matter in other terms than those of a pious fear of God, which not unbeautifully decorates the situation with its emotions, and for example dwells on the fact that when the angel had spoken to Mary the whole creation called out to Mary : say yes, only hasten to say yes etc. . . .

She could then—yes, she could have smiled, like Sarah—there was just as good cause. And if she could not have smiled then she might have felt ashamed at the words addressed to her, and rejected them.

Or she might have said: this is too much above me, it is beyond me, spare me, it is beyond my strength. And it is clear that the angel thought it beyond her strength: therefore the strength of the Holy Ghost shall overshadow her. All that is very well, but it is precisely this believing and being nothing, a mere instrument—which is more difficult than anything a man can possibly attempt.

Cupid and Psyche

Only to-day I was reading the story in Apuleius. The fourth test which Venus sets Psyche is to fetch the casket from Proserpine—and the dangers besetting the road consist in a large measure of meeting such sights and objects as will move her to compassion and so hold her up, and back.

This is something I have also noticed in other myths, that in relation to the Exceptional, what one would have to call in Greek, the divine risk, that which holds one back, or tempts one to remain behind is compassion.

That is perfectly right. For dangers and everything belonging thereto frighten the ordinary man back. But then there are the courageous ones. They are not frightened by dangers and the like. And so the trial is in the sense of compassion. And it is precisely the courageous who are normally inclined to show most compassion towards others. The ordinary man would not perhaps let himself be held back by compassion, if he himself only had the courage to go to meet the dangers; but it is the courageous who are weakest where showing compassion is concerned.

Pascal

Who in modern times has been used so much by parsons and professors as Pascal? His ideas are appropriated—but Pascal's asceticism and his hair-shirt are omitted; or else they are explained away as the hallmark of his day which no longer concerns us. Brilliant! Pascal was original in every other respect—only not in this.

But was asceticism really so general in his day, or had it not been done away with long ago, so that it was for Pascal to reassert its rights in face of the whole age?

Everywhere it is the same; everywhere that infamous and disgusting cannibalism whereby (just as Heliogabalus ate ostrich brains) men eat the ideas, opinions, expressions, and moods of the dead—but as for their lives and characters; no thank you, they will have none of that.

My life's course

In frightful inner suffering I became an author.

And so I was an author year after year, I suffered too for the idea, in addition to what I suffered within me.

Then came 1848. That helped. There came a moment when overcome with blessedness I dared say to myself: I have understood the highest. In truth, that is not given to many in every generation.

But almost at the same time something new rushed upon me: the highest of all is not to understand the highest but to act upon it.

I had certainly been aware of that from the very beginning, and I am therefore something other than an author in the ordinary sense. But what I was not so clearly aware of was that, by having means and being independent, it was easier for me to give existential expression to what I had understood.

When I understood this I was ready to declare myself a poet, namely because I have had means, which has made action easier for me than for others.

But it all comes to this, that the highest is not to understand the highest, but to act upon it, and be it noted, with all stress upon it. Then I understood properly for the first time that "Grace" must be introduced or else men are stifled just as they are about to begin. But "Grace" must not be introduced in order to hinder endeavour, no, it comes again in the form : the highest is not to understand the highest but to act upon it.

The difficulty with our age

June 4. The fact that enthusiasm lies beyond "reason," that is the goal of the struggle.

But oh, for the man who has to awaken that enthusiasm there can be no question of being understood in his own age. Everywhere nothing but these half-experienced, blasé, individualities, who when quite young had a dash of enthusiasm, but who when still almost as young became reasonable. They are so far from allowing themselves to be carried away that on the contrary they immediately supply an envious opposition, and instead of taking part —think they ought simply to "observe" the enthusiastic person, hoping that it will culminate in his either becoming reasonable or ending badly.

Have you seen a boat aground in the mud, it is almost impossible to float it again because it is impossible to punt, no punt-pole can touch bottom so that one can push against it. And so the whole generation is stuck in the mud banks of reason; and no one grieves over it, there is only self-satisfaction and conceit, which always follow on reason and the sins of reason. Oh, the sins of passion and of the heart, how much nearer to salvation than the sins of reason.

About myself

June 19. Understanding myself to be fundamentally different from others, also with a thorn in the flesh, I became an author in great inner suffering.

Thus I had held out year after year in spite of suffering, and in spite of the new sufferings : a rabble's persecution : I can never thank God enough for what has been done for me.

Then came 1848. I was lifted up to a height which I had never before known, and perfectly understood myself in what had gone before, and the past. So I understood my task to be, or I thought of it in this way : to give myself entirely in a pure intellectual enthusiasm to the task of making it clear what Christianity is—yet without defining unconditionally my relation to Christianity, on the other hand to endure everything for the idea in intellectual enthusiasm.

That is how I understand it and myself in my difference. I wished to go into the country in order to stress it even more clearly.

However, that did not happen at once, a suspicion awoke in me, and my worries began. Whether, the first time the cares of life grew really serious, whether I should not regret having so decisively missed the possibility, which always remained to me, of getting a position in the Church. Whether it was warrantable both in regard to the Church and mankind, whether I could not whip things up so that I became the stumbling-block for Christianity. Then the thought of her awoke again strongly in me. . . .

From the moment I gave up the idea of going into the country I suffered greatly and in ways which I have never otherwise known : cares and misfortunes in all the small things of life, all of which has been increased by financial anxieties. I have certainly prayed for some time past for education, and those particular cares grew greater after that time. But I have certainly developed.

————

And now I have returned to the point I was at in 1848, but with a higher understanding. Once again I have been strongly reminded of my difference, and reminded of what I had almost forgotten, that I cannot take ecclesiastical office. Ordination is an obstacle to me. Moreover my idea was rather to get a position at a seminary. And so I understand myself in being different. On the other hand I have a direct relation to Christianity so that what I may suffer in the future does not belong under the rubric of intellectual enthusiasm for the question "what is Christianity" (that was how I understood my task in 1848), but under that of suffering for the doctrine, so that in bearing it I have the direct support of Christianity. . . .

It is the "imitation of Christ" that must now be introduced—and I must be what I am, in being different from others. O my God, it was thou who didst hold thy hand over me so that in the long hours of anguish I should not go and take a step in the direction of becoming like others and thereby becoming guilty of procuring an abortion (to use the strong expression employed in one of the Journals of that date, to describe what I then feared), and furthermore embroiling myself in something which in time I should have discovered to hold nothing but worry, because I am not at home in it, and finally should incur a protest when I come into eternity.

The "imitation" must be introduced. But *without authority,* that is and remains my category.

That has moreover happened, for in *On my work as an*

author and in the preface to *Two Discourses at communion service* and later in *For Self-examination* I declare myself to be a poet.

For " Grace " is the decisive point, but the " imitation " must be introduced; but I am not anxious about my ability or about others, therefore I am only " a poet "; yet my life has already expressed for more than being a poet, and expresses more if I remain different.

The polemical craft which is my natural characteristic and is inseparable from my very being is here again in place. For how ironical—there are 1000 parsons, *i.e.* teachers (which is something far higher than being merely a poet)—and I am only a poet.

O my God, how clearly it now all stands out before me, how endlessly much has already been done for me. It is not difference that I must pray myself out of, that is not the task, but alas, I shall never know security, which consists in being like others. No, I remain different. There I remain with thee—and verily I know its happiness; the only thing that has made me anxious was the thought that possibly the task was another, namely that I should escape from that unlikeness, a thought which may very well have been prompted by the wish to make my life secure.

So I also feel courage and happiness—not indeed with an ebullient joy as in 1848; but then anxiety for my livelihood was more remote—if I were free from that at the present moment I should once again rejoice, for otherwise everything is well. However, I have suffered so very much in the past year and had to consider everything so seriously that doubtless I am a good deal changed.

But even with the financial anxieties I have, and some idea of what I, with my knowledge of the world, can foresee of the rumpus which will ensue, I feel peaceful and happy, perhaps more definitely so and with a more tranquil confidence than in 1848.

Conservatism

What may be explained as a result of something ethical in a man may also find its explanation in a paramount love of pleasure : the desire to retain the old, the established.

It is the very man whose one intention is to enjoy life, and make a brilliant worldly career, to whom it may be of the greatest importance that there should be no disturbances where religion is concerned. Once the "spirit" begins to move, life becomes unsettled, and one cannot concentrate properly on making a career. That is why it is so important that it should be kept as it is, that religion should be taken over exactly as it was transmitted by the last generation, with at the most a few little modifications. For epicureanism always retains something of the old epicurean saying : *nil beatum nisi quietum.*

Marcus Aurelius—Epictetus

How insignificant Marcus Aurelius's works are compared with those of Epictetus! There is nothing real about him, he is almost affected, like a don. But a slave—his works have style and the nobility of stoicism, where truth is the only way out. Marcus Aurelius helped himself along in a lot of little ways—by being Emperor.

The " in-and-for-itself "—and my task

With the N.T. before me I ask myself the following question : how do we men, nowadays, stand in relation to the whole view of life expressed in the N.T.; has there not, by comparison with it, been a whole qualitative change in the race, and what it means to be a man?

Yes there has, and nothing is easier to see.

Where does the change lie? It is that the "in-and-for-itself," the absolute, has gone out of life, and reason has been put in its place so that the "in-and-for-itself," the absolute, has not only gone out of life, but has become something ridiculous in the eyes of men, a comic exaggeration, something quixotic which one would laugh at were one to come across it, though one never does see it because it has gone out of life.

The "in-and-for-itself" and reason are related to one another inversely; where the one is the other is not. When reason has completely penetrated all relationships and everything the "in-and-for-itself" will have disappeared entirely from life.

That is more or less where we stand now. Reason is everywhere : instead of love—a *mariage de convenance,* instead of unconditional obedience—obedience as a result of reasoning, instead of faith—reasonable knowledge, instead of confidence—guarantees, instead of daring—probability, clever calculation, instead of action—events, instead of "the individual"—several people, instead of personality—impersonal objectivity etc.

But the N.T. presents the "in-and-for-itself," simply and solely, and nothing else; and so I ask : what does it mean when we continue to behave as though all were as it should be, calling ourselves Christians according to the N.T., when the nerve of the N.T. the "in-and-for-itself" has gone out of life?

The tremendous disproportion which this state of affairs represents has, moreover, been perceived by many. They like to give it this turn : the race has outgrown Christianity.

I think the very reverse : the race has gone backwards (or is a *mariage de convenance* even though there were 170,000 of the choicest reasons for it; not a step back as compared to a love match), the kind of men Christianity has in mind no longer exist; on the average the human race has progressed, but there are no more individuals who could bear Christianity. That in my opinion is where we stand. And again it is my belief that the race must go through reason to the absolute.

Goethe as the representative of modern characterlessness —the sins of reason more frightful than other sins.

. . . Now take a richly gifted, egoistical nature with a strong desire to enjoy life. He is at the same time too gifted and too highly developed intellectually not to see that without ideas and ideals, and some relation to them, life becomes all too insignificant.

But at the same time he is a complete egoist and sensibly egoistic. So what does he do? He distinguishes. With the help of his imagination he is related to all that is noble, good, unselfish, elevated—and it gives him exquisite pleasure; as he knows well enough. . . . Poetically, then, he seizes hold of the ethical ideal, poetically he exhausts himself—but he is clever where his worldly profit is concerned, and is not such a fool as to step forward in the rôle of goodness. How charming! There is a double profit: first of all the direct worldly profit which one gains by being an egoist; and then the *appearance* of nobility which the poetic works cast over him.

Preaching of the Gospel

Parson: Thou shalt die unto the world.—The fee is one guinea.

Neophyte: Well, if I must die unto the world I quite understand that I shall have to fork out more than one guinea; but just one question: Who gets the guinea?

Parson: Naturally I get it, it is my living, for I and my

family have to live by preaching that one must die unto the world. It is really very cheap, and soon we shall have to ask for considerably more. If you are reasonable you will easily understand that to preach that one must die unto the world, if it is done seriously and with zeal, takes a lot out of a man. And so I really have to spend the summer in the country with my family to get some recreation.

God's guidance

Originally I was in possession of the outward requirements for the enjoyment of life; and within me, that is all too certain, there was desire enough to enjoy life—but there was given to me a thorn in the flesh, a cross : and I could not really succeed in enjoying life.

Then, as the conditions for enjoying life began to disappear, and financial worries came upon me, it occurred to me that it might be possible for the thorn in the flesh to be taken from me. I would then have been able to put the abilities and gifts granted me to my own use, and humanly speaking I should certainly have secured, by acquisition, the conditions for enjoying life, and so all the same have succeeded in enjoying life. . . .

And now things begin to happen as I expected. That thorn in the flesh will perhaps be taken from me; but by then I shall no longer be in possession of the requirements necessary for enjoying life, and I will be so tried in suffering and so far out, that I shall have cut myself off from all possibility of acquiring the conditions.

So perhaps there will be still one more course left for me to go through. The thorn in the flesh will be taken from me—and then suddenly all the requirements for enjoying life will be offered to me, almost forced upon me. And then the task will perhaps be for me to be so dead to the world, so mature a spirit, as to have the strength to say freely : no, I will not accept them.

And so in the end I shall never enjoy life. Oh, my God, that was certainly my qualification; you had something far better for me than that I should waste my life in enjoyment —and repent through all eternity.

But at first I could not understand that and could not do it, and so force had to be used, just as one puts splints on a broken leg. The education consisted in leading me to being able to do freely what at first I had to be compelled to do.

. . . I cannot possibly make it clear enough that the Exceptional has nothing whatsoever to do with ethics; ethically there is nothing exceptional, for the highest is quite simply what is demanded. . . . The " Exceptional " has nothing to do with ethically fulfilling what is demanded, but is a particular relation to God.

Renunciation as it is commonly understood appeared to me to be an attempt to make God out a foolish pedant, and the relation of God to man always petty and mean. And that did not appeal to me. But the real situation is entirely different; for renunciation, yes, the delight of renunciation, is simply a lover's understanding with God. So far as I am concerned, truth obliges me to admit that it was God who gave me the hint. I had not dreamed of it, neither had I believed myself capable of it. But it was as though God had whispered the secret to me : Renunciation is a higher relation to God, it is really a love-relationship : and for me at least an enchantment was spread over renunciation—I have never been so enchanted.

That thought I have loved like my very life—I was on the point of reconciling myself to the notion that I must give it up, that it was my duty to submit to the humiliation of giving it up because I could no longer afford to live for it.

Now—O, blessed fortune!—I am again restored to this thought of mine, but in a far higher sense. It seems as if God said to me: My little friend, I who am love would find the greatest joy in using an expedient to make you independent again; but then your cause will not go forward, then you will not learn to love me in a higher sense. You are now so far developed that, were I to bestow riches upon you, I should almost have to be angry with you if you did not instantly give them back, saying: No, under the circumstances, I dare not. Surely you are too developed not to recognise how unseemly it is to preach the blessedness of doing without while living in opulence, too developed to help yourself out by saying, what it will always be a good thing that you had the honesty to say, that you are only a poet. And so it is; even though humanly speaking I can be said to have been something more than a poet.

September 10

And so it is 12 years ago to-day that I got engaged.

"She," naturally, did not fail to meet me. . . . She looked at me to-day: but she did not bow to me, nor did she talk to me. Oh, perhaps she expected me to do so. My God, how I should like to do so, and do everything for her. But I dare not take the responsibility: she must ask for it herself.

Yet I should have liked it this year; and moreover it is painful to keep something at breaking point like this, year after year.

However, it was well that nothing happened. For there is always the possibility that the effect upon me might have been such that in order to bedeck her with celebrity I might have been tempted to strive for success from a worldly point of view, and make a sort of success in the world.

For that very reason I was profoundly impressed by the fact that to-day everything went, or passed off quietly. I was profoundly and vividly reminded that she has not, after all, the first place in my life. No, no, humanly speaking certainly—and how willingly would I not prove it, she has and shall have the first place in my life—but God has the first place. My engagement to her and the break are really my relation to God, they are, if I may say so, divinely speaking, my engagement with God.

And so September 10 is the anniversary of my engagement; so understood that I remembered it in solitude— oh, and perhaps I was urged on to be reminded of this, to be reminded not to go and become a Sophist, making a success in the world by preaching that it is blessed to suffer, a Sophist who though he does not really enjoy life himself might yet be delighted by enjoying a woman's pleasure at celebrity shining upon her.

Perhaps she will meet me to-morrow and will ask for it herself, perhaps the day after to-morrow, perhaps in a year's time—I shall be willing enough. But oh, the fact that nothing happened to-day of all days was such a valuable lesson.

I might perhaps have misunderstood it as a hint from God in the sense of wishing to enjoy life, a temporal victory—and so I should have disturbed the spirit, but perhaps only at the hour of death would I have become aware that I had taken a wrong turning.

1853

My Prayer

There was a time—it came so naturally, it was child-like—when I believed that God's love also expressed itself by sending earthly "good gifts," happiness, prosperity. How foolhardy my soul was in desiring, and daring—for this is how I thought of it : one must not make the all-powerful petty; I prayed for everything, even the most foolhardy things, yet one thing excepted, exemption from the deep suffering beneath which I have suffered from my earliest days, but which I understood as belonging to my relation to God. But as for the rest, I should have dared anything. And when (for the suffering was simply the Exceptional), everything succeeded, how rich my soul was in thankfulness, so happy in giving thanks,—for I was convinced that God's love could express itself by sending the good gifts of the earth.

Now it is otherwise. How did that happen? Quite simply, but little by little. Little by little I noticed increasingly that all those whom God really loved, the examples etc. had all had to suffer in this world. Further-more, that that is the teaching of Christianity : to be loved by God and to love God is to suffer.

But if that were so then I dared not pray for good fortune and success because it was as though I were to beg at the same time : will you not, O God, cease loving me and allow me to stop loving you. When a desire awoke in me—and I wished to pray, all my former burning inwardness was blown away; for it was as though God looked upon me and said : little child, think carefully what you are doing, do you wish me not to love you, and do you wish to be excused from loving me?

J.   225   H

On the other hand, to pray directly for suffering appeared to me too exalted, and it also seemed to me that it might easily be presumptuous, and that God might grow angry at my perhaps wishing to defy him.

For a long time my prayer has therefore been different, it is really a silent surrendering of everything to God, because it is not quite plain to me how I should pray.

I am brought to a stop by that difficulty. And yet the question presents still another difficulty. For even if I were really frank enough to grasp that to be loved by God, and to love God, is to suffer, for which after all I was disposed by nature, I who from my earliest days believed I was marked out for suffering—what of other men? That is how I had understood my life from this point of view. Now, for better or for worse, I live in the isolated cabin of melancholy—though I may rejoice at the sight of other people's joy and may sanction it from a *Christian* point of view. To be loved by a woman, to live happily married, to enjoy life—well, that has been denied me; but when I step forth from my isolated cabin I may rejoice to see the good fortunes of others, may strengthen them in the conviction that God is pleased at their joy in life. To be strong and healthy, a complete man with the expectation of a long life—well, that was never granted me. But when I step forth from my lonely suffering I come out among happy people; I thought I might have the melancholy joy of confirming them in their enjoyment of life. Oh, but if I have to preach mortification, and that to be loved by God and to love God is to suffer, then I have to disturb others in their happiness. I cannot have the melancholy joy of rejoicing in their joy, the melancholy love of thus being loved by them.

And consequently I am brought to a stop by that difficulty. If anyone can prove to me from Holy Scripture that to be loved by God and to love God is compatible with enjoying this life: I shall accept this interpretation from God's Hand with unspeakable thankfulness, happy on my own account but also on account of others, for I understand only too well what comes so naturally to man. If anyone can make that plain to me from the New Testament : then the position of my cause, if I may so express it, would be so brilliant at that moment that with a little worldly wisdom and confidence in God it would be sure to be victorious in this world. *Aber, aber,* my soul is suspicious of earthly enjoyment and worldly victories. That is why I dare not use worldly wisdom—I am almost afraid of winning a temporal victory; for, from a Christian point of view, to be loved by God and to love God is to suffer. In any case, in order to have confidence in God—for I cannot combine confidence in God and worldly wisdom in such a way as to use wordly wisdom with confidence in God—I must have the frankness not to use worldly wisdom, and if I am victorious temporally, I must be able to say honestly : it was God's will, I attribute it to him—by renouncing the use of worldly wisdom. . . .

However, as I have said, I am held up by this difficulty; as yet I dare not decide absolutely whether God might not wish me to be victorious in the world, whether it is not only true of the chosen ones that to be loved by God is to suffer, whereas like men in general I am excepted therefrom, but then too have not so close a relation to God; I am not yet strong enough to pray for suffering.

But I am brought to a standstill, and resigning myself silently to God I await a nearer understanding. It is so infinitely high, this : to be loved by God and to love God is to suffer—oh, and nothing, nothing makes me so afraid as the thought of approaching too near to God uncalled. . . . And so with the models, the glorious ones, the chosen of God; but this is precisely the difficulty with " Christendom," that there, on a frightful scale, people have made it only too easy for themselves to rid themselves of the chosen ones, to manœuvre them out of the way, to presume that everything strict in the New Testament is said to the Apostles *in particular*. The question is whether the New Testament recognises any kind of Christian other than the " disciple." For the humility which does not desire to be an apostle or a disciple—oh, it can be such a swindle : to wish to be freed from the apostles' suffering and then, as usual in this human thieves' slang, lyingly call it humility and gain two advantages : to be freed from suffering and to be honoured as suffering. Not to desire the gifts of an apostle—yes, that may be all right, that is humility; but that it should be " humility not to desire his sufferings," no, that ends in hypocrisy.

My task. About myself

Feb. 13, 1853. One phase of asceticism, however, may well be considered as over, though not, be it noted, in such a way that subsequent ages do not require to have it inculcated again and again, and in any case how they stand in need of " grace." But in the history of the human race, or of Christianity one phase may be looked upon as finished. First of all Christianity had to fight against violent and wild passions and in that respect educate mankind with what in the strictest sense of the word must be called asceticism.

The fruit of this education is to have produced a Christian culture and civilisation.

To reintroduce asceticism, and consequently in a heightened form, upon the basis of this Christian culture and civilisation is a very nice point. In any case I do not look upon that as my task.

On the other hand this culture and civilisation has at the same time produced a development of rational understanding which is in the process of identifying being a Christian with culture, and with intelligence, desirous of a conceptual understanding of Christianity.

This is where the struggle must come, and will be fought in the future. It will be a question of establishing the validity of Christianity's incommensurability in this respect, of keeping open the possibility of scandal, in short it will be a question of scandal and asceticism in this connection—while asceticism in the earlier sense will also have to be introduced in order to maintain the balance and inculcate the need of grace.

Grace in the first place

This is true even where the objective, the sacraments, the word is concerned.

Communion for instance. Now if I think of wishing to go to communion : well, I admit that up to the present I have never succeeded in going worthily to communion. This I repent, grace is offered me, this is grace in the second place, grace from behind, in relation to what is already past.

But now I am to go to communion again—am I now worthy? dare I now say that I am worthy? And this might after all be demanded of me in thanksgiving for the grace I have received in the past.

There we have it! The sacrament promises and strengthens me in grace, but I must have grace in order to dare to use the sacrament. It cannot be otherwise, unless I have an immediate relation to God and he says to me : to-day at four o'clock you shall receive communion—for then I have no responsibility. . . .

What I have desired

March 25.   As I can now see it.   *Good Friday.*

There is one thought which has been in my soul and occupied it from my earliest years, inexplicably deeply rooted, a thought which has to do with Socrates as a model, the man to whom I have been inexplicably related from my earliest years, long before I really began to read Plato —the thought : how is it that all those who have in truth served the truth have always come out of it badly in this life, *as long as they lived,* and as soon as they are dead, then they are deified?

The explanation is quite simple : the mass of mankind can only relate itself to ideas, the good, the true, through the imagination. But a dead man is at a distance, in the imagination. But on the other hand they cannot endure the living who give them reality, they are scandalised by them, put them to death, tread them down. . . .

About myself

Oct. 13. In all that I have noted about myself in the Journals of 1848 and 1849 something of the literary side often slipped in. It is not so easy to keep all that kind of thing apart when one is poetically productive to the degree that I am. It happens the moment I take pen in hand. For strangely enough, deep within me I am quite otherwise clear cut about myself. But as soon as I want to note it down I immediately become productive. In the same way, and that too is extraordinary enough, I have no desire to note down the religious impressions, thoughts, expressions as I use them myself, they are, as it were, too important for that. Of those I only have a few—but I have produced masses. And only when a word like that is, so to say, used up can it occur to me to note it down or let it become part of the productivity.

1854

Bishop Mynster[1]

March 1, 1854. So now he is dead.

If only it had been possible to persuade him to end his life with the admission that what he represented was not really Christianity, but a mitigation of it : that would have been most desirable, for he carried a whole age along with him.

The possibility of this admission had therefore to be kept open to the last, to the very last, lest he should perhaps make it dying. Therefore he had never to be attacked; and I had to submit to everything, even when he did such desperate things as in the case of Goldschmidt, for no one could tell whether it would not have an effect upon him and so move him to make the admission.

Dead without having made that admission, everything is altered; now it merely remains that his preaching hardened Christianity into a deception.

The situation is also changed as regards my melancholy devotion to my father's priest; for it would be too much of a good thing if I could not talk about him more freely even after his death, however well I know that my old devotion to him and my æsthetic admiration will always continue to be attractive to me.

Originally I wanted to transform my whole thing into a triumph for Mynster. Later, as I understood it more clearly, my wish remained unchanged, but I had to require this one little admission, though not for my sake and

[1]Died January 30, 1854. The Journal (NB[28]) breaks off on Nov. 2, 1853. After a silence of four months, which not even Mynster's death caused him to interrupt, it begins again with this entry.

therefore, so I thought, it could perfectly well be done in such a way as to become a triumph for Bishop Mynster. . . .

And yet it almost came to a point where I thought I should have to attack him. I only missed one of his sermons, that was the last; I was not prevented by illness, on the contrary, I went to hear Kolthorf. To me that meant : it must happen *now,* you must break with your father's tradition : that was the last time Mynster preached. God be praised, surely that is very like providence.

If Bishop Mynster could have given in (which could have been concealed from everyone, and to them it would thus have become his triumph) then my outward position would have been made easier; for Bishop Mynster, who at the bottom of his heart certainly made me certain spiritual concessions, reckoned cleverly from a worldly point of view that in the end I should have to give way to him in one way or another, because I could not compete with him financially. An expression which he often used in conversation with me was very instructive : it is not a question of who has most strength, but who can last longest.

God's Majesty—the only thing which interests him is obedience

It is so easy to see that one to whom everything is equally important and equally insignificant can only be interested in one thing : obedience.

Lutheranism

Lutheranism is a corrective—but a corrective made into the norm, the whole, is *eo ipso* confusing in the next generation (when that which it was meant to correct no longer exists). And as long as this continues things get worse with every generation, until in the end the corrective produces the exact opposite of what was originally intended.

And such, moreover, is the case. Taken by itself, as the whole of Christianity, the Lutheran corrective produces the most subtle type of worldliness and paganism.

"Yea, a sword shall pierce through thy own soul also"

Luke 2. 34, 35. Coming as an interpolation, in conjunction with the words about Christ being a sign which shall reveal the thoughts of many hearts, these words must not only be understood to refer to the pain at the sight of the Son's death, they must be understood to mean that the moment, the moment of pain and agony will come for her when she will—at the sight of the Son's suffering—*doubt* whether the whole thing was not imagination, a deceit, the whole story of Gabriel being sent by God to announce to her that she was the chosen one.

Just as Christ cried out: my God, my God, why hast thou forsaken me—in the same way the Virgin Mary had to suffer something which humanly corresponded to it.

A sword shall pierce through thy own soul—and reveal the thoughts of the heart, yours also, whether you dare still believe, are still humble enough to believe, that you are in truth the chosen among women, she who found grace in the sight of God.

Oh, Luther

Luther; your responsibility is great indeed, for the closer I look the more clearly do I see that you overthrew the Pope—and set the public on the throne.

About myself

Among those who have been ordered out extraordinarily
by providence not a few have had greater abilities, and
greater learning, all perhaps greater zeal and ardour—
but none, none has had a more difficult task, in all Christendom none.

To battle against princes and popes—and the nearer we
come to our own times the truer this is—is easy compared
with struggling against the masses, the tyranny of equality,
against the grin of shallowness, nonsense, baseness and
bestiality.

Outside Christianity Socrates stands alone—noble, simple
and wise, you were indeed a true reformer.

On Arthur Schopenhauer

A.S.* is unquestionably an important writer, he has interested me very much and I am astonished to find an author
who, in spite of complete disagreement, touches me at so
many points.

I have two objections in particular to his ethic.

His ethical point of view is : the individual succeeds in
seeing through the wretchedness of this existence either
through the intellect, and consequently intellectually, or
through suffering ($\delta\epsilon\nu\tau\epsilon\rho\sigma\varsigma$ $\pi\lambda\sigma\upsilon\varsigma$), and then decides to
deaden or mortify the joy of life; this is where asceticism
comes in; and so, as a result of complete asceticism we
reach contemplation, quietism.—And this the individual
does out of sympathy (here we find A.S.'s moral principle),

*Curiously enough I am called S.A. and we probably
stand in an inverse relation to one another.

out of sympathy, because he sympathises with all the misery, which is existence, and consequently sympathises with the misery of others, which is to exist.

Against this I would urge: that I am almost tempted to reverse everything, also be it noted—out of sympathy. Now whether a man reaches asceticism as a result of a profoundly personal intellectuality, because he sees through the misery of everything, or better still the misery of existing, or whether he is brought by suffering to the point where it is relief to let the whole thing come to a rupture, to a break with everything, with life itself, *i.e.* with the joy of life (asceticism, mortification), and where all the small and ever new miseries are concerned this may bring much relief, like breaking into a sweat compared with the painful heat one endures when one cannot begin sweating: in each case I should reverse the question; might it not be that it is this very sympathy which should hold him back, prevent his going so far, sympathy with all the thousands and thousands who cannot possibly follow him, thousands upon thousands who live in the happy illusion that life is pleasure—and whom he would therefore merely disturb and make unhappy without being able to help them up to his level. Cannot sympathy also put the question in that way, though I readily admit it easily conceals a swindle, by not daring to go to the bitter end itself, and so merely gives the appearance of sympathy?

Secondly, and this is the main objection. After reading through A.S.'s Ethic one learns—naturally he is to that extent honest—that he himself is not an ascetic. And consequently he himself has not reached contemplation through asceticism, but only a contemplation which contemplates asceticism.

This is extremely suspicious, and may even conceal the most terrible and corrupting voluptuous melancholy, item: a profound misanthropy. In this too it is suspicious, for it is always suspicious to propound an ethic which does not

exert so much power over the teacher that he himself
expresses it.

A.S. makes ethics into genius—but that is of course an
unethical conception of ethics. He makes ethics into genius,
and although he prides himself quite enough on being a
genius it has not pleased him, or nature has not allowed
him, to become a genius where asceticism and mortification
are concerned.

Here I come to a point which S. scornfully dismisses,
namely this : Thou shalt, item : eternal punishment etc.
The question is whether that kind of asceticism and mortification is really possible for a man if he does not respect
the "Thou shalt," and is not determined by the motive of
eternity, not by genius however, but ethically. S. who
really gives up Christianity always praises Indian Brah-
minism. But those ascetics, this he must himself admit,
are determined by considerations of eternity, religiously,
not by genius; it is put to them as a religious duty.

                    *   *   *

As I have said, A.S. interests me very much. And so
of course does his fate in Germany.

S. has quite rightly learnt and felt that (like the parsons
in religion) there is a class of men in philosophy who under
the guise of teaching philosophy live by it . . . S. sees quite
rightly that these respected gentlemen are the dons : On
this point his rudeness is unsurpassed.

But here we have it again; S. is not a character, not a
moral character, not a Greek philosopher in character, still
less a Christian police-official.

If I could talk with him I am sure he would shudder or
laugh if I were to show him the standard.

S. has seen quite rightly that this donnish meanness
consists mainly in using one method : ignoring whatever is

not of the faculty. S. is really charming, admirable and unequalled in effective rudeness.

But then look how S. lives! He lives a retired life and once in a while sends forth a thunderbolt of rudeness—which is ignored. There we have it.

No, tackle the problem differently. Go to Berlin, force all those swindlers down into the street, endure being famous, known to everyone. Endure personally a sort of intercourse and understanding with the rascals so that people see one together in the street, and so that if possible everyone knows that they know each other. That is how to undermine their mean way of " ignoring." That is what I have done, on a smaller *terrain* certainly, here in Copenhagen : they have been made fools of for all their " ignoring " . . .

But A.S. is quite different; in that respect he is not a bit like S.A. He is, after all, a German thinker, hipped on recognition. To me it is inconceivable that a brain like S., a capital writer into the bargain, can be so unironical where character is concerned (for stylistically he has a lot of it), so wanting in lightness of touch and superiority.

There can be no doubt that the position in Germany is this, that—it is easy to see because all the literary gossips, journalists and authorlings have begun to busy themselves with S.—that he is now to be dragged forward on the scene and proclaimed. And I bet 100 to 1 he will be awfully glad; it does not even occur to him to keep the scum down, no, he will be delighted.

That is surely inexplicable. Representing, and with so much talent, such a misanthropic point of view as he does, he is then extremely happy, really seriously happy that the *Gesellschaft der Wissenschaften* in Trondhjem (Good God, in Trondhjem) crowns his Prize Essay—it never occurs to him that perhaps the Society values it as a rare honour to have an essay sent them by a German. *Pro dii immortales!* And then because Copenhagen did not crown another of his prize essays S. makes an awful fuss, quite seriously, in the preface that accompanies it.

To me that is inexplicable. I could understand S. having to do with these societies in order to play a joke on them —and having laughed at being crowned in Tronhjem, no less than at not being crowned in Copenhagen. Oh, but not the way S. takes the whole thing.

. . . He was scurvily treated, but that did not break him, it developed him into an important writer. . . .

It may therefore be said of S. that in a scurvy way he was the victim of the whole mean donnish racket, but ethically, religiously S. is not a victim—for above everything he wished to be proclaimed.

. . . The important thing is that it should be made perfectly plain that suffering is chosen freely.

That is true, noble tragedy. . . . In pure comedy, elevated comedy, or purified comedy one never laughs at something which in another sense is fundamentally misery. Oh, but in the common run of things, the majority of writers help themselves along by laughing—at misery. And they speculate successfully, because what they are after is bigger sales. . . .

Greek

July. There were philosophers even before Hegel who took it upon themselves to explain existence, history. And it is true of all such attempts that providence can only smile at them. Though perhaps it has not exactly roared with laughter at them; for there was always something honest, human and serious in them.

But Hegel—oh let me think in Greek!—how the gods must have laughed! A miserable don like that who had seen through the necessity of everything and got the whole thing off by heart: ye Gods!

It amused me more than I can say to read Schopenhauer. What he says is perfectly true and then, what I allow the Germans, he is rude as only a German can be.

"Windbag"

An excellent word; I envy the Germans for having it; particularly because it can be used both as an adjective and a noun. A. Schopenhauer makes excellent use of it, I might almost say, what a quandary he would be in if he did not have that word, for he has to talk about Hegelian philosophy and the whole of donnish philosophy.

That is why the Germans have the word, because there is constant use for it in Germany.

We Danes have not got it; but then neither is what it describes characteristic of us Danes. It is not really part of the Danish character to be a windbag.

On the other hand we Danes have another failing, alas, a *corresponding* fault; and for this the Danish language has a word, a word which perhaps the German language has not got: windsucker. It is commonly used of horses but can be put to ordinary use.

That too is roughly the relation between them: a German to produce wind and a Dane to swallow it: for a long time past that has been the relation of the two countries.

Luther

. . . The longer I study Luther the more clear does it become that Luther also makes this confusion: he confuses what it means to be the patient with what it means to be the doctor. He is an extremely important patient for Christianity, but he is not the doctor; he has the patient's passion for expressing and describing his suffering, and what he feels the need of as an alleviation. But he has not got the doctor's breadth of view. And in order to reform Christianity the very first requirement is surely a view of the whole of Christianity.

Denmark

Christianity's first and foremost duty is to return to the monastery from which Luther broke away.

Providence really makes use of only one power, time; it gives time, gives the mistakes time—on a scale which a mere man cannot grasp at all—to unfold themselves in all their consequences.

In order to make the absurdity, the dishonesty, and the corruption of protestantism manifest when—instead of being a necessary corrective at a given moment—it sets up as a religion, as Christianity : in order to get that made manifest it required a country which was not even assisted —as in Germany and other countries—by having Catholicism close at hand.

No, Protestantism had to go its own way, left entirely to itself in a country which even has a language all of its own.

So it required—in order to make everything perfectly plain—a worldly wise, pleasure-seeking, artistically gifted epicurean, a master in the art of conjuring up and maintaining a show—a man of that kind is required at the head of the Church. Then, if he is granted a long life, then practically the whole depths of nonsense and confusion will have been revealed.

This has happened under Bishop Mynster—but naturally the country, the people do not see it, they are very well pleased with that kind of Christianity and with the condition of Christianity in the country.

From a Christian point of view it is just about as pitiful as it could be—indeed, to use the predicate Christian of conditions in Denmark, even though it is in order to add that conditions are extremely poor, is really saying too much. The predicate "Christian" is ridiculous when it is applied to Denmark. Take an illustration. If a man comes dragging along with the most miserable nag of a horse there is nothing ridiculous in his saying it is a horse. If on the contrary he comes along with a cow and says it is a horse, then it is ridiculous. It is no good his being willing to admit that it is a poor kind of horse—it is a cow.

Denmark has fallen so low religiously that it is not only lower than anything hitherto seen of Christianity but lower than Jewry, in fact it can only be compared to the lowest forms of paganism—to such a degree have people forgotten the point in Christianity : self-denial, while worldly well-being and soft-hearted mediocrity are idolised.

Christianity as a regulating weight

. . . And because Christianity has been abolished it has also been possible to muddle up the whole of temporal existence, and consequently it is no longer a question of there being a revolution once in a while—but beneath everything is a revolution which may break out at any moment.

This is closely related to the fact that Christianity has been abolished as the regulating weight, consequently as a weight, but a regulating weight. . . .

There must be a weight—a clock or the works of a clock need a heavy weight to make them go properly, a ship needs ballast. This weight, this regulating weight is supplied by Christianity, which makes the fact that his eternal happiness is decided in this life the important thing in the life of every individual. . . . And this weight was calculated to regulate temporal existence, both its good and its evil days.

And because the weight was lost—the clock cannot go, the ship turns turtle—and human life is a vortex.

The Sexual relationship

The lower man is in the degree of consciousness, the more natural the relationship.

But the more intellectually developed a man is, the more the conscious life penetrates it—the closer one gets to the point where lies Christianity and whatever resembles it in religious and philosophic outlook : where continence becomes the expression for spirit.

Between these two extremes lies incompleteness (half measures) where the sexual relationship has lost its immediacy, and where one does not wish to attain to spirit.

There one feels—this may be considered partly as a kind of bashfulness, partly perhaps it is a little hypocrisy or sometimes a hypocritical refinement—the need to decide to marry—for reasons. The fact that one has reasons is, in a way, going to spiritualise marriage, make it something more than the satisfaction of an instinct.

Rubbish ! Either simply and solely the satisfaction of an instinct, or spirit.

The Vicar of Wakefield begins like this : " I was always of the opinion that the honest man who married and brought up a large family did more service to the state than he who continued single and only talked of population."

There we have one of the reasons for marrying : to produce children to serve the state—*risum teneatis amici!* No, the thing is this, with the increase of culture and the increase of conscious life man in a sense grows out of the instinct, in any case of the immediacy of the instinct. A certain intellectual embarrassment enters in (which must not be confused with the immediate bashfulness, *pudor*) *in specie* in man. That is the reason why he must have reasons behind which to hide, however poorly one may be hidden, as, for instance, behind the very transparent screen of producing children to serve the state. To serve the state! Yet perhaps there is something in that, perhaps the state is best conceived as a stud—and the King ought not to be compared to a shepherd but to the master of the stud.

About myself

Slight, delicate, and weak, denied in almost every respect the physical requirements in order to be able to pass for a complete man as compared with others; melancholy, soul-sick, profoundly and absolutely a failure in many ways, one thing was given to me: a pre-eminent intelligence, presumably so that I should not be quite defenceless.

Even as a child I was conscious of my intelligence and that such was my strength in face of those much stronger boys.

*   *   *

It was intelligence and nothing else that had to be opposed. Presumably that is why I, who have had the job, was armed with an immense intelligence. . . .

The imagination

is what providence uses in order to get men into reality, into existence, to get them far enough out, or in, or down in existence. And when imagination has helped them as far out as they are meant to go—that is where reality, properly speaking, begins.

Johannes v. Müller says that there are two great powers, around which everything revolves : ideas and women. That is quite true, and is intimately connected with what I have just said about the importance of the imagination : women, or ideas are what tempt a man out into existence. Naturally there is this great difference, that among thousands who run after a skirt there is not always one who is moved by ideas.

As for me, it was so difficult to get me out that a girl was used against me in a quite unusual way, as an intermediary, in order to get me out, and in the interest of ideas.

The system

Aug. Personality is aristocratic—the system a plebeian invention; with the help of the system (that omnibus) everybody can get about . . . .

The New Testament

. . . And all this tom-foolery with Bible societies distributing New Testaments by the million, is supposed to be Christianity.

No, I am tempted to make a different proposal to Christendom. Let us collect all the New Testaments there are in existence, let us carry them out to an open place or up upon a mountain, and then, while we all kneel down, let someone address God in this fashion : Take this book back again; we men, such as we are now, are no good at dealing with a thing like this, it only makes us unhappy. My proposal is that like the inhabitants of Gadara we beseech Christ to " depart out of our coasts." That is an honest and human way of talking, quite different from that disgusting,

hypocritical, mealy-mouthed trash about life being of no
value to us apart from the inestimable blessing of Christianity.

. . . Protestantism is the crudest and most brutal
plebeianism. People will not hear of there being any difference of quality between an apostle, a witness to the
truth and oneself, in spite of the fact that one's existence is
completely different from theirs, as different as eating from
being eaten.

About myself

One gift has been given me and in such a degree that
I can call it genius—it is the gift of conversation, of being
able to talk with everyone.
This happy gift was given to me in order to conceal the
undoubted fact that I am the most silent man of my day.
Silence hid in silence is suspicious, arouses mistrust, it
is just as though one were to betray something, at least
betrayed that one was keeping silence. But silence concealed by a decided talent for conversation—as true as ever
I live—that is silence.

All—Nothing

God creates everything out of nothing—and everything
which God is to use he first reduces to nothing.

The sign by which it may be known whether a given
condition is ripe for decline:
. . . If the conditions at a certain time are such that
almost everyone knows *privately* that the whole thing is

wrong, is untrue, while no one will say so *officially*; when the tactics used by the leading people is : let us simply hold on, behave as though nothing had happened, answer every attack with silence, because we ourselves know only too well that the whole thing is rotten, that we are playing false : then in that case the conditions are *eo ipso* condemned, they will crash. Just as one says that death has marked a man, so those conditions are the symptom which unquestionably calls for attack. There can be no question of something truer standing side by side with something which honourably believes itself to be true. It is a battle against lies.

But fundamentally that is the condition in Christendom, particularly in Protestantism, particularly in Denmark.

Tribulations

The tactics are perfectly simple : remain quite indifferent towards them, absolute indifference towards them is victory. Such thoughts aim at making you anxious, they want to make you so anxious that in your cowardice you imagine that you are responsible for them, they want to enter into you by way of anxiety, father upon you the idea that you listened to them and rested in them and so on, and all this in the agony of your responsibility. If once you begin to think that, there is the devil to pay. Therefore absolute indifference ! more indifferent than you would be to a slight rumbling in your stomach. Or else get angry, as angry as you get when a man stands knocking at your door at an impossible hour and you rush out and say : what sort of behaviour is this, etc. *i.e.* get angry so that you are not afraid; for the thing that must be avoided more than anything is fear.

You are right to fight temptation by flying, running away. It does not help against tribulation because the thoughts follow you. Here the proper tactics are : do not be afraid, keep perfectly calm, absolutely indifferent.

But tribulation is unknown nowadays among Christians, particularly the Protestants, particularly in Denmark . . . a progress of the same kind as the doctor's cure in *Barsel-stuen* : the patient died, but the fever left him entirely.

One must take the world as it is

or : life is what one makes it, though of course understood to mean : one must take the world as it is, that is the content of the life of all these millions of sample-men and of life.

Existence does not really notice the existence of all these millions, where existence is concerned the same thing happens to the sample-man as to the stickleback in relation to the net which is set to catch bigger fish, the net is certainly there (and existence is also a net) in order to catch fish—but the sticklebacks have free passage. The fact that sample-men become masses does not help, they do not in consequence weigh any more : one sample-man and a million touch existence, which produces them lavishly out of a horn of plenty, just as little.

But as soon as a man with originality comes along, and consequently does not say : one must take the world as it is (the sign for a free passage, like a stickleback), but saying : whatever the world may be, I remain true to my own originality, which I do not intend to change according to the good pleasure of the world; the moment that word is heard, there is as it were a transformation in the whole of existence, as in the fairy story—when the word is said the magic castle, which has been under a spell for a hundred years, opens again and everything comes to life : in the same way existence becomes all eyes. The Angels grow busy, look about with curiosity to see what is going to happen, for that is what interests them. On the other side : dark and sinister demons who have sat idle for a long while gnawing their fingers—jump up, stretch their limbs : " this is something for us " they say, for they have waited long for something of the kind, for the sample-men give them nothing to do, they no more than the angels.

This is what the apostle means when he says that the Christian's fight is not merely against flesh and blood but with principalities and powers. . . .

The existence of a Christian touches existence. It is no doubt true that he cannot be said to bring with him originality in the sense of genius, but he personally assumes the demands of Christianity with originality, in regard to being a Christian,* and therefore pays no attention to the miserable saying : that one must take the world as it is.

On having an objective relation to one's own subjectivity

The majority of men are curtailed " I's "; what was planned by nature as a possibility capable of being sharpened into an I is soon dulled into a third person.

It is a very different thing to have an objective relation to one's own subjectivity.

Take Socrates ! He is not a third person in the sense that he avoids going into danger, avoids staking his life, which one avoids doing if one is a third person—not an " I." In no sense is that true. But actually in danger he has an objective attitude to his own personality, and when he is about to be condemned to death speaks of his condemnation like a third person. He is subjectivity raised

*And ethically, as is shown elsewhere, originality means to stake everything, to risk everything, *First* the kingdom of God.

to the second power, his attitude is as objective as that of a true poet to his poetic works; he is just as objective to his own subjectivity. That is an achievement. Otherwise one invariably gets one of two things, either an objective something, an objective bit of furniture which is supposed to be a man, or else a miscellaneous hodge-podge of accidents and spontaneity. But the task is to have an objective attitude to one's own subjectivity.

The maximum which anyone achieves in this respect may serve as an infinitely weak analogy of how God is infinite subjectivity.

The sense of majesty

I am therefore suspicious of the way people use the expression " to serve God "; for one cannot serve God as one serves another monarch, who has objects to attain. No, the only adequate way to express a sense of God's majesty is to worship him. Generally one makes a distinction and says that what is involved in worshipping God is feelings, moods, and their expression in words, whereas serving God suggests actions. No, your action is true worship, and it is that most clearly when it is free from all bustle and the notion that God has a cause. To renounce everything as an act of worship offered to God, and so not because he needs to use you as an instrument; but to renounce everything yourself as the most insignificant superfluity and article of luxury—that means to worship.

" Man "

All those who have been exceptional, who have lived sparsely scattered through time, have each of them delivered their judgment on " man." According to the report of one :

man is an animal; according to another : he is a hypocrite; according to another : he is a liar etc.

Perhaps I shall not hit it off least happily when I say : man is a twaddler—and that with the help of speech.

With the help of speech every man participates in the highest—but to participate in the highest with the help of speech, by talking nonsense about it, is just as ironical as to participate in a royal banquet, as a spectator from the gallery.

Were I a pagan I would say : an ironical deity gave mankind the gift of speech in order to have the amusement of watching that self-deception.

From a Christian point of view of course it is out of love that God gave man the gift of speech, and thereby made it possible for every one really to grasp the highest— oh, with what sorrow must God look upon the result.

A personal God

. . . God is certainly personal, but whether he wishes to be so in relation to the individual depends upon whether it so pleases God. It is the grace of God that he wishes to be personal in relation to you; if you throw away his grace he punishes you by behaving objectively towards you. And in that sense one may say that the world has not got a personal God (in spite of all the proofs!) . . .

But while dons and parsons drivel on about the millions of proofs of God's personality, the truth is that there are no longer the men living who could bear the pressure and weight of having a personal God. There is something moving about the way in which a patriarch or an apostle talks of dying tired of life; that can well tire a man. Figuratively : a cart-horse, even though it has worked hard before the plough—has no suspicion of the exhaustion of a highly-trained horse after it has been ridden.—Alas, even if my life were without pain and suffering, this alone would be enough, the disgust which comes over me every time I think of the nonsense in which men waste their time and lives. It would after all disgust one to think of mankind not eating food but living off filth, eating vermin and the like—but it is just as disgusting when one thinks that men consider themselves fortunate in being able to live off and pay parsons and dons exorbitant prices for—rubbish.

Human Education

Providence has given every man certain characteristics. The important thing in life should therefore be to develop that characteristic, strengthened and confirmed by the conflicts which it must produce with its surroundings.

Human education, on the other hand, is demoralising, is calculated to teach a man how not to have an air, not to use a word, not to undertake the least thing without having a guarantee that numbers of others have done the same thing before him. . . .

The human race

. . . Christianity is God's thought. To be a man was, for God, an ideal which we can hardly even imagine; the fall was a guilt which involved a degradation, and in order to feel the painfulness of it one must have an impression of the ideal which went before. . . .

THE DOMESTIC GOOSE

a moral tale

Try to imagine for a moment that geese could talk—that they had so arranged things that they too had their divine worship and their church-going.

Every Sunday they would meet together and a gander would preach.

The sermon was essentially the same each time—it told of the glorious destiny of geese, of the noble end for which their maker had created them—and every time his name was mentioned all the geese curtsied and all the ganders bowed their heads. They were to use their wings to fly away to the distant pastures to which they really belonged; for they were only pilgrims on this earth.

The same thing happened each Sunday. Thereupon the meeting broke up and they all waddled home, only to meet again next Sunday for divine worship and waddle off home again—but that was as far as they ever got. They throve and grew fat, plump and delicious—and at Michaelmas they were eaten—and that was as far as they ever got. It never came to anything. For while their conversation on Sundays was all high-sounding, on Mondays they would tell each other what had happened to the goose who had taken the end set before them quite seriously, and in spite of many tribulations had tried to use the wings its creator had bestowed upon it.

All that was indeed common knowledge among the geese, but of course no one mentioned the subject on Sundays, for as they observed, it would then have been obvious that to attend divine service would have been to fool both God and themselves.

Among the geese were several who looked ill and wan, and all the other geese said—there, you see what comes of taking flying seriously. It is all because they go about meditating on flying that they get thin and wan and are not blessed by the grace of God as we are; for that is why we grow fat, plump, and delicious.

And so next Sunday off they went to divine service, and the old gander preached of the glorious end for which their Maker (and at that point all the geese curtsied and the ganders bowed their heads) had created them, and of why they were given wings.

And the same is true of divine worship in Christianity.

How I understand the future

Certainly things will be reformed; and it will be a frightful reformation compared with which the Lutheran reformation will be almost a joke, a frightful reformation that will have as its battle-cry "Whether faith will be found upon earth?" and it will be recognisable by the fact that millions will fall away from Christianity, a frightful reformation; for the thing is that Christianity really no longer exists, and it is terrible when a generation which has been molly-coddled by a childish Christianity, fooled into thinking it is Christianity, when it has to receive the death blow of learning once again what it means to be a Christian. . . .

Mediocrity

Among the mediocre, individuals are certainly not unreasonable towards each other, they do not provoke impudence, they respect each other's mediocrity.

But contemporary mediocrity, the whole mass of mediocrity, or mediocrity *en masse* is an impertinence to God, because it tries to raise itself up to the highest position, that of the ideal. Just as people insure one another against fire, mediocrity as a whole insures the individuals who go to make up that mediocrity, that mediocrity is the truth.

How came it that Christ was crucified

I can answer that in such a way as to show at the same time what Christianity is.

What is "spirit"? (for Christ is spirit, his religion that of the spirit). Spirit is: to live as though dead (dead to the world).

This way of life is so entirely foreign to man that to him it is quite literally worse than death.

Very carefully introduced for an hour or so in the distance of the imagination, natural man can bear it, it even pleases him. But if it is brought nearer him, so near that it becomes, in all seriousness, something required of him: the natural instinct of self-protection rises up so powerfully in him that a regular uproar follows, as with drink or as one talks of a *furor uterinus*. And in that condition, in which he is beside himself, he demands the death of the man of spirit, or rushes upon him to put him to death. . . .

End of the Journal

Other Fontana Religious Books

MERE CHRISTIANITY

C. S. Lewis. Here at a popular price is a revised and amplified edition of C. S. Lewis's three famous books, *Broadcast Talks, Christian Behaviour,* and *Beyond Personality*, brilliantly presenting the author's modern revaluations of Christian apologetics, ethics and theology.

THE SCREWTAPE LETTERS

C. S. Lewis. This witty and profound analysis of Christian strength and weaknesses outlined in the letters of the elderly devil Screwtape to his young nephew, is a classic of religious exposition.

THE PROBLEM OF PAIN

C. S. Lewis. The author gives his view as a layman on the Christian doctrine relating to all aspects of the problem of pain and explains the existence of pain in a Christian world.
It is really a pleasure to be able to praise a book unreservedly and that is just what I can do with this book."
Manchester Guardian

THE DIVINE PITY

Gerald Vann, O.P. Doubters as well as professing Christians who look for a strong simple statement of the abiding truths of Christianity will find inspiration from this work.

THE PLAIN MAN LOOKS AT THE BIBLE

William Neil. This book is meant for the plain man who would like to know what to think about the Bible to-day. It deals with the relevance of the Bible and restates its message for the Twentieth Century.

THE GOSPELS IN MODERN ENGLISH

J. B. Phillips. "It is all to the good that we should be given a translation in straightforward English, and Mr. Phillips has a flair for doing this that none of his predecessors in the task seem to have had."
Times Literary Supplement

THE PERENNIAL PHILOSOPHY

Aldous Huxley. The author illustrates and develops passages from the writings of those Saints and Prophets who have approached a direct spiritual knowledge of the Divine.
" A mine of curious and erudite learning."
New Statesman

Other Fontana Religious Books

SEX, LOVE AND MARRIAGE

Roland H. Bainton. "Dr. Bainton lays before us the Christian attitude, past and present, to this important subject. He shows us how, amongst others, St. Augustine faced these problems and how it was as real to them as it is to us today. This is a book which no one can afford not to read."

MORE FROM THE PRIMEVAL FOREST

Albert Schweitzer. An unadorned and poignant account of almost incredible difficulties and achievements, this book is based on reports sent home by Dr. Albert Schweitzer during his second period in Africa from 1924-27.

NAUGHT FOR YOUR COMFORT

Trevor Huddleston. The author describes his twelve years ministry in Sophiatown, the coloured quarter outside Johannesburg from 1944-56. Father Huddleston has become world-famous for his championship of the rights and dignity of the non-European races in South Africa.

THE MEANING OF PAUL FOR TO-DAY

C. H. Dodd. Professor Dodd suggests the place of Paul in the history of religion, he has sought to bring out the permanent significance of the apostle's thought, in modern terms, and in relation to the general interests and problems which occupy the mind of the present generation.

SCIENCE AND CHRISTIAN BELIEF

C. A. Coulson. The author sets out to show that, far from outdating and nullifying traditional Christian beliefs, science is essentially a religious activity, playing its part in the unfolding of the nature and purpose of God.

THE SONG OF BERNADETTE

Franz Werfel. The author tells in this simple and moving book the story of the Apparitions and of the little girl who returned day after day to the grotto to honour silently the Lady who appeared to her there—the Lady whose presence it never occurred to her to call a miracle.

LETTERS TO YOUNG CHURCHES

J. B. Phillips. The author's most famous book, this is more than a mere translation of the Epistles. It has already become a contemporary classic of Biblical interpretation, a valuable guide for all those who in their groping towards a maturer Christian faith, encounter and are perplexed by the vital but difficult Pauline doctrines which constitute the foundation of Christian Theology.

PELICAN BOOKS

Children Solve Problems

Edward de Bono was born in Malta and after his initial education at St Edward's College, Malta, and the Royal University of Malta, where he obtained a degree in medicine, he proceeded as a Rhodes Scholar to Christ Church, Oxford, where he gained an honours degree in psychology and physiology and then a D.Phil. in medicine. He also holds a Ph.D. from Cambridge. He has had faculty appointments at the universities of Oxford, London, Cambridge and Harvard.

Dr de Bono is the founder and director of the Cognitive Research Trust in Cambridge (founded 1969) and the Centre for the Study of Thinking. He runs what is now the largest curriculum programme in the world for the direct teaching of thinking in schools. Dr de Bono's instruction in thinking has been sought by many of the leading corporations such as IBM, Shell, Unilever, ICI, Du Pont and many others. He has been invited to lecture extensively throughout the world.

He has written twenty-two books which have been translated into nineteen languages. He has also completed two TV series, 'The Greatest Thinkers' for WDR, Germany, and 'De Bono's Course in Thinking' for the BBC. Dr de Bono is the originator of the term 'lateral thinking' and also the inventor of the classic L-game which is said to be the simplest real game ever invented.

His books include *The Five-Day Course in Thinking* (1968), *The Mechanism of Mind* (1969), *Lateral Thinking* (1970), *The Dog-Exercising Machine* (1970), *Technology Today* (1971), *Practical Thinking* (1971), *Lateral Thinking for Management* (1971), *Eureka!: an illustrated history of inventions from the wheel to the computer* (1974), *Teaching Thinking* (1976), *The Greatest Thinkers* (1976), *Wordpower* (1977), *The Happiness Purpose* (1977), *Opportunities: a handbook of business opportunity search* (1978), *Atlas of Management Thinking* (1978) and *De Bono's Course in Thinking* (1982). Many of these have been published in Penguin. Dr de Bono has also contributed to many journals, including the *Lancet* and *Clinical Science*. He is married and has two sons.

Children Solve
Problems

Edward de Bono

Penguin Books

Penguin Books Ltd, Harmondsworth, Middlesex, England
Penguin Books, 40 West 23rd Street, New York, New York 10010, U.S.A.
Penguin Books Australia Ltd, Ringwood, Victoria, Australia
Penguin Books Canada Ltd, 2801 John Street, Markham, Ontario, Canada L3R 1B4
Penguin Books (N.Z.) Ltd, 182–190 Wairau Road, Auckland 10, New Zealand

First published by Penguin Books 1972
Published in Pelican Books 1984
Reprinted 1984

Made and Printed in Great Britain by
Butler & Tanner Ltd, Frome and London
Set in Monophoto Century Schoolbook

Contents

Preface

Almost all the drawings in this book were obtained in the course of a design project which I ran in the educational journal *Where*, which is published by the Advisory Centre for Education. I am very grateful to Beryl McAlhone, the editor of *Where*, for her cooperation in running the design project. At that time there was no intention of publishing the drawings in any other way. It was at the suggestion of Martin Lightfoot of Penguin Education that the drawings were put together in a more complete way in this book. I myself agree that the drawings are so good that they deserve this further publication.

The drawings showing improvements in the design of the human body were obtained from Sawston Junior School through the help of David Johns and his staff. I am very grateful to Audrey Davies who transcribed a very hurried tape recording into this book.

I would like to take this new opportunity to thank all those teachers and parents who sent in designs for the original series in *Where*. Since there are thousands of designs, it has never been possible for me to thank them as personally as they deserve. It is always encouraging to be reminded that there really are teachers who are enthusiastic and who do care. Unfortunately, even in this book it is only possible to use a fraction of the drawings sent in. They are not necessarily the best ones, but simply the ones that can be most easily reproduced. For instance, very detailed drawings and coloured drawings were not suitable.

The proceeds from this book go to the Cognitive Research Trust, which is concerned with the study of thinking, and which is working towards the point when it might have enough funds to carry out a research programme in this important but largely neglected area.

Introduction

We can learn a lot from children, and especially from watching children think. Children can be brilliant thinkers. When children were given the 'political' problem of stopping a cat and a dog from fighting their ideas went far beyond the approaches used by politicians. It is not that we judge children with indulgence; they are genuinely more fluent with ideas. It is this fluency that gives children an advantage over adults in creativity and lateral thinking. On several occasions I have asked a lecture hall full of highly-educated and highly-paid thinking men to design a dog-exercising machine. They take the request in good humour but the ideas produced are nothing like as good as those produced by children. From time to time every creative person wishes he had the outlook of a child so that he could find his own perceptions and escape from the ones that have been imposed on him. This book is intended to provide an opportunity to look directly at the thinking of children.

A child enjoys thinking. He enjoys the use of his mind just as he enjoys the use of his body as he slides down a helter skelter or bounces on a trampoline. This enjoyment is reflected in the following comments which came in just some of the covering letters with children's designs:

Too late I suppose! But the children concerned so enjoyed doing them that I didn't have the heart not to send them. (Know College, Jamaica)

The enclosed was completed in a high state of excitement within half an hour of my suggesting to Philip that he 'had a go'.

They obviously enjoyed doing this. The younger one kept happy for quite a while and the elder one finished his design in twenty minutes.

I am now sending you some of the inventions designed by my class of nine year olds. They thoroughly enjoyed this and we are having an inventions corner to display the other designs they thought up.

They enjoyed doing them enormously.

In going through this book I hope you will be as impressed as I always am by the sheer ability of young children to think. At first sight the drawings may appear to be no more than cute, crazy and amusing, but if you study them more closely and put yourself into the position of the child you will suddenly appreciate the thinking involved in each case. A child's knowledge and experience are limited and so the problem solutions are often impractical. But what matters is the way the child's mind uses the limited material at its disposal.

If children can already think so well at this age, then surely the long years of education must develop this ability to a high level. Not so. At the end of education there has been no improvement in the thinking ability of children – in fact there has actually been a deterioration. This opinion is based on experiments involving several thousand people all of whom had benefited from higher education. It is an opinion which seems to be shared by others who have considered the matter. Why should education have this effect on thinking ability?

Education has always regarded its prime duty to be transfer of knowledge and those who have doubted the wisdom of this approach have usually been brought to their senses by the practical responsibilities of examinations. In transferring knowledge teachers are keenly aware that the only valid criterion of success is for the pupils' output to match the teacher's input. Although the extreme example of this – the example of rote learning – is dying out (more slowly than many imagine) the emphasis is still on doing things 'as they should be done'. This emphasis not only makes it unnecessary to think, but is also dangerous for the unfortunate pupil who comes up with an unacceptable, new point of view. To be fair it should perhaps be added that this method of transferring knowledge is sometimes quite effective if that is what you want to achieve, but the knowledge may not outlast the exams for which it is stored.

The amount of knowledge that has to be transferred is increasing all the time and as a result the student today has much less time to think than ever before. It is true that in some specialized areas, and in passing exams, knowledge is more useful than the ability to think but it may be of little use outside those areas or in helping a person to live with himself and with society. The emphasis on orthodoxy and the amount of knowledge required inhibit the development of thinking ability but may nevertheless be necessary with the education system as it is at the moment. What is worse is that no time is deliberately set aside for the encouragement of thinking ability. If thinking ability were being actively encouraged in one oasis area then its neglect in other areas would not matter so much. The absence of any such direct attention to thinking is to my mind the main cause of the deterioration of thinking ability during education.

The idea that thinking can be treated as a learnable skill is already taken for granted in two other areas of human activity. These are the business world and the computer world, both of which have to deal with reality, unlike the self-satisfying world of education which measures its own success for itself. In business poor thinking means bankruptcy and in the computer world it means a waste of expensive computer time. In education, alas, it is undetectable. For some time now the business world has been paying direct attention to such aspects of thinking as decision-making, planning, innovation and problem-solving and treating them as learnable skills. From the computer world comes the idea of 'heuristics', which includes all those aspects of thinking which cannot be fitted into mathematical formulations. The paradox is that it required the logical efficiency of the computer to demonstrate that logic is only part of thinking. In the computer world increasing attention is being paid to the thinking that has to take place before a situation is parcelled up into neat concepts that can be worked on with logic. This switch from logical thinking to what might be called perceptual or lateral thinking is a much more important change in thinking about thinking than most people in education realize. Most of them continue to assume that sufficient excellence in logic is all that is required in thinking.

I have often been told that there are four sorts of people in education: fools, knaves, the passive and the impatient. I have met several of the impatient ones but it is clear that they do not run the system and indeed they soon get edged out. As to the other categories I believe that there are not many fools and knaves though they may have an effect out of proportion to their numbers. The majority fall into the passive bracket – not because they are passive in themselves but because the self-preserving character of the education system is so strong as to make them despair of the usefulness of activity. It has been said that education serves two functions supremely well: it preserves its own jobs and it keeps children out of the home. The reaction of most teachers to the idea of teaching thinking as a specific subject is not a negative one. On the contrary, they are enthusiastic about it but are doubtful about how it can be done.

There would be very little problem in developing and testing a method of teaching thinking directly as a specific subject in its own right. I have already started a project (TAP: Thinking-Ability Project) whereby teachers in different schools try out various formats for the teaching of thinking. It is not a question of creating a body of dogma that has to be learned (like geometry) but of creating special situations which develop thinking ability directly because they are learning situations. The situations do have to be carefully structured so that students can learn from each other, for if the situations are loose the students are working on projects so different that this important aspect of learning is lost. Principles, strategies, guidelines, awareness of error, are all fed in along with the direct-thinking experience. Since the impetus to carry out such a project is unlikely to come from the educational establishment – which is too tied up in the administration of education to be concerned about its content – there is a need for some foundation to take the lead. The importance of the subject and the rewards are great – but so is the boldness required. But when thinking is finally part of the curriculum I believe we shall look back and wonder why it ever seemed a strange idea.

In this book children are shown solving a variety of problems. Problem-solving may seem to be a rather specialized part of thinking. But if we change the name to 'dealing with a situation', 'overcoming an obstacle', 'bringing about a desired effect', 'making something happen', then it can be seen that the thinking involved is very much the thinking that is involved in everyday life even though the actual problems may appear exotic. The convenience of problem-solving as one format for practising thinking is that there is a defined objective. Problem-solving is by no means the whole of thinking but the processes are not essentially different from other thinking processes and it is a convenient way of demonstrating these processes. (In spite of this, not everyone in education has had much to do with thinking. One educational journalist for instance declared himself unable to see what designing a dog-exercising machine had to do with thinking.)

Each of the problems in this book was chosen because it has some special feature. The cat-and-dog problem is a political problem involving psychology and motivation. The elephant problem involves dealing with magnitude and also dealing with matters well outside personal experience. The house-building problem involves making an existing complex process faster and more efficient. The fun machine involves choice and direct experience. The policeman-and-bad-man problem involves moral judgements. And so on.

Finally, a word about drawings. Many people ask me why I seem to prefer drawings to words as a thinking medium for children. There are several reasons. Young children are not always very good at expressing their ideas in words and it would be a pity if their ideas were to be restricted by insisting that they use words. Again, words can sometimes be difficult to understand and interpreting the meaning behind them may become a matter of guesswork. Drawings, however, are clear and relatively unambiguous. To make a drawing you have to commit yourself to a definite idea: you cannot say 'the bricks are put in position more quickly than usual' in a drawing because you have to show exactly how this is done. There are more advantages. With a drawing the whole idea is visible all at once and you can work at it with addition, alteration, modification, change, etc. With words you have either to remember it all in your mind or else read through your description each time you want to see what you have got. It is significant that in a recent survey of inventive people the only uniform characteristic was their use of drawings and sketches in their thinking. Finally, there is the fact that children from disadvantaged backgrounds are often handicapped when it comes to the use of words. But preliminary work suggests that there is no such handicap with visual expression.

To my mind it is a waste of time to flip through this book making 'how cute!' exclamations before moving on to the next drawing. The more you look at a drawing the more you will find in it. Each drawing is a laboratory in which to study. The study of how children think is the best basis for *understanding* how children think. This is obvious. But what is less obvious is that such a study is also a very good basis for understanding how adults think. The differences between the way children think and the way adults do it is much smaller than most adults believe.

1 Stop a Cat and a Dog Fighting

Show how you would stop a cat and a dog from fighting.

This is *the basic* political problem. How to stop people with differences from fighting each other. The differences may be racial, religious, ideological, or based on nationality. Cats and dogs are as racially and culturally different as any two human groups, and traditionally they are supposed to be always fighting each other.

The starting situation is very definite – there are cats and dogs which are distinct and which fight each other. The objective is also very definite – how to stop them fighting. What means would children use to try to achieve this objective? Would they take into account the psychology of a cat and a dog, or would they try and use purely physical means? Even if they used physical means, these could only work in the end if they had psychological effects. As there are no traditional, stereotyped ways of stopping a cat and a dog from fighting, the children would have to solve the problem on their own. They would have to come up with their own ideas of how to stop the fight.

How practical would the children's ideas on fight-stopping be? Would these ideas reflect the political thinking that adults have tried throughout the ages, or would they show different approaches. The language and the ideas used by children might be simple because they have to fit in with the limited experience of a child. And yet the principles involved may themselves be very sophisticated: all one needs to do is to change the names a little to find that they may apply directly in adult political thinking.

Cat and dog – 1

The ghetto concept. The
traditional way of stopping two
different groups from fighting
is to put them in separate cages
or within national boundaries
and keep them apart. In this way
they cannot get at each other
to fight. It does not always work,
especially when the two groups
cannot be separated in this way.

Cat and dog – 2

A variation on the ghetto concept. The cages here are balls and
chains which restrict free movement. For instance, the need for
visas, special passports and so on, which achieve the same effect
as a cage-type or wall-type ghetto.

Put Slippery and magnetic material on their feet So when they start fighting they slide apart. Take more off each time they meet.

OH!

Slippery material.

Cat and dog – 3

An ingenious idea which constitutes an automatic ghetto. The slippery material on the feet of the dogs and cats presumably would not inconvenience them in general, but as soon as they start to fight then they slip apart and are unable to get at each other's throat. Certainly worth considering in its political implications.

Put a very strong see through wall beteen the cat and the dogs feeding ~~placein~~ places so they can see eachother but they ~~canot~~ can not fight. Later take it away

Cat and dog - 4

The arm's length concept. The cat and the dog are not completely separated but held at arm's length so that they cannot get at each other's throat. But they can see each other very clearly and get used to each other, and in the end they may come to love each other. Probably does not work because the more you see of your enemy perhaps the more you get to hate him. Optimistic!

A metal Bar dips along
with the dog on the
end and the dog gets
tired of barking.
That when very raise
the cril and dog they
will be used to eachother.

Cat and dog – 5

A variation of the arm's length concept. This time there is no
physical barrier but the two have a certain range of movement
and can get quite close to each other but not really close enough
to fight.

Cat and dog – 6

Another variation of the arm's length concept with the cat and
dog each at the end of an arm. They can circle round and round a
track and go past each other's home, where there is in each case
a jar of scent to 'scare' the cat or dog. Thus they can get used to
each other's home ground without ever being allowed to get close
enough to fight. Note that individually both of them are well
looked after. For instance there are individual hutches in case
either of them gets tired. Each is also protected from the weather
by an umbrella. Two special hands are provided, one in case the
dog bites and the other in case the cat spits. These are additional
protection.

Cat and dog – 7

The exact opposite of the ghetto concept. This could be called the 'let them get on with it' concept. The cat and the dog are separately tricked into jumping into the same enclosure. Their movement in entering the enclosure makes the lid come down very firmly. And then they are left to get on with it, and to fight it out or get used to each other.

First of all I put them in cages and then talk to them and I say, "Now Dog, you're going to meet a cat", and "Now Cat, you're going to meet a dog". And I get them out on a nice sunny day, both together, and what I do is, I have a game of ball with them.

Cat and dog – 8

The distraction concept. Athletics stop all fights. The cat and the dog are kept in their separate ghetto cages, and then they are brought out on a nice sunny day to play ball together (Olympic Games). So they make friends and live in peace happily ever after.

Cat and dog – 9

An extension of the distraction concept. Keep both cat and dog happy and they will have no time to fight each other. To keep the (Edward Heath-looking) dog happy, all you have to do is to provide a bone for him to chew, a tin of Pedigree Chum and a pair of postman's trousers for him to worry. The cat is kept happy with a tin of Kit-e-Kat, a clockwork mouse and a cushion to sit on.

You tie a Fish to the cats tail and a steak to dogs, and by the time the have finished running round in circles they will be too dizy to fight. And they will be good company for each other

Cat and dog – 10

The 'self-interest' variation on the distraction theme. You allow each group to get so tied up with their own affairs and interests that they have no time to fight. The cat is too busy chasing the fish at the end of his tail, and the dog is too busy chasing the steak on the end of his tail. Since self-interest probably has a priority over fighting other people the system might well work.

Cat and dog – 11

The third-party concept. In this case the third party takes the form of the big super-power ally. The dog is chasing the cat and then a great big lion comes out and makes noises at the dog, and then suddenly the dog decides that he might as well be friends with the little cat after all. Principle: if you have big friends you have fewer enemies.

Cat and dog – 12

A variation of the third-party concept. The cat and the dog are
fighting each other so the third party in the shape of a child or
baby comes along and pulls both their tails. They then stop
fighting each other and gang up on the child. This could also be
considered as a variation on the distraction concept.

The cat and dog fight
each other.

A Child or ~~Baby~~ pulls
There tales
            and then
they join togther
and

fight the
child or Baby
and so the
are friends.

Cat and
            dog
            fighting

~~CHILD~~ Child pulling
cats tale.

dog and cat
fighting child.

Cat and dog – 13

The cultural-assimilation concept. In other words, get used to your
enemy and then you may find that he is not so terrifying after all.
Put a toy dog in the cat's apartment, and a toy cat in the dog's
apartment. When they have finished barking at the toys and
chewing them about they suddenly realize that they are pretty
inoffensive and start learning to live with them. Then when the
cat and the dog meet in real life they will not have so much trouble.

Real Pretend Cat

The Toy dog

The brick wall built so they cannot fight each other

That is the real dog

Toy cat

This is a plug to close the tunnel

This is the tunnel which they can go through to meet, after they have got used to the toy animals.

First of all the real dog gets used to the toy cat and the real cat gets used to the toy dog They are separated by a brick wall.

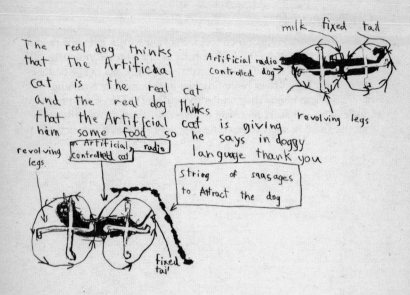

The real dog thinks that the Artificial cat is the real cat and the real dog thinks that the Artifficial cat is giving him some food so he says in doggy language thank you

an Artificial radio controlled cat

revolving legs

milk   fixed   tail

Artificial radio controlled dog

revolving legs

String of saasages to Attract the dog

fixed tail

Cat and dog – 14

In this idea instead of there being toy cats and dogs there are
artificial radio-controlled cats and dogs which can walk about
using their circular legs which are painted on a revolving disc.
The real dog thinks that the artificial cat is the real cat, and the
real dog thinks that the artificial cat is giving him some food. So
he says in doggy language 'Thank you', and rather comes to like
the artificial cat. This liking is of course then transferred to a real
cat. You could only get an artificial radio-controlled cat to give
a dog some food.

Cat and dog – 15

A more sophisticated variation of the 'cultural-assimilation'
technique. Instead of having toy or radio-controlled cats and dogs,
you have the real thing. But you disguise the real thing. So the
cat is fitted out in a dog mask with false ears and also a false dog
tail for when it meets the dog. Similarly the dog is fitted out with
a cat mask and a false cat tail. So the cat looking from inside its
dog mask sees what appears to be another cat, and similarly the
dog looking from inside his cat mask sees what appears to be
another dog. So since the obvious cultural differences and points
of differentiation have been removed they can get on quite well
and discover the real personalities.

Cat and dog – 16

A more gradual process of cross-cultural assimilation. Cat and
dog live in separate apartments. But there is a tube from the cat
which comes out near the dog's food, and a tube from the dog
which comes out near the cat's food. This means that when the
cat goes to eat he gets the scent of the dog around his eating and so
learns to associate the dog's smell with good things. Similarly
when the dog is eating he can smell the cat and so learns to
associate the cat's smell with good food.

1 Smear your dog with cat food.

fishy treet

2 Smear your cat with dog food.

doggie licks

3 leave them alone as they scent each-others food

AND

Friends!

Cat and dog – 17

A further extension of the cultural-assimilation concept, but tying it in more directly to self-interest. The dog is smeared with cat food and the cat is smeared with dog food. When they meet each other they smell their own food, and so they get to licking each other and soon become friends. The principle is that business self-interest, if allowed free rein, may well overcome national or traditional animosities.

Mathew

Sophy

THE CAT
WITH ITS TONGUE
OUT
THE DOG DIVI-
ING IN

A pond full of Milk

Cat and dog - 18

Instead of there being some outside person who paints the cat with dog food and the dog with cat food, this is done automatically by the individuals concerned. There is a pond full of milk and into it the dog (wearing swimming trunks) dives. On the bank stands the cat with its tongue out waiting to lick the dog clean as soon as he comes out.

Cat and dog - 19

Nothing much is left to chance. A great deal of care is taken to make absolutely sure that the dog is acceptable to the cat. First of all he is dumped into a basin full of milk, and then he goes through a pipe which is smeared with treacle. He comes out of the treacle pipe and falls into a basin full of fish ends. From this he emerges to go through a tube full of minced mice. Finally, exhausted, he falls out of the tube to lie on a mat by the fire. The cat, unable to resist this mixture of goodies, immediately licks him all over and they become good friends. Possible principle: if you really think it worthwhile for people to become friends, and spare no effort to make it worthwhile, you may perhaps be successful.

The owner starves the animals. The cat food is on the dogs tail and the dogs food is on the cats tail so they have to make friends to eat.

Cat and dog - 20

The mutual-aid concept. The cat is starved and so he is hungry. But the only way he can get his food is to eat it off the dog's tail. Similarly the only way the dog can get his steak is to eat it off the cat's tail; so they have to learn to get along with each other to get any meals. It might of course be argued that if the dog simply set off in pursuit of the cat he could get rather nearer to that steak.

BOWL For cream when the the cat goes on long Journeys.

Trough for od Dog Food for Dog.

STRAP STRAP To keep To TROUGH keep ON TROUGH on

MOUTHPIECE To BONE COLLAR.

BONE COLLAR. FILL IT UP WITH BONES SO THE DOG CAN EAT BURY THEM.

STRAP TO KEEP TROUGH ON

STRAP TO KEEP TROUGH ON.

STRAP TO KEEP TRO

Strap to keep trough on.

Strap to keep trough on.

STRAP To keep TROUGH ON.

BOTH ANIMALS HAVE TROUGHS FULL OF THE OTHER ANIMALS FAVOURITE FOOD. SO TO GET TO THEIR FAVOURITE FOOD, THEY HAVE TO BE FRIENDS TO SIDLE UP TO THE OTHER ANIMAL TO GET THEIR FAVOURITE FOOD.

Cat and dog – 21

Instead of simply tying the food to the tail of the cat or dog, this time there are special troughs, which are strapped alongside the bodies of the cat and dog. Since each trough contains the food of the other animal, they have to get alongside each other in order to eat. For some reason there is a bowl of cream attached to the cat's tail for when it goes on long journeys.

YOU PUT A CAT
IN ONE PART AND A DOG IN THE
OTHER WHEN THE CAT
STEPS ON A SMALL
BAR THE DOGS BONE
COMES DOWN AND
VICE VERSA . SO
WHEN THEY GO
NEAR EACH OTHER
THEY GET FOOD
SO THEY BECOME
FRIENDS

Cat and dog – 22

The whole mutual-aid thing here is formalized into a psychological training cage, rather like a Skinner box. The only way they can get fed is for one to feed the other by pressing on the bar. The cat quickly learns that if he presses the bar the dog gets fed and looks pleased. In return the dog learns that if he presses the bar the cat gets fed and he looks pleased. So they now work very hard to please each other, because they realize that it is only by pleasing the other one that they end up by pleasing themselves. A view that is perhaps cynical but immensely realistic.

The dog fishing for the cat with un under water gun

Butcher

Bones

The cat holding up the butcher for Bones

Or give them love pills if the other method wont work

Cat and dog – 23

The mutual-aid thing is here carried to extremes. In the upper part of the drawing the dog equipped with aqua-lung apparatus is seen with a harpoon gun catching fish for the cat's supper. In the bottom half the cat, with a sub-machine gun, is seen holding up the butcher to obtain bones for the dog. If this method does not work then you give them 'love pills'.

Cat and dog - 24

This could be called the 'inadvertent' mutual-aid concept. Or it could more simply be called the gratitude concept. What you do is beat the drum and this makes the dog jump about. The dog jumping about makes a string jump about, and so the cat thinks it is a mouse. The cat takes hold of the string and pulls it. This pulling on the string rescues the dog from the well. The dog is then immensely grateful to the cat and so from this gratitude springs a true friendship. Note that the designer has thoughtfully provided a sponge just in case the cat botches the rescue and the dog falls to the bottom. She also insists that the dog should be fairly thin otherwise the strain on the cat's mouth might be enough to hurt it.

I am holding the cat and the dog nose to nose and strocing them

Cat and dog – 25

The direct-love concept. You hold the cat and dog nose to nose and stroke them and so induce them to love each other. In fact the preaching and practising of love.

Cat and dog – 26

If you don't trust your love-inducing power then you take the cat and the dog along to a society which is a 'Friendly Society' and therefore functions to make people friends. Unfortunately the friendly society (like the United Nations) is a bit of a misnomer, and does not serve to impart what it appears to promise.

Cat and dog – 27

Another variation on the direct-love concept. This time instead of
relying on human exhortation one relies on science. Both cat and
dog are put on the brain-washing machine. Note the packet of
washing powder at the base of the machine. Note also the bubbles
which come out whenever anything is washed. Cat and dog will be
brain washed into loving each other. Is that so awful?

.LOVE. MACHINE.
FOR . FIGHTING. CATS. AND. DOGS.

CAT AND DOG
TAKE IT IN TURNS
TO SIT IN CAGE
WHILE BEING GIVEN
DOSE OF THE
'LOVE RAY'

FOR SLOW ELEVATION OF BONE, SO THAT DOG SITS UPRIGHT ALL THE TIME.

HEIGHT OF PLATFORM

FOR SLOW ELEVATION OF FISH, SO THAT CAT SITS UPRIGHT ALL THE TIME.

1' 2' 3'
LENGTH OF RAY

Cat and dog – 28

Another love machine. Cat and dog take it in turns to sit in a cage and then they are made to sit upright when the bone (or fish) is hoisted up. When they sit upright they are exposed to the full force of the love machine, which induces in them this feeling of love – presumably for everything in the world, since there is no actual dog or cat in sight.

Variety

Perhaps the most striking thing about the attempts of the children to solve this political problem is the variety of approaches used. Each child decided in his own mind how he would tackle the problem, and then set out to tackle it in a definite way. Difference of approach is a very characteristic feature of children's thinking. If you put a group of adults in a room and ask them to tackle a problem they will have relatively few approaches distributed among them. But a group of children will come up with a much greater variety of approach. I have tried this out on a number of occasions and each time it is the same. It is probably not that children have a special ability to look at things in a different way, but simply that adults have almost completely lost this ability. So adults are always looking for the best and most sensible way and this only means the way which fits in best with their current ideas or experience. Since children have so little of this 'current' element in their experience or ideas, they are much freer to try out new ideas. Such ideas, though they may not seem very successful at first, can actually be carried further to give a useful and practical solution.

Direct

In tackling the cat-and-dog problem the children came immediately to the point. In each solution they show a simple and direct way of carrying out their idea of peace-making. There is no hesitation or messing around. If there is an effect to be achieved, then there is a simple and direct way of achieving it, and this the child shows.

Psychology

It might have been thought that the children would try and stop the cat and dog fighting simply by taking each one into a corner and giving it a good scolding, or else by shouting at them as they were fighting, and telling them 'to stop it at once'. It is after all the universal adult and political approach to stopping people from fighting. Indeed in the adult political world it is almost the only approach used. It is condemnation and exhortation. The psychology of children, however, seems to be a good deal better. They place little reliance on exhortation, or indeed on punishment. Instead they prefer to work through such things as the self-interest of the cat and the dog. Many of the designs were based precisely on this self-interest, and making it worthwhile for the cat and the dog to stop fighting simply because someone else has told them that it would be a good thing to stop fighting. They only expect the cat and the dog to stop fighting because the cat and the dog have realized that they can get what they want (e.g. food) much better if they stop fighting and cooperate.

The second psychological principle used by the children is that of distraction. If the cat and the dog are both fully occupied, and enjoying themselves, then they will have much less time for fighting. In other words the children realize full well that fighting is often the result of intense boredom, and that fighting provides the only interest and amusement in the lives of many people who are involved in such fights.

The third psychological principle used by the children is that of getting one side used to the other, and if necessary providing disguises or artificial aids for this purpose. Children are aware that it is often simple physical things like appearance and smell that become symbolic of the opponent you dislike (like skin colour). You can get the cat or the dog used to the other in a situation where he is not in any danger and is not terrified, and then gradually he will come to accept the difference and not be afraid of it. To my mind the thinking of children in tackling this problem shows a much better understanding of psychology than you find in politics either today or throughout the ages.

2 A Fun Machine

Design a fun machine.

Fun, pleasure, enjoyment are very abstract concepts which it is difficult to define. But fun is when you are having fun. It may be difficult to define, but fun is a very definite thing and you can recognize it at once. Fun is also very much part of a child's world. A child's world is fun centred. This is probably not the same as pleasure centred which is a much more adult thing. Given an opportunity to design a fun machine, would children choose a lot of 'fun' apparatus, or simply things which they enjoyed doing? Would the emphasis be on the hardware of fun or on the software (the mechanics of the situation or the mental response to a situation).

How greedy would children be? Would they want to have all the fun things they had ever known, or would they settle for one simple fun machine which they would use over and over again? What is fun for children? Is it a physical thing like jumping about? Or is it more like eating something you like? The basic problem is whether children would sit pondering the *definition* of fun, as most adults would, or whether they would regard it as a very real thing which can be brought about in a very real way, and then set out to design a machine that would have the effect of making it come about.

Fun – 1

A fun machine that goes along when you press a button. The machine is a sort of store of all sorts of fun things like a box of Lego, a box of bricks, a box of Meccano, a box of general toys and a bookstall. (One of the compartments is simply the works of the machine, to make it go when you press a button.) Here the emphasis is on the fun machine being a collection of all sorts of fun situations, and in this particular case mainly toys. Fun is having something to play with.

Fun – 2

A fun factory on wheels by a very young designer. The factory does all sorts of fun things like selling you sweets and biscuits and making toys. Why should the factory be on wheels? Because most fun things are on wheels, or at least they 'do' something in some way, and movement is the simplest way of doing something.

horns that hoot when button pressed and a car is pulling factory along

Fun factory on wheels.
Sells sweets and biscuits.
makes toys.

Fun - 3

Another 'collection' type of fun machine. You put together all sorts
of fun things and then you get what you want. Hanging from strings
on a ceiling are all sorts of goodies like toffee, peppermints,
sherbert, orange juice, Smash ice lollies and chocolate. 'If you want
a sweet go and ask the engineer for a long sword to cut the strings.
The cushions are for stopping the jars from breaking. If you want
trifle, all you need to do is press four buttons, one after another.
The rest you probably know.' In addition at the side there seems to
be a set of wings, for the person to fly up and take the things down,

just in case the sword approach does not work. As everyone knows
trifle is made of cream, jelly, custard and hundreds and thousands
put together in a special way. So if you want a trifle you have just
got to press each of the buttons which releases one of these
ingredients, but unless you want them all mashed up together you
had better press the buttons in the right order. Since you are going
to be up in the air most of the time, you might as well have a
helter-skelter to enjoy coming down to ground again.

Fun – 4

A highly concentrated fun assembly. There is even a comment that
really there should be lots more things, but there is too little space
to put them in. There are luxury armchairs, a robot to obey your
commands, a switch panel which you press for any sort of food you
want, and a whole lot of books on the bookshelves (as an author
this is gratifying, because one knows that adults don't read books,
so it is nice to think that children still regard them as fun). It is not
quite clear how the Big Dipper or the football pitch come into the
picture, but since they are part of having fun it is as well to put
them in.

FUN MACHINE.

(P.S. LOTS MORE THINGS— TOO LITTLE SPACE)

Fun – 5

Another assembly of fun things, but this time more in the sense of a
fun palace. On the ground floor there is a see-saw with careful
provision of cushions to stop you from getting that nasty judder
when you hit the ground. Also the swing and the tickler box which
provides tickling hands to tickle the kids and make them laugh.
Another tickler box is provided on the upper floor. An unusual
aspect of the fun to be had in this fun palace is the water sprinkler.
As you tread on the white string a rod goes up and lets water pour
through on top of your head – naturally this is a lot of fun.

Fun - 6

The fairground approach to fun.
You go down a slide on to a
bouncer and then on to a
roundabout. Since it is a fun
machine all the parts must fit
together and it isn't a matter of
walking from one enjoyment to
another. They are all linked up in
some way. So all you have to do is
sit at the top of the slide and then
everything happens to you in
sequence.

Within the drawing:

you climb up ladder and slide down the slide, and go into the truck which slides up and down

the truck gets stuck and you fall onto the trampoline

swimming bath

you bounce on the bird which flies and drops you into the swimming bath
It will lay a chocolate egg.

Fun – 7

Another sequence fun machine. You bounce on to the bird which flies and drops you into the swimming pool (the bird will lay a chocolate egg if you wish). Then from the swimming pool you climb up a ladder and slide down into a truck which zooms up over a hump and then comes down and stops rather suddenly, which means that you fall off on to the trampoline with its great springs and then back on to the bird again. So you go on going round and round on this fun trip of sliding and bouncing and flying. You probably eat the chocolate egg as you go along, or at least give it to a friend. Bouncing and sliding and slipping seem very much to be basic ingredients of fun.

Escalator

Springboard

trampoline

hole in stair unit

swimming pool

GROUND LEVEL

underground helter-skelter

trapeze

Netted frame topped by platform with hole in

GROUND LEVEL

FUN - SET EQUIPMENT.

This can be taken advantage of in any way, each piece of equipment being adaptable to many kinds of use. Part of the equipment is underground to add interest to it.

2nd trampoline

UNDER GROUND GAMES ROOM.

mattresses

Fun – 8

More bouncing and sliding. Up an escalator on to a springboard, off that to a trampoline, then down a helter-skelter on to a second trampoline which shoots you up from on the ground on to a trapeze, and then on to a platform with a hole in it through which you fall down on to mattress underground. This time you have to find your own way back up to ground level and the start of the escalator.

Fun - 9

A very ordinary looking toy car,
with pedals which you turn to
make it go, but then there is a
unique feature. The unique
feature is the keyboard with lots
of buttons as shown in the
drawing. You press a button and
you get anything you want. For
instance if you want a tree house
then 'somehow' the tree house
appears.

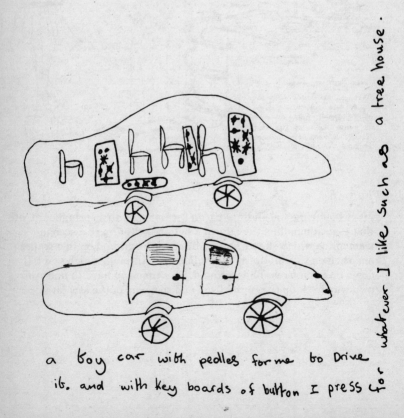

a boy car with pedles for me to Drive
it. and with key boards of button I press for
whatever I like such as a tree house.

Fun – 10

The ultimate simplification of press-button omnipotence. You simply
have a bracelet which you put on your wrist. Then when you want
something you just press the right button. This is perhaps the purest
form of the press-button idiom in any of the problem-solving efforts.
You press a button to get a television picture, and you press a
button to change that television picture, so why should you not be
able to press a button to get anything you want. All you have to do
is to buy the right machine, or for someone to make the right
machine. That is not your responsibility. All you have to do is to
know which button to press once you have got the machine. As I
have stated elsewhere, I think the growth of the press-button idiom
in thinking, is probably one of the most significant changes in
thinking for centuries. Its impact on adult thinking is much more
significant than is ever realized.

this is a thing wich you put on your rist and when you want eny serten thing you press a diffrent button

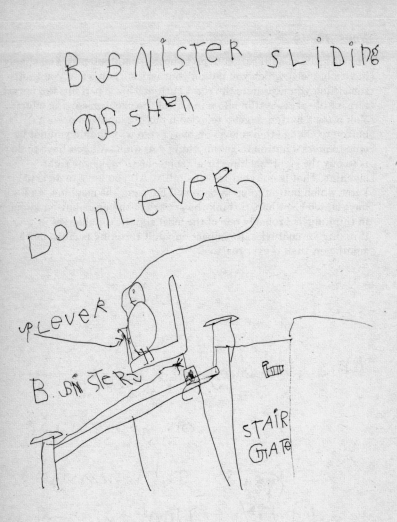

Fun - 11

In contrast to the previous designs, this designer has concentrated
entirely on one single aspect of having fun. Sliding down bannisters
is fun so if you have a machine to slide down bannisters, that is a
fun machine. The machine is operated by a lever.

Fun - 12

Tree-climbing is also fun so if you have a special machine to climb trees that will be a fun machine. The tree-climbing machine actually takes all the hard work out of tree-climbing, because it is operated by a battery. The machine operates by throwing a brass arm around the tree trunk and then proceeding upwards on its brass feet, rather like a lumberjack climbs a tree by throwing a loop of rope around it and then climbing up on his nail-studded boots.

Fun - 13

Another single-minded design. This design comes back to the joy of
bouncing about. There is a silver bar (presumably chrome) which is
supported on springs, and this makes it very bouncy. So you bounce
from the bar to the spring mat and then up to the bar again and
down again, and go on bouncing for as long as you like.

Theres a dip in the mechanical horses neck
and theres a puzzle. The horse gallops along
and talks to me nicely. It never wants
to stop. Unless i want it to.
And it tries to buck me off.

Jigsaw
puzzle

blanket

grips so
horse
doesn't
fall over

track

grass so it won't
hurt when I fall off

Fun – 14

Not quite so single-minded as the previous designs. This girl wants
to have her cake and eat it. Jigsaw puzzles are an indoor activity.
Horse riding is an outdoor activity. What you do is have a
mechanical horse with a jigsaw puzzle built into its neck. So as the
mechanical horse goes along its pre-set track you can get on with
the jigsaw puzzle. Because falling off a horse is not very pleasant
there are grips so that the horse does not fall over, and indeed if you
fall off there is grass so that you don't get too badly hurt. The
advantage of a mechanical horse is that it never wants to stop
unless you want it to stop, and also you could arrange it so that the
horse talked to you nicely.

Fun – 15

Cricket is fun too, only you have to go through all the bother of having a lot of other people about, and if you are quite young it is often difficult to get someone to bowl to you for hour after hour. So a fun machine would be an automatic bowling machine which bowls at you. And it works off a battery. A system of pistons and weights catapult the cricket ball towards you and then you bat it back and the whole thing starts over again.

Fun Machine (one man cricket)

Piston pushes Net with ball in, up very quickly so ball goes flying to batsman. He hits it back and it repeats again.

Fun – 16

Most of the previous designs for fun have been rather vigorous
activities. This is really a water-music machine, with glasses and
bottles partly filled with water, and depending on how full they are
with water, they make a different note as you tap them. So by
having all these different glasses you can play music.

There are to circles one has planks and the other
has archs. You must walk up the planks—or
archs hold on and walk round and round.
And as you walk round music comes out.

Fun - 17

Another music machine but this time combining the joys of music
and some of the joys of physical activity.

Ready made

For their fun machines the children borrowed existing ready-made
fun apparatus: some Lego, a box of Meccano, helter-skelter,
trampoline, roundabout and so on. These were proven fun devices
and their only defect was that they were not readily available the
whole time. The child's only contribution to designing the fun
machine was to think of the fun apparatus, or to assemble it with
other fun apparatus in a particular way. Even when a new machine
was designed, as for sliding down bannisters or climbing trees, this
was to perform a fun activity which itself was very well known.

Collection

Most of the designers saw the problem as one of getting to, or
having, fun machines. A natural way to solve this problem was to
bring together all the fun machines that one could think of in one
place, and this one place would be the fun machine. Many of the
designs as a result were simply collections of fun ingredients
brought together. The choice of fun ingredients varied from child to
child. Some children might prefer playing with Lego or Meccano
while other children might prefer watching television, or a football
match or sliding down a helter-skelter. I doubt whether the choice is
of any significance at all, but simply reflects what first came into the
child's mind out of the multitude of opportunities for fun that he
was aware of. Some of the designers worked hard to try and think
of every conceivable source of fun and put them together. Other
designers, however, took the easy way out and all they did was to
assemble a collection of press buttons. This saved them the trouble
of having to think of all the things that could be fun. Instead of
actually providing the things you provided 'opportunity', which
meant that as soon as you thought of something that could be fun
you would simply have to press the right button and you would
have it. But this is in fact quite an important design principle. Do
you design for an actual situation, or do you design for flexibility
and opportunity and a change of mind or use?

Satisfied

The fun-machine problem probably shows less actual originality or
innovation than any of the other problems. This may be because
children are themselves well satisfied with the fun machines that are

available to them. The only snag is that these machines are not available often enough, and so they never really get a chance to get tired of them. If you have something that works very well why should you try and invent something new? In any case fun is such an abstract thing that you cannot invent a fun machine unless you know that it is going to be fun. The only way you can tell whether something is going to be fun is if it has already been fun in the past, or at least if that kind of activity has been fun in the past. It is not difficult to imagine an apparatus for building a house more quickly, but it is quite difficult to imagine a new apparatus which you believe would be fun. Fun is very much an experience, and in an experience you tend to go for what is tried rather than to generate something new about which you can tell very little. It may also be that, in tackling problems that are very familiar, the chances of coming up with a new approach or novel solution decrease the more familiar the problem is.

3 Weigh an Elephant

If you were the zoo keeper and wanted to find out how heavy an elephant was how would you do it?

Elephants are very large and very heavy. The purpose of this problem was to see how children dealt with this matter of size and weight. Would they treat the elephant like any other object to be weighed or would they take the great weight into special account? Magnitude is difficult to think about. You can distinguish very easily between a dog and a cat because they have different features but it is much more difficult to distinguish between a small box and a big box because they are both boxes.

But elephants are not boxes or lumps of concrete: they are living animals with personalities of their own. How would the children deal with this personality problem? Would they ignore it or make special provision for it? Would they treat the elephants as large inert weights or as large animals with feelings and wishes? Then there is the actual process of weighing. The idea of weight, balance and measurement is a difficult one but not uncommon in everyday life (kitchen scales, bathroom scales, etc.). Would children grasp the actual principles involved or just borrow complete machines for the purpose?

I would make a **huge** Weighing mashine and weigh the elephant

Elephant – 1

A downright, no-nonsense solution to the problem. If you have something very big to weigh then you simply make a HUGE weighing machine. The sort of answer you might expect from the chairman of a large company or a government minister, both of whom would leave more exact solutions to their technicians.

Here is How I would buy a very big kichen Scales and make the elephant go up a ladder by puting A bun in the tray

Elephant - 2

Kitchen scales are for weighing things so for a very large thing you need to buy very big kitchen scales. But the problem is not yet solved because you have to get the elephant up into the scale pan. This is done by providing a ladder for the elephant to climb and a bun to tempt him to climb. A mixture of pound and ton weights will tell you how much the elephant weighs.

Elephant – 3

This problem of getting reluctant elephants up on to weighing-machines was regarded by many of the children as the major problem. These psychologists paid more attention to the intentions and inclinations of the elephants than to the mechanics of weighing. Reluctance to do something other people want you to do is not unknown to children as a behaviour pattern. A well-dressed keeper with a whip urges the elephant up the tin plank on to the mighty strong table.

winch for pulling
harness with elephant

ELEPHANTS
WEIGHT

Harness.

CONVEYOR BELT

0
1
2
3
4
5
6
7
8
9
10
T
O
N
S

Pull for
elephant
To rise

WEIGHT
MEASURED BY
SPRINGS going
Down.
ARROW POINTING
TO WEIGHT. ~

PULL

Elephant – 4

Another inclined ramp but this
time the elephant is winched up
as he stands on a free running
conveyor belt. The elephant steps
on to the weighing platform
which sinks down as the springs
are compressed. At the end you
have to pull a lever to bring the
elephant back up.

Elephant – 5

Instead of winching the whole
elephant up the ramp, you simply
haul up a bun on the bun railway
and the elephant follows after it
just as greyhounds follow the
the electric hare. The platform is
made of 'metal or steel'.

Elephant – 6

This problem-solver knows that even when you get an elephant up
the ramp he can still hesitate at the edge of the weighing machine
(like a reluctant horse being loaded into a horse-box). The elephant
is tempted up a ladder by a bunch of bananas and then finds himself
sliding willynilly down a chute and on to the weighing machine.
The elephant may seem rather small in relation to the men but that
is because if you draw the chute first the elephant has to fit inside it.
In any case, he weighs two tons.

Explanation
The elephant climbs
up the steps while
he is doing that, he
eats the bananas
and then he slides
down the slide and
at the bottom there is
a weighing machine
and that is how
it gets
wieghed

Elephant – 7

Instead of trying to make the elephant walk on to the weighing
machine you pick him up with a crane and put him there. You need
a crane because elephants can be quite heavy. The
sideways/forwards looking elephant looks a bit like a flying duck.
There is a bun to soothe his feelings.

Elephant – 8

A single crane could overbalance so you had better have two - one on each side.

Elephant – 9

Cranes are used in industry to lift heavy weights but so are
fork-lift trucks. Not three elephants but the same elephant in three
stages of the process. As in previous drawings the weighing
machine works by the compression of springs.

THE ELEPHANT GOES DOWN ON A PLATFORM ON SPRINGS AND NEEDLE SHOWS WEIGHT. PEOPLE GO DOWN TO SEE WEIGHT ON STAIRS

ELEPHANT

ANOTHER PLATFORM WITH WHICH TO PULL THE ELEPHANT OUT.

GROUND LEVEL

WEIGHT

WEIGHT IS SHOWN ON THIS SCALE

WEIGHING AN ELEPHANT

Elephant – 10

The lateral-thinking solution. Instead of going to immense trouble to get the elephant up on to the weighing machine you simply bury the weighing machine in the ground and let the elephant stroll on to it. At the end the platform is raised again to let the elephant get off. The actual mechanism of the weighing machine is shown in detail.

This spring is inside the brass encase and the needle is free between the white scale+ encasement.

1 – BEING THE ZOO-KEEPER A.U NOT REPRESENTED IN MY CRANE CABIN.

A WEIGHING MACHINE WITH A SPRING INSIDE – IT MEASURES IN NEWTONS.

THE ZOO-KEEPERS CRANE

THE ELEPHANT.

Elephant – 11

This time a crane is used not to put the elephant on to a weighing machine but to suspend the elephant from a spring-balance. Details of the spring-balance are given in the adjacent drawing. As the spring is stretched the pointer moves down the scale to give the weight of the elephant.

HELICOPTER.

LONDON Zoo

Zoo Keeper

Conection to helicopter

Gaint fish weigher.

HOOR

Strong straps

Elephant stands on here.

Giving the signal.

keeping stand steady

Elephant – 12

Another spring-balance but not any old spring balance but a 'giant fish weigher'. This makes sense because fish are certainly the heaviest 'living' weight to be weighed. Instead of a crane to suspend the balance there is a helicopter or 'sky-crane'. The elephant simply moves on to the platform and the helicopter rises a little. Great attention to organizational detail with one man giving the lift signal and another steadying the platform which would otherwise swing about.

Elephant – 13

A new design for a spring weighing machine. The springs are clock- (or clockwork-) type springs and they can be wound up with a handle. As you wind up more and more springs the tension increases until the weight of the elephant is balanced. The number of wound-up springs then gives you the elephant's weight in tons.

When the man turns the handle round once it it is one ton and twice on around two ton and so on. And When the elephant gets o to the top of the rope it tells you what the a elephant weighs

Elephant – 14

Another new invention for a spring weighing machine this time
using the tension of a bending metal sheet. The elephant goes up
the stairs and walks across the sheet which bends under his weight.
You keep on lowering the plank of wood until the bending metal
sheet no longer rests on it. You can then read off the elephant's
weight from the level of the plank – as in a high-jump competition.
Although the plank is really just an indicator it has to be a 'very
thick plank of wood' since to begin with the elephant's weight
rests on it.

First the wood is put on the ½ ton shelf. Then the elephant
walks up the stairs. When he is on the metal it will bend under
his weight. If it touches the wood you know the elephant is more
than ½ ton. Then you take the elephant off and move the wood
on shelf down. Give the elephant something nice to eat, then
make him go onto the metal again. When the metal does not touch
the wood you know he is however many tons the last
shelf was.

Elephant – 15

A change from springs to a well thought out hydraulic weighing system. Water is pumped from a tank into a cylinder to raise the ramp supporting the elephant platform (like a hydraulic lift in a garage). The pressure which supports the ramp is indicated by the gauge and this gives the elephant's weight. The rear view of an elephant is rather easier to draw than the front view.

Water tank

Motor for Pumping

PRESURE GAUGE IN POUNDS

ELEPHONT

Ramp

Arows outside
is when it is
being weyed

Arows inside
is when it is
being pumped up

Elephant - 16

Another water-filled system. It seems to be based on the
conventional scales with the two pans connected by water instead
of a beam. Readers can try and figure out whether the system would
actually be usable or not. The answer is not easy.

Elephant in
Sling

Rocking-bearing

Beam

Basket for
Weights

Elephant – 17

The conventional beam scale. A fork-lift truck is used to get the
heavy weights up on to the pan. The available weights range from
one to three tons and give some idea of the expected weight of the
elephant.

Elephant – 18

A two-stage process. Tempted by buns the elephant walks up the ramp. Then several 'strong men' who have already weighed themselves on the human scales swing from the beam. More men join the swingers until the elephant takes off. A measuring stick tells when this is happening.

Elephant - 19

A special 'trunk lifter' to prevent the elephant from cheating by
holding on to the food or the ground and so giving a false weight.

Elephant – 20

This elephant weighs himself by making use of the unique
advantage offered by his trunk. Judging from the weights he is
using he seems to be indulging in some wishful thinking.

Elephant - 21

A very simple and very clever solution. The elephant is too big for ordinary household scales. So you get four such scales and make him stand with one leg on each – then you add up the four weights (about half a ton could be weighed in this way). I have used the method myself with people too heavy to be weighed on ordinary scales. The elephants tusks seem to curve the wrong way.

Elephant – 22

A figure-conscious young lady who has got girth and weight mixed
up. The corset is pumped up and then a plug pops out so indicating
the pressure in the corset. For a given air input this pressure will
be related to the girth. It may well be that as with humans fat
elephants are heavy elephants.

baby
elefant

Elephant – 23

Someone has ducked the main problem by choosing to weigh a baby
elephant. Or it may be easier to identify with a baby one.

Magnitude

On the whole the children appreciated that elephants were big and heavy. This could be seen by the specification of steel or 'mighty strong' platforms, by the use of ton weights, and by the need for such devices as cranes and fork-lift trucks.

Psychology

A lot of the children seemed more concerned with the psychology of the elephant and the difficulty of getting him on to the weighing machine than with the actual weighing which was taken for granted. Buns, bananas and branches were offered as temptation.

Mechanism

A few children simply borrowed available weighing devices such as a fish-weigher or kitchen scales but most of them actually designed special weighing machines using springs or water pressure, etc. Such designs showed an extremely good grasp of the principles involved.

Function

When children want to achieve a certain function they are very good at borrowing machines which give that function even if it is not the main function of the machine. Helicopters, fork-lift trucks and clock springs are examples of this sort of function borrowing. This ability to actually separate out the function from the total idea of a machine is strong in children and surprises many adults.

4 Build a House Quickly

If you wanted to build houses more quickly, how would you do it?

The problem is to do something that is already done, but to do it 'more quickly' – to speed things up, to achieve some sort of new efficiency. The speeding-up process might be a speeding up of the whole building process, or it might be a speeding up of some part of it. Another way would be to take some part of the process and change it, or maybe even drop out some part of the process. Or would the children decide that instead of speeding up the existing process they would like to change it and invent a new process or invent a new way of building houses completely?

Speed is a fairly abstract concept. You can tell whether a car is going faster than another car, but how do you tell that you are building a house quickly? Is it simply the rate at which you put the bricks down, or the convenience with which you put the bricks down? Is it the number of stages you have to go through, or is it simply a matter of speeding up the transport of different bits and pieces to the place where you need them?

Achieving speed and efficiency in processes are very real problems, both in business organization and in organizations in general. In particular the building of houses more quickly is a real problem to virtually every government.

if you had magik.

a wizerd he cood do abc ba pre!

House – 1

A direct conceptual solution. If you had a wizard and he could do magic, and he said 'Abracadabra!' then you could build a house very quickly. This is not as mad and impractical as it may seem. In Chicago recently, where a building schedule was as much as two years behind time, the constructor hired a 'wizard' foreman and within a few months the construction was ahead of schedule. (In fairness it should perhaps be mentioned that the Mafia is suspected of having had something to do with the affair.) On the whole this sort of problem-solving is too much neglected in business and government.

House - 2

This time you make the houses the size of matchboxes, and then
the people shrink themselves down to fit the size of matchbox
houses. The machine shown deals with matchbox houses and
matchbox cars, and does everything that needs doing to them. The
general concept from this is that you do whatever can be done
quickly and simply and then you adapt yourself to the result. In
practical terms perhaps not a bad principle.

BIG
KILN
FOR BAKING
WHOLE
.HOUSES

House - 3

The houses are baked intact in a big kiln, and then a mechanical
arm takes them out and puts them on their site complete, down to
smoke issuing from the chimney. The idea is that the house is built
as a single unit, just as a jar or other piece of pottery is put
together, placed in the oven and comes out complete. Unlike all the
other designers, this designer has chosen to make houses as a
complete unit, rather than build them up from bits and pieces.

Aim. is to have a mechanical bricklayer and so speed up the building work The cement and bricks are pre-mixed and they move along a belt to the site.

House – 4

One part of the house-building process is speeded up. The most time-consuming job is laying the bricks, so to speed up house building you have a mechanical bricklayer. In this bricklayer the cement and bricks are pre-mixed and then they move along a belt and get put on the wall. In addition there is an automatic scraper, which prepares the bed on to which the bricks are going to be laid. So the bricks move directly from the lorry to the site where they are to be placed without any human intervention. There is no indication as to how the machine decides where to place the brick.

House – 5

Another automatic brick-laying machine. This time using waving antennæ for taking the bricks off the pile and putting them on the building. A separate tube pours out a quantity of cement just underneath where the brick is going to be placed. This time the bricks are placed according to a large control board. The control board can also be seen to have a little oscilloscope window with the usual sort of patterns you see on an oscilloscope.

Machine to put bricks on conveyor.

Part built house

Stock of bricks.

House – 6

There is a crane-like machine to put bricks on a conveyor belt.
The bricks are then hauled right up into the air, and then come
down again on the other side to start building the house. It seems
that the designer thought that the conveyor-belt idea would be
good, and then got rather carried away by the idea, so that the
conveyor belt becomes almost an end in itself. It seems to introduce
a rather unnecessary journey on the part of the bricks. One must,
however, bear in mind that the height of the conveyor belt is to
allow you to build rather high houses, even though the conveyor
belt at the moment is shown laying bricks at a rather low level.
Presumably the down slope on the conveyor belt can be raised to
whatever is the height of the house. In my experience I don't ever
recall having seen a conveyor belt giving bricks to the man who is
laying them. This would seem quite a simple idea which could be
put into practice immediately – if it does not already exist.

House – 7

The conveyor-belt idea multiplied up to deal with all the ingredients of a house – such as nails, beams, floor-boards, wires, plugs, switches, plumbers' equipment and so on. Each one of these is stocked on its own shelf and can move to the house along a pre-set channel. The designer has clearly focused on transport as that part of the building process which slows things down. If you can get the necessary materials you need to the place you need them quickly, then the house-building process would be speeded up very much. It is certainly true in major construction works that one of the most important problems is to get the vast amount of material needed to the site when it is needed. Delays in this are certainly a major factor in building speed.

This shows the driver that the bricks are dropping properly

This shows the diagram of the house about to be built

These are the wings

Diagram of house

These are the wings

These That door is the entrance to the machines

Machines

These buttons route how fast the machine go's

The machine drops a brick in its place as it flys along.

House – 8

Brick transport this time is by a flying brick-layer. The machine
flies over the site and carefully drops bricks where they are
required. The driver is provided with a diagram of the house that
is to be built, and also with a little television monitor screen to
show him that the bricks are dropping where he intends to drop
them. There is a row of buttons which tell you how fast the
machine is going, and also a row of indicators to tell you the speed,
the pressure and so on. On this occasion the designer is not only
concerned with how to get the bricks quickly to where they should
be placed, but also with strict control of how they are being placed.

House – 9

This is a design showing how bricks come to be coated with cement
before they are put in place. The box of bricks goes along a conveyor
belt and the bricks get coated with cement which drips through a box
with holes in the floor. A hand then picks up the bricks and puts them
in layers. Something of the sort could presumably cut building
time because much of the time in brick-laying is spent on laying
the mortar on to which they are going to be laid. If one were to
have some sort of pre-coated bricks, or bricks which did not need
cementing in place, then building would indeed be speeded up.
The designer has focused on a very definite part of the building
process, which though it may seem rather small is certainly very
significant.

House - 10

Further attention to this problem of getting cement on to the
bricks when they are put in place. The cement is poured out of
a large jug by a mechanical arm. Another mecahanical arm is
laying the bricks. You pour the cement into a hopper and then it
travels up a pipe and comes out in a tube just over the jug, so
that whenever the jug is empty it can be refilled immediately.
An interesting point is that in order to get the cement travelling
up the tube cement magnets are provided. These magnets act
through the walls of the tube and attract the cement upwards.
In order to keep the cement properly mixed there is a mixer which
puts an arm into the pipe and stirs the cement around.

House – 11

New materials. A crane with a
special lifting mechanism lifts
glass-fibre panels into position.
Once they are in position then
the outside of this rather flimsy
glass-fibre house is sprayed with
cement which sets hard and
gives you a solid house. The
speeding-up process here comes
about because there is complete
elimination of the slow brick-by-
brick-laying process. Were
house building not such a
traditional industry, it seems
likely that something of the sort
would be in effect already.

a fibre-glass house.

this moves out

inside

a cement sprayer

crane

As pure oxygen has more pressure than ordanairy air
it holds up the plastic structure very well.
When the concrete has stuck the plastic is peeled
off. The rest of the building and the appliances are built conventionally.

REINFORCED PLASTIC COVERING (NO SUPPORTS AIR PRESSURE HOLDS STRUCTURE UP.)

FAN

PURE OXYGEN

AIR PIPE

REINFORCED CONCRETE (BLOCKS MAKE THE WALLS)

EXTRACTOR

THIS MOTOR EXTRACTS AIR AND SEPERATES CARBON DIOXIDE FROM THE OXYGEN.

MOTOR

CARBON DIOXIDE CYLINDER

ADHESIVE CEMENT

House - 12

Another coating system. Pure oxygen which 'has more pressure
than ordinary air' holds up the plastic structure very well.
Adhesive cement is then sprayed on to the walls, and when the
concrete has set the plastic is peeled off. The basic idea is similar
to the previous design, except that this time an inflatable
structure is used as the base to which the concrete is attached
instead of a constructed glass-fibre structure. This would, in fact,
make house building even quicker. On a lesser level inflatable
shuttering for conventional concrete work would seem to be a
good idea.

inflatable house

plastic windows; cheap plastic

inflation + heater.

in the holidays we blow the balloon up full then we go away.

House – 13

Direct inflatable house which is blown up full in the holidays
and then allowed to collapse when 'we go away'. Inflation is
achieved by means of hot air coming from a little heater, and the
house is inflated just as a hot-air baloon is inflated. The bottom
half of the drawing shows the house being inflated by this hot air,
and the top half shows the house as it is completely inflated. Note
the change in shape, in the size of the windows and the doors of
the house, as it gets inflated. Initially they are small and they
become bigger as the whole house expands in size.

Windows are made with
a single layer of plastic and
walls and doors are made
with two layers.

Extra rooms can be
added.

When the balloon is blown up it is transfered to the
next machine which blows the heat lining in.

House – 14

More inflatable houses, though this time on a rather more
permanent basis. Neutral plastic is poured into a container, and
then it is blown along by air, colour is added and finally the plastic
is blown into a balloon. When the balloon is blown up it is
transferred to another machine which then blows the 'heat'
insulation lining into the first balloon. The balloon sets solid.
Houses are then an assembly of these balloon-like structures. If
you want a bigger house, or more rooms, you simply add another
balloon. This is an immensely attractive idea. One might imagine
large plastic balloons being put together and then going inside to
cut out the pieces that are redundant in order to give you as much
space as you like inside.

① Choose huge balloon with nice wallpaper pattern.

②

Spray with Concrete. all over.

Final result

③ cut in half, and cut out doors and windows Then glue together again to reform this is →

⑥ Bring furniture.

④ Roll to side

⑤ Dissolve glue

Another satisfied customer.

House – 15

You choose a huge balloon with a nice wallpaper pattern and blow it up, and then you spray it with concrete all over. This gives you a solid sphere which you cut about a bit, and then reassemble.

House – 16

A direct and very simple idea.
You have a square coil of rope
which you lay in an igloo fashion
putting glue between each layer
and when this has set you have a
solid house. One might imagine
this system actually working with
concrete impregnated rope which
is coiled round and round to give
a structure. When the structure is
complete you 'cut out' doors and
windows.

Coil of square rope

Glue

Cut out doors and windows.

Concertina or Chinese lantern

pull up

Fire

House – 17

A concertina-type house, which is very easy to pack and transport
and when you get to where you want you open out the concertina
and provide some central support. In a sense like a tent but much
more permanent. After all, one only wants walls for weather
protection, and the weight-supporting part of the house can be
quite different. The beauty of the concertina house is that there is
no assembly work at all to be done on the site, not even the fixing
of panels to a basic structure.

House - 18

You can buy little sheets of cardboard from which you cut out the shape of a house and then you fold the flaps as indicated and you have a house. So why not do this on a large human scale by using sheet metal instead of cardboard? A direct transfer from immediate experience to a larger scale. This is in fact a building system which does work on somewhat similar lines, with walls that are folded in on a flat base and then the walls are folded out on site and fixed into position.

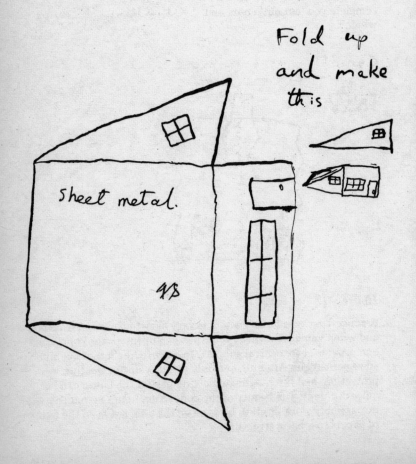

House – 19

Away from traditional materials like bricks and cement to a
plastic house. Outside plastic walls are moulded at the factory,
and then inside plastic screens are used to divide the house into
bathroom, bedroom, dining room and kitchen. The advantage of the
circular structure is that the walls can be moulded in one piece,
or at least in identical panels which can be fitted together. In this
design there is no attempt to try and speed up the existing
technology, but simply to provide a new technology.

VECLEY
Bricks

ThATBig

LiKE LEggo

8 ft.

4 FEET

Br bricks are one made of
plastic. hollow filled with
fileglass wool.

House – 20

Another design that uses plastic. This has two central features.
First that the bricks themselves are very big. They are four feet
by eight feet. But they are not very heavy because they are made of
plastic, and they are hollow and filled with fibre-glass wool, which
acts as insulation. The advantage of having very big bricks is
clearly that you can build a house very quickly with them. The
big bricks are rather like Lego bricks which mean that they have
knobs on them, and you can fit them together simply by pressing
them together. This gets rid of the bother of having to put in
cement and so on. Another example of 'transfer' or 'scaling up'
in problem-solving.

House – 21

The house is built of ready-made panels which are fitted together
in rather a special way. Each panel is edged with strong magnetic
metal, and so all you have to do to fit them together is simply to
put them in position, and then the magnets will hold them together
for ever. This is certainly very much quicker than having to screw
the panels together or nail them together in some way. It might be
argued that the magnetic metal would be very expensive or would
soon wear out, and yet one could go on from this idea to some
sort of temporary magnetic band which one would use to hold the
pieces together while some longer acting material like glue or
cement was allowed to set. Even this would speed up the
attachment process considerably. Note the use of magnetic adhesion
as a type of instant adhesion which can be stored permanently and
which comes into effect immediately – there are not many other
adhesives which have these qualities.

Magnetic House
(The magnetic metal is only
on the edges ~~not over~~ of the building)

The houses
can be made
any shape or size.

The roof is fitted
on separately
with tiles fitted
magnetic
on afterwards.

strong
magnetic
metal

spaces
ready for
windows.
— magnetic
metal.

magnetic metal
dug deep in the
ground
with house attached
to it

handles

magnetic
lock.

magnetic
metal

Outside
Doors (sliding)

— inside
of doors

House – 22

Follow the sequence of construction. Basically the construction
consists of prebuilt units which are placed in position by a
gigantic crane. The walls are fitted together and then picked up
by the crane and put on the foundations. Then the roof is put on.
Note that the next operation is to take the roof off again and put
in the whole of the downstairs at once. This is followed by putting
in the downstairs ceiling leaving a space for the stairs. After this
the upstairs is put in, then the actual roof is put on again. Note
the significance of putting the roof on and then taking it off again.
This is exactly the sort of operation that at the moment does slow
down building so very much. You do something and then you have
to undo it in order to do something else. This is seen very clearly
in road building, where you build a road and only after you build
it do people come along and dig it up and put down drains and
cables. In fairness to the designer, when the roof is finally put on
it is referred to as 'the actual roof'. This may suggest that the first
roof to be put on was only a temporary roof so that people could
work underneath it and get on with finishing the interior of
the building.

SHEET TWO

7 The ceiling is put again with a space left for the stairs.

5 Then the roof is taken off again.

9 Then the actual roof is put on.

8 The upstairs is put in

6 The whole of the downstairs and some stairs is put in at once by a crane.

Improve

The designers looked at the existing process of house building and
decided that they were going to improve it in some way. Most of
them chose to improve it by providing a more speedy transport of
materials to the place where they were needed. Another method
of improvement was to get rid of human labourers who might
slack, be lazy or just tire, and replace them with an automatic
machine which never tired and never needed tea-breaks.

Focus

Several designers chose to speed up the house-building process by
focusing directly on one single aspect of that process and
improving this aspect. For instance, if you pre-coated the bricks
with cement then this would speed up the process by eliminating
the need for using cement or mortar at the actual moment of
brick-laying. In improving any process this is a very effective
principle: look at a part of the process which provides the major
source of inefficiency, and then tackle just this single aspect of
the process, instead of trying generally to tart up things all round.

Change

There were those who were not content to improve the existing
process but preferred to introduce completely new technology.
Outstanding among this group were those who suggested spraying
concrete on to basic structures or blowing up houses, which could
either be left as inflated houses or then coated with concrete.
Another type of innovation was not so much in the way in which
concrete was used, but in using new materials, for instance plastic.
Surrounded by plastic and concious of the way it can easily be
moulded in a factory, many children wonder why plastic is not
more often used in house building.

Effective

It is quite easy to change a process or to provide a new process
instead of existing ones. It would have been easy for the children to
come along with some other way of building houses. But in fact
every single one of the designers kept carefully in mind the
specification of the problem – that the new way of building the
house should be quicker than the old way. Every one of the

suggestions at first sight seems to provide a change for the quicker. There is no design which is change for the sake of change. The ability to keep the problem specification in mind is impressive.

5 Invent a Sleep Machine

Design a special bed for people who have difficulty in going
to sleep.

Very few children have difficulty in going to sleep. The problem
is essentially an adult problem. How would the children tackle it?
Would they produce their own ideas on what makes a person go
to sleep, or would they simply borrow sleep-making devices from
the adult world which they had experienced perhaps in their
parents or read about? Would the emphasis be on things that made
a person go to sleep, or on removing those things that kept the
person awake? The problem itself is not a mechanical problem like
some of the other problems but the production of a very definite
state. Would the children use mechanical means to bring about this
state, or would they use psychological means, or a combination
of both.

The big difference between this and the other problems is that in
the other problems there was always a man 'doing something',
arranging something, controlling something. But in this case it is
the man himself who is the object. Something is happening to the
man. How then is this going to be brought about, if it is the man
who is going to do something to the man, and once it is done, the
man is no longer able to control anything – because he is asleep.

He is wearing a masks, and when his
eyes close when he falls asleep
They operate a the leaver so that
the bed slids down, To
a horisontal position.
Being up sidowwn make his eyes
Klose and he fals asleep.

BED

leaver

slids down here

Sleep – 1

Perhaps suggested by those dolls which close their eyes when you
tip them up. The idea is that if you tip up the bed then the man's
eyes close and he goes to sleep. When he is asleep however there
is not much point in leaving him standing on his head. So one needs
some sort of mechanism to turn off the sleep-inducing machine
once the man is asleep. This is achieved by having a mask and
through this mask the closing eyes operate a lever, which can be
seen in the drawing. Once this lever retracts then the bed slides
down under its own weight and assumes the horizontal position.
Note the practicality of the design, for instance in the large
headboard which prevents the man sliding off the bed when his
feet are near the ceiling. Note also the board at the end which
prevents the bed itself from sliding off the support when it slips
down into the horizontal position.

double
a rocking bed

Sticky bed

Socket
to heat
bed

Lathe tub to cool down in

Sleep – 2

The movement this time is more
conventional, being an ordinary
rocking movement. The ends of
the rockers can be seen projecting
from the sides of the bed. Since
it is a rocking bed you might
well slide off, so the bed is a
special sticky bed. An electric
wire goes to a socket to provide
heat for the bed, but at the same
time there is a tub to cool down
in, so you can get your
temperature just right.

Bed to make you go to sleep.
Cats tied to rockers

cats try to catch rubber mice attached to spring.

cats harness

Spring Palls mice
back and forth
wich makes cats pull
rockers

Sleep – 3

Another rocking bed, though this time the rocking is fore and aft.
Rocking however is not left either to chance or to your own
movements. Instead a very carefully designed animal-power rocking
mechanism is provided. Two cats are attached to the rockers, and
as they chase after mice which pop in and out of a hole, they rock
the bed. The mice are special rubber mice attached to a spring, as
shown in the drawing. This spring makes them go back and
forwards so bobbing in and out of the hole. Since it is very unlikely
that the cats would exactly synchronize their movements, or for
that matter that the mice would, the resulting motion would most
certainly provide a rocking movement for the bed. Presumably the
person goes to sleep and after a time the cats also get tired and
go to sleep.

Sleep - 4

Up and down movement with large bouncy springs. Energy is
provided by some sort of motor which you wind up with the handle
provided. This gives you a limited amount of movement and when
that movement runs out you are either asleep or you have to jump
out of bed and wind it up again. Really rather a practical device.
There seems no reason why such a device should not be in actual
production, even if only in the form of a rocking cradle for children.

You wind up the mot—or befor geting into bed. Then you get in and the bed bigins to bouns up and Down which sends you to sleep Then the mot—r stops.

motor

Handle

Boxes hold springs when bed is down

Sleep – 5

Here the movement part consists only of a springy mattress, but there are several other things in addition to movement to make the person go to sleep. For instance there is the 'Boots' hot-water bottle filled with hot perfume to soothe the person. There is also an automatic lullaby coming from a radio, which is switched on as soon as the person's head touches the pillow. Thoughtful provision of blankets as well, since being cold can certainly keep a person awake.

The tape is worked by The pressure
of The person geting in to to Bed

Sleeping drugs

tape that says S-l-e-e-p

Sleep – 6

Another example of automatic operation. This time the weight of
the person getting into bed operates a tape recorder that says
'S-l-e-e-p, sleep, sleep'. It is not quite clear how the tape recorder
gets switched off, when the person has actually gone to sleep, or
perhaps it just goes on and on as a sort of loop in case he wakes
up during the night. If the tape recorder is not sufficient some
sleeping drugs are suspended quite conveniently over the person's
head.

computer bed

sleep sleep sleep sleep sleep sleep sleep sleep sleep

computer giving out sleep instructions and sounds

Sleep

rokar

rounder

computer making roundurs go round and round and move them and rocker rock

rokar

Sleep - 7

This is another automatic design, with a tape recorder calling out 'Sleep - sleep - sleep' in a hypnotic manner. This time the process is controlled by a computer. But in addition to this tape recorder there is also a rocking movement. This rocking movement is provided in an extremely ingenious manner. There are spiral springs as shown, and as these spiral springs go round and round they very gently lift the bed up and down. This is a highly original and inventive design for a rocking mechanism, since the mechanism will be very smooth and undulating because of the nature of the springs. In effect the child is using springs as a sort of cam mechanism, but it is very much better than a cam mechanism because the action is so much smoother.

Sleep – 8

A 'total' type design – that is to say a design where everything that
can be thought of is put in. There is a cross to pray to, eau de
cologne, books to read, a mobile to look at, and sleeping pills in
case everything else fails. In addition there is a space hopper,
which can be looked at as it hops out of the door. The emphasis
seems to be on comfort and having everything you want around
you and then you go to sleep, a bit like the burial of the Pharoahs
in ancient Egypt.

Sleep – 9

It is interesting to see how many children do not rely on a single sleep-inducing mechanism, but want to have additional mechanisms. Here there is also a rocking movement and the provision of sleeping pills. Unlike the previous designs the rocking movement is not achieved by balancing the bed on rockers, but by having it suspended from the ceiling by thick ropes. This gives rather a different kind of rocking – a much more gentle one from side to side. If you want the sleeping pills you don't have to get out of bed to get them, you simply pull on a rope, and this releases a sleeping pill right into your mouth. Most of the designers seem to be aware that if you have to get out of bed to do something then this destroys any sleepiness you may already have. So provision is always made for bringing whatever you may want right to you in bed.

roof

thick ropes

Sleeping Pils

If you want a Sleeping pill Pull this rope.

If you hang the bed from the ceiling, It will rock. So you Sleep.

If person is still awake   camera
projects sheep jumping over a fence
the sheep have to be counted
if person wants sleep

Sleeping pills

Arm.

Camera

Sheep jumping over fence
on screen

When eyes open
arm puts sleeping
pills in persons
mouth

Sleep – 10

There could be trouble here. A camera projects sheep jumping over
a fence, and the sheep have to be counted if the person wants to
sleep. On the other hand if the person's eyes are open, then an
arm dumps sleeping pills in his mouth. So as long as he is watching
and counting the sheep he is getting a steady supply of sleeping
pills. The reasoning is perfectly sound – either you are awake and
watching the sheep, in which case you need some sleeping pills, or
you are asleep, in which case the sheep are turned off and
everything is as it should be. Unfortunately there is a slight danger
of an overdose, since the sleeping pills would take some time to
act, and if you were a very avid sheep counter you might get a
great number of pills dumped into your mouth.

Sleep - 11

Another sheep-counting system, or at least one in which you
watch sheep jumping over a fence. As you do this there is a
pendulum ticking slowly from side to side to soothe you to sleep.
Finally there is soft music which is playing above your head. In
many of the previous designs the sleep-making mechanism was
turned off in some mechanical manner. In this case, however, the
automatic music is turned off by the sound of your snores. Careful
attention to the sheets, blankets and pillows to make sure you are
very comfortable.

When he moves
he shakes. his bed which
Makes the chain move which
Makes the ~~other machine on~~
"out" line move so the bed goes
to the tree's and bird's which
Send him to sleep.

The Rocker does not
Move until it
hears a bird singing.

out line

chain

Roker

Sleep - 12

A highly complicated and effective design. Instead of having 'canned' music to make you go to sleep, this time there is the real thing. Instead of bringing the world into your room you get taken out into the world. The mechanism is operated by the movement of the restless non-sleeping person who shakes the bed. This shaking of the bed makes the chain move, and this chain takes the bed out into the open air, where birds are singing in the trees. The singing of the birds puts him to sleep. To enhance the singing of the birds there is a rocker which rocks the bed. So he lies in bed being rocked and listening to the sound of the birds. However the rocker does not get going until it actually hears the birds singing. An extremely pleasant way of being put to sleep.

Sleep – 13

This time the entertainment is more indoors although a telescope
is provided to look at the stars. In addition there are drinks,
television and a camera, and a switchboard to let you choose
exactly what you want to do. The rocking mechanism for the bed
is shown in considerable detail. There is a motor with a cog wheel
at the end. This meshes with another cog wheel, which in turn
meshes with a serrated semi-circle on the underside of the bed. So
that as the motor runs first one way, then the other the bed tilts
up fore and aft.

Sleep - 14

The idea of the sleep machine being a sort of entertainment complex, which was hinted at in the previous design, is here carried to its logical conclusion. There are a number of buttons to press, and if you press the right button, you can have virtually anything you want. By pressing the right button you can get any film, or theatre, or food you want. You can also make the bed swing or go backwards and forwards in time. By pressing the right button you can also see anything you want to see in the world or go anywhere you like. In other words this is an automatic dream machine. So while you are still awake you can get anything you want, instead of having to go to sleep and just dream about it. It is not too easy to see why if you were getting whatever you wanted you would wish to go to sleep. Though perhaps this is a better understanding of child psychology than most adults - including myself - have. Perhaps you go to sleep when you are happy and you have everything you want.

gas makes a man go to sleep. When he's asleep the gas turns off itself

← gas

Sleep – 15

A very simple sleep machine which uses gas. The gas puts the man
to sleep, and when he is asleep the gas turns itself off, because if
it didn't turn itself off the man would probably be killed. Unlike
the previous designs this use of gas actually puts the man to sleep
in a very positive way. There is nothing he can do to resist it.
Whereas in the previous designs the idea was to create a setting
which would make it easy for a man to go to sleep, or try to
persuade him to go to sleep. Here he is actually forced to go
to sleep.

Sleep – 16

Another design in which sleep is actually imposed on the person.
It is achieved by the use of sleeping gas which comes out of a
nozzle just above the pillow. But it dosen't seem to matter whether
this is effective or not, because as soon as the head touches the
pillow it operates a lever which releases a weight which drops
down on the head of the person and puts him to sleep. As always
with children, the designer is very practical and knows very well
that if a lead weight hits you on the head it is going to make a
nasty mark, so the weight is covered with foam rubber.

foam

Lead weight
with foam on
the end so
there is no
mark made
One the head.

Sleeping
Gas

lever
to
release
weight

This bed is designed so you
can get to sleep within seconds.
A large lead weight above the
headboard can be released to
knock you on the head and knock
you out, there is foam at one end
of the weight so you are not
cut. Behind the headboard is a
cylinder of sleeping gas which
comes through the outlet on the
headboard and puts you to
sleep easily.

Borrowing

The children treated sleep as something definite that could be achieved in a definite manner if you used the right apparatus. Many of the sleep-making devices were borrowed from the adult world, for instance sleeping pills and drink. Some of the others appear to have been borrowed from the world of comics, for instance the weight that thumps you on the head and possibly the sleeping gas. Some other devices might have been more familiar to children, for instance the rocking devices and the music/lullabies. It is perhaps surprising that children should have been so aware of different ways of putting people to sleep – the designs cover just about every device in use.

General atmosphere

Some of the designers rely on one single thing to put the person to sleep, for instance gas or rocking. Other designers however preferred to include two or more sleep-making devices, for instance rocking plus sleeping pills, or a voice saying 'sleep' plus rocking, or gas plus a hammer. Several of the designers, however, did not seem to be just adding different devices together. They seemed intent on creating a general sleep-inducing atmosphere by making the surroundings as comfortable and as pleasant as possible. The designers perhaps thought of sleep not as a semi-mechanical state which could be achieved in a mechanical way, but more as a psychological relaxation. In adult life this second group would be more in favour of psychotherapy, whereas the first group would be more in favour of drugs.

Automatic

Children showed a surprising awareness of automatic operations. In this problem because the operator was putting himself out of action he obviously could not control all of what was going on. Many of the children provided specific means for the sleep-making activity to stop as soon as the person got to sleep. This could be achieved by having a device which sensed the closing of a person's eyelids or a device which simply reacted to the sound of his snores. Other designers were also interested in automatic operation but this time in automatic operation that got turned on inadvertently. For instance the weight of a person getting into bed operates a tape recorder, or else the movement of a very restless person in bed sets off something else, or as the head touches the pillow it activates a lever. All these are very sophisticated uses of control mechanisms, for something is not actually brought about by the intention of the operator but happens when it is triggered off by some other event. There is a big difference between a man switching on a tape recorder before he gets into bed and a tape recorder being switched on automatically by his weight as he does get into bed. Understanding and use of automatic control mechanisms, feedback and feedback cut-off by children shows a surprising grasp of processes that are really quite complicated.

6 Design and Equip a Space Rocket

Design a space rocket in which astronauts could live on the moon for three weeks.

The problem this time is not to achieve a single specific effect, but to furnish a rocket for the three weeks' stay on the moon. It is no longer a matter of being able to find a right answer, but of providing whatever you want. This is a matter of choosing things, choosing some things in preference to others, establishing priorities, finding out what is unnecessary and so on. How would children tackle this problem? Would they carefully assemble the requirements of the astronauts, or would they simply transfer another situation which provided these requirements, and simply install it in the space rocket? On what grounds would children establish priorities? Would they establish priorities in terms of the things that were important to them, or in terms of things that were important to adults or to astronauts? Would they try to imitate what they already knew about space rockets, or would they design their own rockets for use on the moon? The main problem is to provide the living equipment for the rocket on the moon. There is the additional problem that the rocket and the living equipment must take into account the special circumstances of being on the moon. How would children react to this? Would they ignore the fact that the space rocket was on the moon and treat it as though it was on earth, or would they pay a lot of attention to the special circumstances on the moon?

The basic problem is one of deciding what is important, deciding what to put in and deciding what to leave out.

The craft shown here resembles the lunar module used in the Apollo mission.

It will carry 3 astronauts. Out of the crew of five, two are left orbiting the moon in the capsule.

When the landing craft takes-off from the lunar surface, only the upper stage will leave. The lower stage will be used as a launch-pad.

The upper stage will redock with the capsule in orbit and will stay in orbit for as long as it lasts.

NOT DRAWN ON SAME SCALE.

Rocket – 1

Good drawing of the existing moon-landing vehicle. NASA and the United States flag are prominent on the sides. Note the docking collar and the rendezvous rocket (which are functioning in different directions), and the astronaut in his space suit at the window with the radio aerial on his back. This is a good example of what might be called the 'reproduce' type of design, where a child carefully reproduces what he knows to be the actual state of affairs. Since children were not specifically asked to design a new space rocket, the reproduction idiom is perfectly valid and as valid as any more creative attempts. Being aware of how things are actually done is just as important as inventing fresh ways of doing them. In this particular design it is assumed that the existing space capsule can be internally modified to allow astronauts to live for three weeks on the moon. There is no reason why this should not be so. We know that it can support life for a few days and there is no reason why it should not support life for longer. So here the designer has simply indicated an existing mechanism which solves the problem. The designer does not actually go inside the rocket to show the detail of what is provided and how it functions.

Rocket – 2

Another 'external' design,
showing the outside of the space
rocket. The remarkable
resemblance to the human head
with eyes, nose and hair is
unlikely to be accidental.
Provision of the ladder is
thoughtful, but the air holes
which allow communication with
the outside are probably not such
a good idea. Again the designer
does not go inside the rocket to
show what is provided.

Radio

Eat

Sleep.

Rocket – 3

This young designer removes the outside of the rocket so that we
can see what is provided inside, and inside are provided all the
essentials for life on the moon, which are simply stated as radio, eat
and sleep. Each of these is delegated to a specific and separate
compartment. 'Eat' is indicated by a table with things on it, and
'sleep' by a bed. The last compartment, although it is unlabelled,
seems to indicate the engine or mechanism. Although simply stated
the idea is comprehensive. Radio is for communication, eat and
sleep are for life support. That is, after all, what the problem
demanded.

Rocket – 4

Another statement of the furnishing of the space rocket. This time it is so simple as to be laconic. The designer is perhaps a little more practical than the last designer, because she provides bed, food and a toilet.

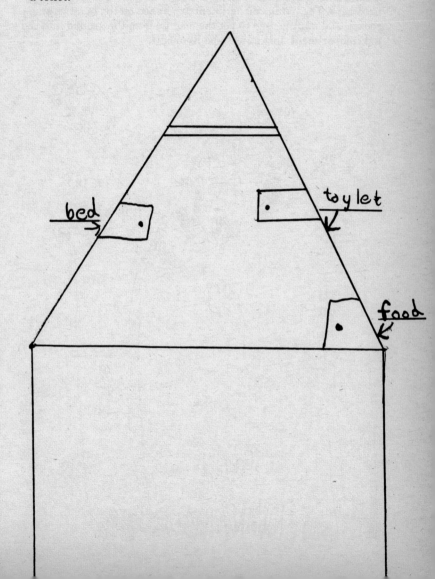

Rocket – 5

In this design the furnishing of the rocket is described in a little
more detail. Instead of there just being a label saying 'food' or 'eat',
there is a listing of different sorts of food, like meat, cake, bread,
special moon sandwiches, and the tablets that are going to be
necessary. The living compartment is perched on top of a two-stage
rocket, and a lift is used to get the man up from the ground into the
top compartment, just as at Cape Kennedy.

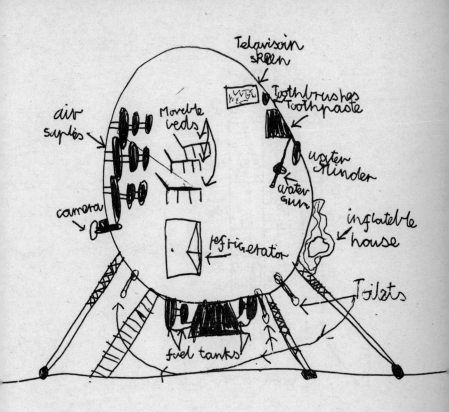

Television screen
Toothbrushes Toothpaste
air suplys
Moveble beds
water clinder
water gun
inflateble house
camera
refrigerator
Toilets
fuel tanks

Rocket – 6

Yet more detail, with three movable beds, a television screen, a refrigerator, camera, water gun, and of course separate compartments for important things like toothbrushes and toothpaste. What is important to a child is not necessarily the same as what is important to an adult. On the side of the vehicle can be seen a rather useful design, the inflatable house, which could of course work quite well on the moon, as quite a low air pressure inside would serve to inflate it. The house might for instance be used to protect the astronauts, not from the weather, but from the intense glare of the sun.

Rocket – 7

This seems to be the doll's house approach. The inside of the space
rocket is furnished just like the inside of a house. Each room is
provided with a lamp and a shade in the middle of the room. It
seems that at the moment only the lights in the engine room are
switched on. The furnishing of the rocket is transferred straight
from the furnishing of a house, so there is a sitting room, a bedroom,
toilet and a room for storing food and water, and other rooms for
radio controls and the engine. Access to the different rooms is
provided by lifts, and the rooms at the top of the rocket seem very
like attic rooms. This is a 'transfer' kind of solution. If people need
houses to live in, then there must be a house inside a space rocket
if they are going to live in it on the moon.

Rocket – 8

Another house with dining room, kitchen, library, bathroom and so on. There is, however, an awareness that this is not an ordinary house on the surface of the earth, but a space rocket on the moon, for in the store room the food is mostly 'in tubes'.

Rocket – 9

The beds are stacked as bunks. As in most of the designs there are three beds for three astronauts, because the American space ventures have usually featured three astronauts. The gas cooker is carefully provided with the different gas mark numbers. In the centre of the floor is a mat to make it just like home. An unusual feature of this particular design is the map of the moon, which is stuck on the wall so that the astronauts can find their way around. In this particular drawing there is no attempt to suggest that the contents are situated within the outer shape of a rocket. The contents are given directly just as though they were furnishings in a house, and apart from the map of the moon, there is no indication that it is a space rocket at all.

Rocket – 10

This design gets away from the straight 'doll's house' approach, and here the items that are needed are scattered around, for instance a row of cups and some books and also a grandfather clock with a pendulum. On a shelf are three guns, one for each astronaut. The astronauts themselves, wearing their space helmets are sitting down quite comfortably, one of them with a newspaper and the other one apparently about to pour from a teapot. In the food compartment there appears to be a large turkey just ready for serving. At the bottom of the vehicle are three shoes, or more likely, three pairs of shoes, one for each astronaut. A Union Jack is also provided.

Rocket – 11

In contrast to the simplicity of the furnishing in some of the previous designs, this design shows considerable detail. The larder seems to stock quite a lot of the kind of food you might expect to find in a more earthly larder. On the other hand there is the comment that most of the food is powdered or made into pills. The interior of the rocket is surrounded by a vacuum. There is thus a strange juxtaposition of furnishings which are very directly earthbound and yet a lurking awareness that this is a different situation that calls for a vacuum to retain the heat just as in a thermos flask, and for the food to be powdered or in the form of pills. Two mice have been brought along as mascots, and they can be seen living in the larder alongside the water tank. The spacemen are out of the vehicle wearing their space suits, but obviously they have a spare set of space suits, which can be seen hanging on a rail. There are practical points of detail, for instance all the living rooms are provided with emergency lights, and the whole vehicle itself is provided with a rubber tip on the end as protection against a nose-dive.

Rocket – 12

Most of the designs so far have tried to provide a balanced
environment, in terms of food, sleep, communication and so on, but
some designs seem obsessed with one particular requirement. For
instance in this design, the requirements seem limited to a variety
of food ranging from 'taties' to desserts. These are stocked in sort
of drawers and you can have what you want. When you are not
eating you are sitting strapped in chairs in front of this food panel.
The only additional equipment is a drawer for toilet bags.

Rocket – 13

This time the concentration is on providing proper air for the three
astronauts as they sit in front of a gigantic control panel. The air
can be seen to come in from the back and go through the first stage
of processing and then on to the second stage of processing before it
reaches the astronauts.

← Computer

← Capsule

← "Happy" exploren and escape craft

Leg →

FUEL

The fuel ignites when it meets oxygen.

The rocket lands parallel to the moon's surface.

Hover jets →

OXYGEN

Steering jets →

Combustion chamber

Parachutes →   ← Parachutes

Leg →

Rocket - 14

Here the concentration is on providing fuel for the motors. Each motor has its own dual chambers of fuel and oxygen. In effect this is a rather realistic view since the actual rockets which go out in space do consist mainly of fuel.

INSIDE OF A SPACE-ROCKET

one line of drawers contain
   a huge quantity
of too bottles with
water in for
   washing.

Sun reflects in, to make a light

drawers
lining the
wall.

folding in
Clothes drawers

nailed down record
player.

wash-
basin

TRAP-
Door

tube to
plastic-bag

bottles
of drink.

Cellar

exit from
Space-ship

Rocket – 15

Not perhaps a very comprehensive furnishing of space rocket, but
the designer does have an eye for detail. In the roof there is a
reflector so that the sun can make itself into a ceiling light. The
wash basins and toilet are each connected to separate plastic bags,
instead of having tubes just ending in the air below the space
rocket. The record player is nailed down so it can't move about. On
the other hand there is a huge stack of drawers which contain a
quantity of bottles of water just for washing. The overall design
looks a bit like a hat, though it is probably more closely related to a
flying saucer.

Rocket – 16

Another designer with a practical eye for detail. Note how one of the legs of the rocket is used as the drain for the toilet. There is a special indoor garden for growing cress. This is really a very practical idea, and some of the groups working on advanced space travel are seriously interested in ways of providing food which actually grows within the space vehicle, instead of just transporting stored food.

SPACECRAFT

Rocket – 17

This designer is well aware that being on the surface of the moon is
not the same as being on the surface of the earth. So she has
attached lead weights to the beds, to the storage cupboards, and
even to the dustbin. At first sight this might seem a silly idea, for
weightless conditions, lead itself would also be weightless. Therefore
this might seem less effective than nailing things to the floor as in
one of the previous designs. In fact there is a force of gravity on the
moon, although it is considerably less than that on earth, so the
addition of these lead weights would serve a very practical purpose,
in making the objects to which they are attached moveable but
much more stable and less likely to be kicked about.

Transfer

Several of the designers simply transferred the idea of a furnished house to the inside of the space rocket, this procedure solved the problem in one go. Because instead of having to try and build up a living environment piece by piece, all that they needed to do was to indicate that the inside of a rocket was like the inside of a house and, as we all know, houses are good places to live in. Transfer, in fact, can also be seen in those designers who simply drew an existing space vehicle, and implied that with this drawing they transferred the full use of that vehicle.

Importance

Where the designers actually built up the living conditions in the space rocket, what features did they consider important? Three things which the designers obviously felt to be the most important were sleep, food and toilet arrangements. The sleeping accommodation was either in the form of a bedroom, or at least in the form of very solid looking beds, one for each astronaut. In real terms this is perhaps a bit surprising because one would imagine that the astronauts would sleep just about anywhere, but it may arise from the fact that with television showing the actual astronauts in their space craft, they are often to be seen in their sort of couches which serve both as seats and as beds. It may also be that sleep is an important part of a child's life. Eating was dealt with both by the provision of a dining room with a full complement of tables and chairs, and also by the provision of rather extensive larders, showing the various sorts of food that were to be consumed. In a design which showed little else carefully listed were meat, bread, cake and moon sandwiches. With the provision of toilets and wash basins one designer even went so far as to provide a huge set of drawers containing bottles of water for washing in.

Apart from these major living considerations various designers included other things they thought to be important, such as a medicine cupboard or first-aid kit, books for entertainment, mascot mice, grandfather clock, mat and so on.

Difference

Many of the designers seem to be torn between trying to provide a living environment such as might be found on earth, and yet being aware that this was the moon, and therefore things would be different. One of them overcame this problem in a simple way, for instance by providing a map of the moon in the room. Others carefully indicated that the food had to be powdered or in tubes, though it looked as though it was very much earth-type food. One designer had a very simple furnished spacecraft, but put each of his astronauts in space helmets to indicate that he was aware that they were indeed in space. A more specific awareness of the problems created by space was shown by the designers who nailed the gramophone to the floor or provided lead weights for keeping the furniture on the floor. On the whole the designers were probably more influenced by experience of real earth shapes than by their ability to design specially for space, for instance beds and chairs look very much like earth-type beds and chairs. It must of course be admitted that the children may only have wished to convey the idea of a chair, and the best way to convey the idea of a chair is to use that shape of a chair which everyone would recognize. If, for instance, you were to invent some very special type of space chair which had no legs, then how would the reader know what you meant? This argument does not really hold up because in several of the designs, the tables and chairs are very carefully labelled as tables and chairs, even if they are unmistakeable.

7 Improve the Human Body

Draw a picture showing how you could make your body better.

In many of the problems given to the children there was some definite 'end-point' which had to be achieved: weigh an elephant, build a house quickly, invent a sleep machine, etc. This time the problem is open-ended. There is no specific end-point to be achieved just the vague idea of making the body better. The children are left to decide for themselves what improvement they want. Does an improvement consist in being able to do something new that could not have been done before? Or in doing what could be done before faster or more easily?

Our bodies are so familiar that they seem perfect and it is difficult to think how they could be improved. You can improve a design by picking out the obvious faults and correcting them. Another way is to find a gap and fill it. You could also try and add some entirely new function.

Would the children think of an effect they wanted to achieve and then find a way of achieving it? Or would they just make a change for the sake of it and then look around to see what use it could be?

Would the children want to achieve fantastic things like flying to the moon or practical things like getting to school more quickly?

Stephen and I would like a bigger mouth so we can eat a bit more food at a time. And we could drink a drop more

Mouth →

Human design – 1

The improvement consists of a small change in an existing feature in order to bring about a definite advantage: 'I would like a bigger mouth so we can eat a bit more food at a time. And we could drink a drop more.' Someone who had sensibly noticed that when you are very hungry the mouth is just not big enough.

I would like ears that
record what other people
said. Then I would not have to
go and ask them what
they said.

I said I am
going to the
Foot ball Match

Human design – 2

The same designer with another change to give a definite advantage.
The suggestion is that recording a conversation should be a function
of the ear (as in a tape-recorder) rather than of the brain. This is
one of the few design changes that are not accompanied by a visible
alteration in the feature itself (the ear does not change shape or
size).

I think it would be better If my finger's could grow longger and Shorter. Because then I can pick big things up when my finger's are long. And I can pick up Small things when my finger are small.

Human design – 3

A most excellent improvement to give a definite advantage. A coarse working hand and a fine working hand so people would be just as good at embroidery as at digging ditches.

I would like to change my hair to very pretty hair and so that I could change it short or long when ever I want to. To save mummy taking me across the road to have a hair cut. And so that if I want long hai badly I can just change it to long hair and to save the money from mummy buying a wig for me to chang my hair.

Human design - 4

The advantage to be gained here is one of money and convenience. The matter is one of real concern to the designer who is after all not asking much. Being able to change appearance at will is not unknown in the animal kingdom (birds with ruffs, etc.).

Human design – 5

More of most things except
fingers and toes. But no reason is
given for this multiplicity and no
advantage claimed.

This is a young man I would like him to have
two mouths. 2 noses. 2 eyes. 2 ears 1 neck
three arms. 3 legs. 4 or 5 fingers and toes.

Human design – 6

Not just more of the same but direct improvements as well. Spring feet for a more agile goalie. Expanding-tong-type arms for grabbing things and people. Supersonic ears. And of course an aerial to call for help if someone attacks you. Three eyes and noses but only one mouth, doubled up arms but a third leg. Most children are inconsistent in the way they multiply up the features and it seems that aesthetic considerations are just as important as mathematical or mechanical ones.

Airial for if some one attacks you.

Supersonic ears

3 eyes for good eye sight

3 noses for good smell

Good arms for grabbing things or people.

Spring legs for a good goalies

Human design - 7

Another multiplicity example with a rather unexpected and not
entirely convincing reason given: 'so that I could get to school
quicker'.

This is a boy these are the thing
that I would like to have 4 eres.
4 eyes 2 noses 2 mouths 3 hands
and arms and 3 legs so that I
could Get to school cwiker.

Human design - 8

Even the dog has benefited from the generous improvement in the human shape. On one side the double arms mean that he can get all the shopping 'in one go'. But on the other side the extra arm is only used to hold an extra lead to the same small dog.

He can get all the shopping in one go.

I would like tow more pears of arms so that I can use things more quitkely and to feel more easily. I would like tow on the back and tow on the front and tow on the side. And I would like five more fingers on each hand. And my arms. So they can bend back, this will work by praessing a button and the arms will go backwords and forwards

Human design – 9

This time only the arms are increased in number but with octopus-like lavishness: 'press-button' effect suggests mechanized arms rather than natural ones. In time people may indeed come to be fitted with additional mechanical arms. In this case, unlike the previous examples, the multiplicity seems to be for a definite purpose.

This is a Picture of me.
I have three eye's becuse
If i go blind in one eye
I Still have two to See with.
And i have three leg's becuse
If one gets tied i still
have two to walk with.

Human design – 10

This time the multiplicity is not to give any special advantage but to provide a 'reserve' capacity. The arms remain unmultiplied suggesting that in this case as well the multiplicity is for a definite purpose.

I would like to have two heads, when I was looking at a book if my other pair of eyes did not like the they would look at work the other page.

Human design – 11

A most unusual design since two heads are usually placed side by side not one above the other like storeys in a house. The designer seems to have a strong sense of duty which requires one head to do what it is told and the other to move on to something more enjoyable.

MY maw has Too pairs
of eys so when one
Pair goes To sleep the other
Pair wakes up. he has
To mowthes one happy
one sad. he has Two
Pairs of arms so when
he gets into a fight one
Pair holds the VICTIM while
The other pair punches.
and he has two Pairs
of legs so if one pair
slip the other puir will
hold him up.

Human design – 12

The reasons given for each additional feature are specific, sane and
practical. A fearsome creature indeed.

Human design – 13

The essence of multiplicity. Just three additional fingers which will obviously make the owner do her work quicker.

I would want more fingers on my hands then I could do my work quicker

I would Like to
change my nose. I
whant my nose on my
legs. so that I can
Smell if any bad men
have come. that way.
and I the would Like
my nose a very
Strong Smelling nose. and
a very Long nose.
So I can Smell
a Long way Like
a cat.

It will work
when you press a
boton evrething hapens.

Human design – 14

'I would like to change my nose. I want my nose on my legs so that
I can smell if any bad men have come that way and I would like my
nose a very strong smelling nose and a very long nose so that I can
smell a very long way like a cat. It will work when you press a
button everything happens.' A very sensible transposition of the
nose from its useless position up in the air to being near the ground
where all the interesting action is. Note the 'press-button'
mechanism again.

Human design – 15

A combination of both the multiply strategy and the transpose
strategy. Clearly a girl with a strong mind and revolutionary
tendencies. Double ears mean better hearing.

This is a girl with double ears I have
put double ears on her because she will
be able to hear things she ~~sould~~
should not hear. and I have
put fingers on her head so she
can grab anything what is on
a top shelf and her mother
has told her not to get.

Human design – 16

Another design to improve hearing this time by putting the ears on stalks so that they can get closer up to what is being listened to. Naturally these special ears are activated by a button – most things are nowadays (TV, radio, hoover, washing machine, etc.).

I would like to change my ears

I would like to press a button and my ears would shoot out

Then I would not have to strain my ears

I think it would be a good Idea.

Button that I press to make ears spring out.

Here

DAIL TO. DAIL THE NUMBER
SWITHES.

RECEIVER. TO TACK TO PEOP
ON.

AERIAL TO WORK RADIO

RADIO IN BULLET PROOF
SKIN, FOR EMERGENCY CALLS

DOUBLE HEARTS, FOR
LONGER LIFE.

BULLET PROOF
SKIN, TO PROTECT
HIM FROM MURDER.

Human design – 17

The super-policeman. The child was very concerned about crime,
violence and danger, and his design was for the specific purpose of
providing better protection. Communication facilities are part of
protection. Although the skin is made bullet proof the heart is not
and protection is achieved with a spare heart.

Multiply

The simple increase in the number of features is very characteristic of children's attempts to improve the human body. Two sweets are better than one and in general more means better. So more also means faster, easier, stronger and any other advantage you wish. In only a few cases do the additional features have a real reason (one pair of arms to hold the victim and the other to punch him). I have given the same problem to adults and they also favour this multiply strategy more than anything else. Even with sophisticated professional designers more or bigger is supposed to be better (for instance, fins or chrome on American cars).

Transpose

Another simple design strategy used by adults as well as children. Put the eyes in a different place to see better, put the nose near the ground to smell better, put fingers on top of the head to achieve more.

Reason

In most cases it seems that the change in the number of features comes first and it is assumed that the increase is an obvious advantage (if two legs are good three must be better). Even when reasons are given it often seems that they are a sort of rationalizing after the change has been made. This is not unlike much human invention where the design comes first and then you find a use for it. In a few cases there seems to have been a genuine attempt to solve a real problem.

8 A Bicycle for Postmen

Design a special bicycle for a postman.

It is often thought that children are inventive and original simply because they are ignorant. If you do not know how something is usually done, then you have more chance of coming up with a new way of doing it. Bicycles, however, are very familiar objects to children, and the purpose of giving this problem was to see how children would alter what was already a familiar object in order to make it better.

Problem-solving is quite easy if you are given a definite objective which has to be achieved. Problem-solving is also quite easy if there is some obvious deficiency in a design and you are asked to get rid of that deficiency or fill in some gap. Problem-solving is rather difficult when all you are given is a general idea that you should improve an existing design. This becomes even more difficult when the existing design seems to be a very satisfactory one, as in the case of the bicycle. How would children decide to improve the bicycle? There do not seem to be any obvious deficiences in the design as it has been around such a long time. Nor is it easy to see in what way one could actually improve the design. What could be added to a bicycle to make it better? What could be removed from a bicycle to make it better?

The children were asked to design a special bicycle for a postman, so that their improvements in the bicycle design would be directed to a specific purpose and would not just be general improvements, or change for the sake of change. The child is well aware of the function of a postman. How would he set about re-designing a bicycle in order to let a postman carry out his function more efficiently or more pleasantly?

On what aspects of a postman's function would a child concentrate? Is delivering letters all that there is to a postman's life?

Seat for girl Friend
Pump
Plastic covering for rain
Put letters in
Sack for letters
Press this letters go in letter box
Rubber to bounce along on
Spare Wheel

Bicycle – 1

Being a postman is a lonely business because you spend hours all by yourself riding along. A simple and humane improvement in a postman's bicycle would be to provide a seat for his girl-friend. Since it is rather undignified for a girl to sit with her back to the postman, she can sit side-saddle on the seat which is placed sideways. Note the spare wheel which is towed along behind in case of puncture. Note also the clever positioning of the bicycle pump above the handlebars.

teliscope to
see house
humbers

Buttbn to
make the
seat go up
an down

Aeroplane to
take letters

horn

Box for lunch for
when he goes
along way

Spare wheel

letters

Bicycle - 2

Several improvements including the very practical one of a
telescope through which to see small house numbers. Also a button
to make the seat go up and down at a touch, a box for lunch for
when he goes a long way and also a spare wheel. A rather more
exotic touch is the aeroplane that is going to take letters to the
houses and make it unnecessary for him to get down from the bicycle.

Bicycle – 3

A simple change with provision
of letter baskets for him to put
the letters in. These baskets are
rather like the letter baskets that
might be found on an executive's
desk.

Bicycle – 4

At first sight a very ordinary bicycle with 'Sturmey Archer' gears and a rear-view mirror. But if you look more closely you will find that there has been a change; it is now a front-wheel-drive bicycle. There is no indication why the change has been made from back-wheel drive to front-wheel drive, though of course the front wheel is very much bigger than the back wheel. At first sight there might seem to be disadvantages in this design, because the front wheel has to steer. But in practice, if there did turn out to be any disadvantage in front-wheel drive, this could be very easily overcome.

Rear view mirror

Horn

Sturmey Archer gears

MAIL

Front wheel drive

BICYCLE FOR A POSTMAN

I THINK THAT HOUSES SHOULD HAVE A LITTLE TRACK COMING RIGHT UP TO THE DOOR FOR THE POSTMAN.

TRAILER FOR MAIL

MAIL

SEAT

HANDLE BARS

PEDALS

THICK WHEELS FOR EASIER RIDING

Bicycle – 5

A very sensible designer. He has gone a bit outside his brief in order to suggest that houses should have a little track coming right up to the door so that the postman doesn't have to get down. His design for a bicycle seems most comfortable. It is a sort of armchair bicycle in which you recline back and your feet turn the pedals in the air. This is a good deal more comfortable than having to sit upright with your weight partly supported by the pedals. The wheels are also provided with thick tyres for easy riding. Another innovation is the idea of towing the mail behind on a little trailer. On the whole a design which just looks extremely comfortable.

Bicycle – 6

Further refinements such as a transparent hood over the rider so
that he doesn't get wet in the rain, and also a drink machine, where
you put a coin in the slot and then choose whether you are going to
have tea, coffee or soup. To save the postman's energy there is a
telescopic hand for putting letters in letter-boxes. There is also an
engine in case his legs get tired, but if there is going to be an engine
it is hard to see why the postman should not use it all the time. But
perhaps the designer thought that, if the bicycle was motorized
throughout, then it would no longer be a postman's bicycle but a
postman's motorcycle, so the engine is only provided as a sort of
reserve, just as yachts have little reserve engines without ceasing to
be yachts.

Bicycle – 7

This time the motor is definitely described as a secret motor for
going up hills. The idea is that the postman must not be seen to be
using his motor, because that would be cheating, just as if a boat
sculling down the river in the Henley Grand was seen to be using a
motor. Solid rubber tyres are provided in order to stop punctures.
There is a long pole to deliver letters without getting off the bike.
This really is quite a sensible idea. It may appear that this would be
awkward to use – it probably would be at first, but in getting used to
it it might indeed save the postman from getting off the bike to
actually put the letter through the letter-box. He could stop at the
edge of the pavement and use his tong to put the letter through the
box. An essential part of the improved design is a dog-repellant
spray for nasty dogs.

long pole to deliver letters
without getting off bike

soft
seat

dog repellant spray
for nasty dogs

secret motor
for going up
hills

solid rubber tires to
stop punctures

Bicycle – 8

A lot of the designers were very much concerned with the 'nasty-dog' danger to postmen, and they provided a variety of devices to overcome this danger. This particular design provides an instant ghost with which to scare off dogs. The design is not all fantastic, for instance there is a centrally heated sheepskin seat which sounds as if it would be very comfortable. There is also a combined fog and headlamp in one. Wheels have rubber foam tyres to make for extra easy riding, and there are also twenty-four gears, so that there should be no trouble with hills. As in the previous design there is a telescopic arm to drop letters through the box. There is no reason why the instant ghost should not be some sort of inflatable device.

Bicycle – 9

A design to try and make a postman's life very easy by the use of various devices at the end of extendable arms. The dog danger is taken very seriously. One dog is shown being KOed by a punch, another one is seen being attracted first by a joint of meat and then knocked silly by another punch. One gloved arm delivers letters to the letter-box and another one picks up letters which have somehow dropped to the floor. A peculiar innovation provides for attack by badmen. A couple of guns somehow go down underground and then take the gunmen in the rear. The erroneous notice on the handlebars 'No Postman's Leg Left' is supposed to indicate to dogs that there really is no point in pursuing the matter further.

Conventional model: 1970

POSTMANS WINTER BICYCLE

PROPELLOR TO HELP BIKE UP HILL

-ARIEL

POST EARLY FOR CHRISTMAS
GPO

COVER

WINDSCREEN

HEATED HANDLE BARS

QUIET RADIO

HOT CUP OF TEA

FRONT LIGHT

BACK LIGHT

PARCELLS
1 2 3 4 5 6 7 8 9 10 11 12

LETTERS
G.P.O

TO GET RID OF FIERCE DOGS

Bicycle – 10

There is provision of an engine and a propellor, but once again this
is only to help get the bicycle up the hill, otherwise the postman is
supposed to pedal in the ordinary way. There is the usual boxing
glove on Lazy-Jane tongs to keep off fierce dogs, and a hot cup of
tea. An interesting innovation is the quiet radio just behind the
postman, so that it can amuse him without upsetting everyone else.
Mail is carried already sorted in a trailer.

Bicycle - 11

This is a flying bicycle, and the small drawing below shows what
happens when the wings are extended. Two small propellors drive
the bicycle forward. The designer, however, is a realist and when he
recommends that the advantage of a flying bicycle is that you can
drop the letter down the chimney, he very carefully specifies that
you would have to put them in an asbestos bag, otherwise they
would get burnt. An alternative would be to put them in through an
open window. The Post Office does not want to go on supplying
asbestos bags endlessly. The postman would collect the bags at the
end of the week.

This Keeps the Rain off

Spot light

post Obag | This, posts the letters.

for Kicking   fierce dogs

wheel

wheel

This is for Juping over puddeles

Bicycle – 12

This design is equipped with a device for kicking those fierce dogs that chase along after a postman's bicycle. An unusual feature of this particular design is the device for jumping over puddles. So when you come to a puddle in some way you put down the device and you sort of pole-vault over the puddles. There is also an umbrella to stop you from getting wet at the other end.

Bicycle – 13

An unusual suspension device reminiscent of the puddle-jumper in
the last design. Instead of having suspension on the wheels
themselves you have two separate wheels on the ends of springs,
which serve to take a lot of weight off the main wheel and
would in fact provide quite a useful smooth ride. There seems to be a
bit of an obsession with springs. There is a tomato firer and egg gun,
a letter shooter and an ejector seat for the postman who has
inadvertently used it (which saves the trouble of having to draw
him). There seems to be a sort of tape-recorder device for uttering
those useful syllables 'er', 'um', 'er', in answer to any questions.

spring winedup
when POSt
man is going
So he come
back by spring
Power

delicate PiPe
house
letters
cooter
spring

Bicycle - 14

The young designer is very concerned about the postman getting
tired. There is a delivery pipe which takes letters from the bicycle to
the house, but an even more thoughtful provision is the spring on
the front wheel. This spring winds up when the postman is going
out, so that then he can come back by 'spring power'. This is really a
very useful concept. It might not actually work on the basis of
storing energy in the first part of the morning to give it out in the
second part of the morning. But it could certainly work in storing
energy when one has to come to a halt at a house in order to deliver
a letter, and then requires extra energy to get going again. Using
some sort of clutch mechanism the spring would be wound up as you
wished to come to a smooth halt, and then when you got back on
the bicycle you switched the spring back in, and then it gave you a
sharp push off, to save you having to stand on the pedal to get
going. This principle under the more technical sounding name
're-generative braking' is in fact a part of the thinking of advanced
transport groups, who intend to apply something of the sort in the
design of modern buses.

Bicycle – 15

An unusual idea for the quick delivery of letters. You have a metal
stamp on a letter, and then the householder wishing to receive his
letter stands outside with a magnet, and this attracts the letters out
of the postman's bicycle as he goes past. This makes life very easy
for the postman, because all he has to do is to drive past the houses
and it is up to the householders to collect their letters by long-range
magnetism. It seems likely that the letters would get rather mixed
up. On a more sophisticated scale however, magnetic character
recognition is the basis for a lot of cheque sorting in banks.

your wheers sort the the letters into alpherbetical order; you
press the rights knobs for the house name & the right letters go
down the letter slide & into the house.

Bicycle - 16

The letter-sorting aspect of a postman's job occupies this designer's
attention. A special bicycle wheel is provided for sorting the letters,
which somehow whizz round in this wheel and then come off it at
the appropriate moment and go down a letter slide and end up
directly through the letter-box. The postman has a sort of control
panel and what he does is to press the appropriate knob. Presumably
this operates some sort of scoop mechanism, which scoops the letters
off only a certain part of the bicycle wheel. Note the coat hanger
behind the seat on which the postman sits.

EACH HOUSE HAS ITS OWN CONTAINOR OF LETTERS WHICH CAN BE TAKE TO THE DOOR SEPERATELY →

LARGE LAMP

YOU CAN HAVE A plastic cover to go over the letters if it rains.

LETTER RACK WITH SURNAMES OF THOSE OF COMPARTMENTS

PLACE FOR A MAP

LETTER RACK WITH SURNAMES OR THOSE OF COMPARTMENTS

LARGE LAMP

SPRING

SPRING

PUSH HOB TO RELEASE STANDS

To get stands up again kick them up with your foot and hook them overe this hook

STANDS

MAP OF POST MANS ROUTE THAT CAN BE TAKEN OFF IF ROUTE CHANGES

A Special Bicycle for a Postman.

Bicycle - 17

Further attention to the sorting problem. This time the letters are pre-sorted and placed in little containers, each of which has the appropriate surname on the side. You then take the container to the door, remove the letters, put them through the letter-box and take the container back to the bicycle. In this way you sort out all the letters right from the beginning. A special map stand is provided for the postman, so that if the route is changed he can just put on a new map instead of having to learn it all by heart. The designer has other points which are very practical. For instance, you can pull a plastic cover over the letter racks if it rains. There is also attention to the bicycle stands, because a postman more than anyone else spends all his time getting off the bicycle and trying to prop it up, so he really needs a sort of efficient stand which all bicycles at the moment lack.

of saddle bags spare
Letters in case there is lots
cushions
so that
the postman
can get off
when the bike is
going fast

Bicycle – 18

A long series of trailers to carry letters and some spare trailers in case 'there is lots'. Note the special feature of a cushion which is attached to the bicycle just beneath where the postman sits. This cushion is carried along with the bicycle so that if the postman has to get off the bike when it is going fast, instead of landing on the hard ground he will land on the cushion.

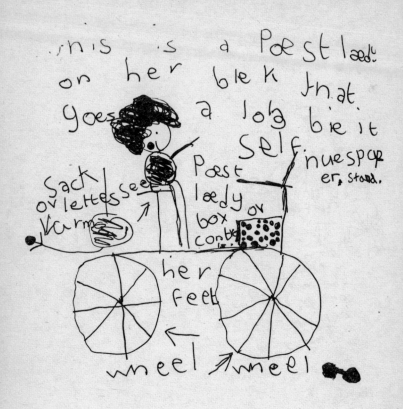

.his is a Pœst lœd!
on her blek that
goes a loj bie it
          Self. nuespap
Pœst   er, staad.
lœdy ov
box
conb

Sack
ov lettes see
Kurm

her
feet

wheel   wheel

Bicycle – 19

Two major innovations. First of all the postman is not a postman at
all but a postwoman. This is not too hard on her because this
particular bicycle goes by itself. So efficient is its control system
that a newspaper stand is provided so that the postwoman can read
the newspapers as she goes on her round. Everything is controlled
from the control box.

Bicycle – 20

Automation is carried a stage further here with a full-scale robot
with metallic-looking robot hair, who actually drives the bicycle,
while the real postman sits behind and controls the robot. A pair of
skies are carried on the back and there is an overhead parcel shelf
with a multi-tone horn. An interesting provision is the bumper in
front of the front wheel. This in fact sounds like quite a good idea,
so that when you do run into something, instead of knocking your
wheel out of shape you simply absorb the shock with the bumper,
which could be very simple and very light.

Bicycle – 21

The usual press-button paradise. You press a button and everything happens. This time there are three buttons. If you press one of them you will get something to eat. If you press another one you will fly, and if you press the third button you will get a slave, who presumably will run and post your letters for you.

This is a button

if you press this button you will get a slave

Presi if you press this button you will fly

if you press this button you will get some thing ro eat

The real problem

The children had little difficulty in deciding what were the real
problems in a postman's life. Nasty and vicious dogs were obviously
a very real problem. Getting wet through by the rain was another.
Getting the bike up steep hills was another problem, and even
merited the addition of 'secret engines'. Then of course the postman
might get hungry or thirsty, so it would be as well to provide him
with instant cups of hot tea, or a choice of tea, coffee or soup, and
also some lunch or sandwiches. Postmen have a long way to go and
they could get tired so it might be an idea to try and help them with
engines or by putting a spring on the front wheel. What especially
tired out postmen was having to get down off the bicycle to go and
put letters through the letter-box. To save the postman the trouble
of doing this there were all sorts of devices whereby the postman
could remain in the saddle and then extend a long telescopic arm
which would drop the letters inside the letter-box.

Different solutions

Different designers picked out different problems in a postman's
life. But even when they picked out the same problem they often
adopted completely different ways of overcoming it. For instance
with the real problem of nasty vicious dogs, some designers came
up with the solution of boxing gloves at the end of an extendable
arm which would simply sock the dog. Other designers preferred a
dog-repellant spray, or an instant ghost. This difference of approach
in solving a problem is characteristic of children thinking, and
indicates in a very clear manner that children really do think and
do not simple repeat standard ways of dealing with standard
situations.

Simplicity

Most of the designs seemed a good deal more complicated than the
ordinary postman's bicycle is at the moment. Most of the
improvements consisted of adding some additional feature to the
existing bicycle, and sometimes at the end the bicycle was so
covered with additional features it was hard to discern the original
shape. Children are never as concerned with simplicity, economy
and elegance as adults, because these things have no real meaning
to them. They only have meaning to someone from an aesthetic

point of view, from a cost point of view, or from a design point of view in terms of ease of assembly or maintenance. To a child, effectiveness is much more important than simplicity, and if you have the problem of repelling dogs, then you must have a device to repel dogs, even if it looks ugly or costs more to include. As a general design point it is very difficult to start out looking for simplicity. First of all one looks for effectiveness and completeness, and then when one has got to that stage one tries to slim down the design and look for simplicity and elegance. You can only prune something that is there. If you do not have it there to prune you run the risk of neglecting it entirely.

9 Policemen and Bad Men

If you were a policeman how would you deal with bad men?

Unlike many of the other problems this problem is very remote from a child's life. Children are certainly very aware of policemen, but they are only aware of bad men in an abstract sense. They know bad men exist, but the chance of a child actually seeing a criminal or a criminal being caught or a criminal being tried is very remote indeed. The child's experience of the way policemen deal with bad men or the way bad men ought to be dealt with is derived almost entirely from second-hand sources, such as films, television and comic strips. In these second-hand packaged situations the relationship between bad men and policemen is very prominent, in fact quite out of proportion to its relation in real life. Thus to the child the problem of how to deal with bad men is a real one in terms of his second-hand experience, but a remote one in terms of real-life experience. In tackling the problems would the child just repeat what he knew to be the stereotyped problems from his second-hand experience, or would he do some thinking of his own?

The problem as stated is very open-ended because no indication is given of what particular aspect of dealing with the bad men is intended. Is it a matter of how to catch bad men, or what to do with them when they are caught? In fact the problem is so very open-ended that no particular problem is actually stated. The children are asked how they would deal with bad men if they were policemen. They were not asked to solve the problem of how to catch bad men or to solve the problem of how to make bad men better, or indeed any actual problem. They were simply given a situation and left to deal with it. In tackling the situation, what aims or objective would the children set up for themselves? Would efficiency in catching the bad men be an aim? Would efficiency in punishing the bad men be an aim? Would efficiency in returning the bad men to society be an aim? The ability to define aims, objectives and specifications for oneself may be an essential part of a problem-solving situation. In some problems the aim to be achieved is set out in a very definite fashion, but in other problems there is simply a general situation and within that general situation it is left to the problem-solver to define the problem and to decide for himself what he would regard

as a satisfactory solution to that problem. That situation is exactly
the case with this particular problem.

There is also the moral aspect of the situation. Are bad men to be
regarded as thoroughly bad, or are they to be regarded as bad but
improveable. How would the children regard the police – as all
powerful and all good, or as relatively human?

Policeman and badman.

rope rote

Bad men - 1

The problem here has been seen as the basic one of catching the bad man in the first place. The policeman is the man wearing the helmet, and he has lassoed the bad man in the age-old fashion. If you have a bad man the first thing to do is to catch him. Note the tummy button which is often characteristic of the drawings of quite young children.

Net opened out

NET

CRIMINAL

Lasso Thredded through the bottom of the net

POLICE MAN

Bad men – 2

Another approach to what might be called the 'mechanical'
approach to catching bad men. A net is thrown over the bad man
and then the lasso at the base is drawn tight. The drawing at the top
shows the net opened out. The policeman in this particular drawing
shows a flat hat, which is extremely unusual, for just about every
drawing shows the policeman in the traditional policeman's
helmet, and this is used as a very strong mark of identification to
show who are the policemen and who are the bad men.

Bad men – 3

This more modern approach to
capture could be called the
'chemical' approach. The
policeman wearing a gas-mask
throws a cannister of gas, which
so upsets the bad man that he
drops both the knife and the
money he is carrying and becomes
immobilized.

use pretty girls as
decoys. Say a gang has ten
members, well ten pretty girls
go off saying "come on" to
each individual member of
the gang, then the girls
walk off in different directions,
and the gang is seperared.
the police then captur the bad
guys who are in a trance.

in trance

Bad men – 4

This approach to capture could be called the 'psychological'
approach. The psychology is subtle and works in two ways. The
first way is to split up the gang by giving each one of them his own
objective, and separating these objectives out so that the gang
splits up as one of them follows one of the ten pretty girls. The
second part of the psychology is that the bad men are so entranced
by the girls that they can lead them anywhere, and in any case the
policeman will have no difficulty in catching them. A strategy that
has proved remarkably effective in capturing bad men, though on the
spy level rather than the petty criminal.

Bad men – 5

What could be called the 'physiological' approach to capture. The policeman sends the radar-controlled homing leech who injects the bad men with a paralysing substance. This is rather a fanciful elaboration of the idea of shooting small darts at wild animals, so that when the dart pierces the animal's hide it releases a tiny amount of substance which paralyses and immobilizes the animal quite painlessly so that it can be captured and in captivity can be operated on. It seems likely, however, that this particular elaboration was derived directly from some second-hand source such as a comic strip. In practice the method seems to have a great number of advantages. For one thing it is quite harmless so even if the wrong person got hit by the dart it would not matter because they would recover without any ill effects. Also it is very much more satisfactory than gunfire, because gunfire will only immobilize a man if it hits him in a vital spot, whereas the paralysing dart will immobilize him if it hits him anywhere at all.

Bad men – 6

We move on now from the problem of how to catch the bad man to what to do with the bad men once they are caught. This particular design shows the traditional method of putting the bad man in prison. The bad man can be seen behind bars, while the policeman outside the bars looks in.

police watchtowers

— high wall

Persistent offenders or criminals on life imprisonment are transferred from normal prisons to a special prison town, with shops houses hotels & public services etc but it is all run by criminals who earn wages and do jobs. Police are on watch 24 hours from watch towers and observation posts.

plan

car park

bungalows

garage

poly

block of flats

semidetached houses

roads

shops

hotel

car park

to town

gate

Bad men – 7

An extension of the prison concept. Here persistent offenders are kept within a sort of prison town with shops, houses, hotels and public services, all of which are run by the criminals who earn a wage and do jobs. The point here is that criminals are not so much punished as kept apart from society which cannot cope with their inclinations. There is no reason why the prison towns should not be comfortable and efficient, because their main purpose would be to keep the prisoners from the outside, and they would probably serve this purpose better if they were comfortable rather than uncomfortable. The idea is of course that the criminals would stay there for life, not just for a period of punishment.

First catch the badmen and Put them in Jail.

The holes are for the Policemen who are standing on ladders to spy on the badmen

holes

The badmen read all the charts which are on all the good things you do.

The JAIL

The badmen read the charts and come out of Jail as goodmen.

Bad men – 8

A view inside a prison. Five policemen's helmets can be seen as they look through the spyhole to observe what the prisoners are doing inside the cells. The cells are plastered with wall charts which tell you how to be good. It is a bit like the propagandist approach of Red China. People are exhorted to be good by material which is fed to them through their environment. There is no reason to believe that this approach would be totally ineffective.

Bad men – 9

The essence of rehabilitation. The prison as a school that is for
making bad men good. In the school can be seen the cells where the
bad men live. A large room for physical exercise, because physical
exercise is a useful part of rehabilitation. Then there is the school
proper and sick bay, dining hall, kitchen and all the other things
one might expect in a school. A large wall surrounds the school
since it is after all a prison, and in one part of the outer
courtyard can be seen the judge's house.

If I was a Police
man I would take them
to this prison. The school
is for making bad men good

Bad men – 10

The 'temptation' approach to rehabilitation. The prisoner is in his
cell with only water, a candle and stale bread. He can look through
a window into a room furnished with a table, chairs, a television
set and wine. He is told he will be allowed a house like this if he
swears not to be a criminal any more. There might of course be
some chance of its working if indeed the criminal was promised
this and could be given this, because it may have been his inability
in the first place to have found this that put him in prison. The
inclusion of wine and a television set as some of the basic goodies
of life is interesting.

Prisnor is kept in cell with candle,
window looking into a comfortable
room. Lx He is allowed a house with
rooms like it If he swears not to
be a crimnal any more.

Bad men - 11

Here the robber is getting better by example. He is sitting
watching a television set showing '*Jackanory*', and he is saying to
himself that he wishes he could do it. When one hears so much
about the harmful effect of television it is nice to see that one child
actually believes that it has an uplifting effect. Outside the prison
are gathered the usual sort of people who make it their business to
discuss what is happening to prisoners, or what should happen to
prisoners. On this occasion at least they seem to be decided that the
particular prisoner in question is being reformed.

Bad men – 12

Here rehabilitation is on the direct hypnotic basis. The policeman
is hypnotizing the bad man and putting him to sleep, and when he is
asleep suggesting to him that he will never commit another crime.
It is interesting to speculate that if the hypnotic method was
effective whether society would in fact approve of it, or whether it
would be termed 'brain-washing'.

Screen showing crime film

Film projector

Receiving hammer on head every time a crime is shown. This makes him connect crime with pain and so stops him committing it.

Badman

Policeman operating hammer box

Bad men – 13

This time the therapy is more orthodox behaviour therapy and is what might be called aversion therapy. The criminal is being shown a crime film and there is a policeman operating a hammer box, so that when a crime is shown on the screen, the policeman drops the hammer on to the head of the bad man. In time the idea is that the pain of the hammer blow would be associated with crime and thereafter the criminal will be less inclined to commit the crime. Orthodox aversion therapy would probably use an electric shock instead of a hammer, but otherwise the principle is exactly the same.

This is the rope that holds the Badman up

This is a spanker

This is a Shaker to shake heads.

police-man

Badman

When you shake his head it changes his badness into goodness.

The spanker makes him realise what he has done.

Bad men - 14

This time the bad man is being shaken and spanked on a special machine. The purpose of this shaking and spanking is not apparently punishment, nor is it a version of behaviour therapy, the idea is simply to make the criminal realize what he has done. There is also a claim that when you shake a bad man's head it changes it automatically from badness into goodness. It is interesting to speculate how society would react to some sort of physical mechanical method (perhaps even brain surgery) to change bad men into good men.

Bad men – 15

Here instead of a good head-shaking there is another method of
making the criminal good. This is by means of electrical impulses,
which are imparted to his head as he sits in a chair. These electric
impulses are 'good medicine'. The machine is operated by a
policeman who is concerned to make him good.

Bad men – 16

This particular design does seem to be concerned with punishment, or at any rate with trying to make life extremely uncomfortable for the prisoner. There is a robot (complete with plug into an electric wall socket), whose job it is to shout 'bleep-bleep' and to clobber the man from time to time. There is a very large pair of pinchers with which to pinch him, a duster to tickle his toes, and a 'thing to pull his hair'. In addition there is a lever which comes down on the bad man's head and a special machine which pops balloons just behind him. In short this is a collection of all the most unpleasant things that a child can conceive of. Although it must be admitted that most of the unpleasant things are more uncomfortable than physically harmful.

Bad men - 17

Another discomfort machine. In one of the chambers a bad man is
punched and kicked and knocked on the top of his head. In a
second chamber he is treated rather as a car might be treated in a
car-wash. There is a squelching thing that comes down on his head,
and then all sorts of tickling arms which tickle him; as in a car-
wash jets of steam come out at about the height of his knees.

an staying
he hot water
so he will
tell the truth
about what
happened

very very
hot water

cage

Bad
Man

lady

Bad men – 18

This time the discomfort verges on torture. The bad man is held in a
cage and then he is sprayed with 'very, very hot water', so that he
will tell the truth about what has happened. The function of the
lady sitting at the desk in the corner is not quite clear.

Bad men – 19

More punishment. The policeman starts off by hitting the bad man over the head with a truncheon and giving him a headache. He is then taken to prison, and while in prison there is a big stone which continually comes down on top of the bad man's head and hurts him. Like some of the previous examples there is no actual indication of what this treatment is supposed to acheive. Then it may not be supposed to achieve anything, but to be part of the general idea of punishment.

Bad men – 20

A no-nonsense, uncompromising approach to the treatment of bad
men. They are taken up by police in what appears to be an RAF
plane and then simply dropped into the sea somewhere. In that
somewhere sea sharks' fins appear to be numerous. Dealing with
bad men in this particular case seems to be disposing of bad men in
as direct a way as possible.

Bad men – 21

In this solution to the problem the two opposite attitudes to bad
men are summarized very neatly. You take them to the 'head
dealer' for a chat. The head dealer is clearly the psychiatrist. That
is to give them pyschotherapy or to rehabilitate them in any other
way. The alternative is quite simply to hang them.

Bad men – 22

This design is completely different to the preceding ones. All the preceding designs were concerned with catching criminals and then with how to treat them in prison. This particular idea is concerned not with catching criminals but with catching motorists. There is a mechanism of lines and lights on the road and under the car. And what happens is that if the car goes across the lines at more than the regulation speed, then the lights flash. This is a highly ingenious and highly practical system. It would be very easy to have lines buried just under the road surface so spaced that if you cross them at more than a certain speed a light would flash and this would instantly reveal that you were above the speed limit, and your car could then be stopped by the police.

The lights and the lines gerkik if it is over the speed limit it is a machanism under the car and on the road

Identification

It seems likely that all the children were not tackling the same problems. Some of the children seemed to be tackling bad men in the sense of nursery naughtiness, which could be put right by being put in an uncomfortable situation, such as having balloons popped behind your head or your feet being tickled with a duster. Other children seem to be dealing with the stereotype of the criminal as dealt with in the cartoon strip – even to the extent of hurling him out of an aeroplane into shark-infested waters.

Change

While some of the designers seemed to accept that criminals would always be criminals and that the only way to treat them was to keep them separate from society or punish them, others felt that somehow it would be possible to make a bad man into a good man. This could be achieved either by dissuasion, or temptation, or more likely by some purely physical means such as electric impulses or aversion therapy by means of hammer blows to the head.

Pure image

Throughout the designers accepted that the policemen were on the side of the good and were always good, and that the baddies were always bad. Both the police and criminals had pure images, in black and white on either side of the fence. It might be interesting to see whether this same effect would hold in other countries. It may be peculiar to the regard in which the English police system is held, or it may arise directly from second-hand experience (TV, cartoon strips, etc.) in which the policemen are indeed always good. It is interesting that no distinction was made between policeman whose job it was to catch the criminals, and the prison system whose job it is to look after the prisoners, or to reform them. Catching the criminals and dealing with them after capture was assumed to be entirely the responsibility of the police force.

No trial

The way the problem was worded gave the impression that the men who were being dealt with were already classified as 'bad men'. This is probably why none of the designs showed any trial process in which the bad man was actually proved to be a bad man. This was more likely to be a fault in the problem wording which pre-judged the issue, rather than to any lack of interest in justice on the part of the children. In second-hand experience (comics, TV, films) the bad men are of course so classified as bad men because one can look in on them as they go about their bad activities. One can see them committing crimes and plotting crimes, so that in the mind of the viewer there never is any doubt that a bad man is a bad man.